KINGDOM COME

The local church as a catalyst for social change

Malcolm Duncan

MONARCH
BOOKS

Oxford, UK & Grand Rapids, Michigan, USA

First published in the UK in 2007 by Monarch Books
(a publishing imprint of Lion Hudson plc),
Wilkinson House, Jordan Hill Road, Oxford OX2 8DR.
Tel: +44 (0)1865 302750 Fax: +44 (0)1865 302757
Email: monarch@lionhudson.com
www.lionhudson.com

ISBN: 978 1 85424 798 8 (UK)
ISBN: 978 0 8254 6151 4 (USA)

Distributed by:
UK: Marston Book Services Ltd, PO Box 269, Abingdon, Oxon OX14 4YN;
USA: Kregel Publications, PO Box 2607, Grand Rapids, Michigan 49501

The board and text paper used in this book have been made from wood independently certified as having come from sustainable forests.

British Library Cataloguing Data
A catalogue record for this book is available from the British Library.

Printed and bound in Wales by Creative Print & Design.

To
Ken and Marjorie Hunter
Robert and Alison Miller
Dave and Laura Vann
Adrian and Naomi Frost
Liam and Collette Hannah

Thank you for your obedience to Christ, love for people and willingness to be where God has called you to be. May you be blessed.

Contents

Foreword

When the local church is working, there is nothing like it. It is dazzling in its beauty and powerful in its simplicity. Lives are transformed and God's grace and love drizzles into countless communities like a gradual rain of hope, slowly and beautifully transforming lives. As local churches live out their calling to be communities of hope focussed on the truth and presence of God's kingdom, they become catalysts for change and conduits of transformation. Yet local churches are made up of individuals – leaders and congregations – who must make a choice about their focus and must decide what kind of community they want to be. Local congregations can do what government programmes, statutory agencies and other groups cannot do because at the heart of the local church is a deep seated conviction that God is at work through us. But the answer is not for the church to be a substitute for the role of government, but rather to be a vital partner with the state, and sometimes to be its prophetic interrogator.

In *Kingdom Come: The Local Church as a Catalyst for Social Change*, my friend and colleague, Malcolm Duncan, outlines a fresh, exciting and achievable vision for the local church. There are plenty of books that criticise local churches and point out their failings, but few that actually see the challenges of the local church as well as the possibilities. Malcolm achieves this balance. He is not a theorist, nor is he an idealist with his head in the clouds. Both as the leader of the Faithworks Movement and as the pastor of a local congregation, Malcolm sets out a way forward for the local church that remains true to our Christian identity and, at the same time, re-imagines our role at the heart of the local community. This is not a comfortable book, but it is a challenging and inspiring one. It is addressed to local church leaders by a local church leader and invites them to paint on a bigger canvas. It shows that there is not just an opportunity for the local church to engage in the community but to engage right at its very hub, inviting local congregations to re-discover the unique and Jesus-defined role that they have to play.

Malcolm is pleading with us to consider who we are, what we do and how we do it. He is reminding us of all that is good in the local church – the commitment to love God with all of our hearts and to love our neighbours as ourselves – and offers practical suggestions to re-connect us with our communities. He displays a clear understanding of the need for what we say in our pulpits to overflow and influence the way that we live and behave on the pavement. He inspires, challenges, and reminds us that the task of the local church is incomplete as long as there are those in need and that the heartbeat of the local congregation should be justice and righteousness. He is calling us to re-discover a commitment to human dignity and to integral mission as part of who we are.

Finally, by inviting us to consider the great image of God's kingdom, Malcolm shows us that we are part of a vast army of people working together and that our ties are stronger than our divisions. Instead of an insipid unity that leads to ineffectiveness, we are invited to consider a unity of mission, purpose and action, to take up our cross and follow the way and example of Christ – and to do it together.

I have been challenged by *Kingdom Come* – I think you will be too. But if we do nothing with that challenge, then this is just another book about the local church. If, however, we do something with what we read here, the story could be very different. May those of us who love God and know the privilege of being part of His church, re-discover the power of service, love and prophetic engagement with society – with those around who desperately need to know that the God we love also loves them and has a purpose for their lives.

Jim Wallis,
Author of *God's Politics* and *A Call to Conversion*
President and CEO of Sojourners/Call to Renewal

Acknowledgements

It is always difficult to know where to start when thanking people for their contribution to a book, but it is important at least to try. I should make it clear that the views expressed in *Kingdom Come* are my own and do not necessarily reflect the views of either the church I lead or the Faithworks Movement. The positive parts of this book are a result of many people, the errors, however, are my responsibility alone

My appreciation goes to Tony Collins, Penelope Wilcox, Simon Cox, Sarah Giles and all at Lion Hudson and Monarch. Your commitment to this book, to me and to the kingdom of God is breathtaking and it is a privilege to work with you. Thank you for your patience, support, criticisms and critiques. Particularly you Penny – this book is a thousand times better because of your partnership.

Thank you also to the whole Faithworks Support team and the Oasis family. It is a privilege to work alongside you and I count it a joy to know that we stand together. My thanks to Hannah Horton and to Sarah Stevens particularly – may God bless you both as you move to new spheres of kingdom influence.

Thank you to Jim Wallis, Tony and Peggy Campolo,

Jonathan Dutton and Helen deVane, Joy Madeiros and Steve Chalke for your words of encouragement, prayers, support and friendship. Thanks go particularly to Jim Wallis for the foreword.

My gratitude also goes to all the members of the Faithworks Movement for your encouragement and example – this book could not have been written without your inspiration. A special word of thanks to the students at Regent's College in their last year in 2006. You were willing listeners and our dialogue helped shape what you now hold.

Thank you to the Mortimer West End Chapel family. How amazing that God would call us together and bless me with your friendship, love and support. I am astounded at the honour of being your pastor and speechless at the things that God is doing among us.

Lastly, thank you to Debbie, Matthew, Benjamin, Anna and Riodhna. God has given me the best team of all right at home – you show me the kingdom in a thousand different ways and I am blessed to be part of our family.

Malcolm Duncan

Soli Deo Gloria

Prologue: A Different Kind of Thinking

There are some dates that you never forget. The day President John F. Kennedy was assassinated; the day Diana, Princess of Wales, died and the day the twin towers of the World Trade Centre fell in New York are just a few examples. These all stand out in our memories because of the despair and heartbreak of each event. They are moments when as a nation, or as human beings, we share in a common sense of loss and despair. There are other dates which are memorable for different reasons – such as the days on which our children are born and we realise the enormity of parenting. It feels like being asked to learn how to dive, just after you have jumped from the diving board!

I will never forget Saturday 7 October 2000. On that evening, I saw something that crystallised for me what the good news of Jesus Christ is all about. The kingdom of God was lived out before me in a more powerful way than I had ever seen. It was one of the most profound experiences of my life thus far. This book is an attempt to put into words some of the impact that event has had on me, an event that has both mesmerised and haunted me ever since. The depth of its challenge lies in its simplicity, and the profundity of its impact is measured by the fact that it still captivates my imagination and inspires me to give more of myself to God and His purposes. It has, in many ways, led to the life choices that I have made ever since.

Archimedes is reputed to have said, 'Give me a fulcrum and a place to stand and I will move the world.' A fulcrum is a small thing that has a big effect. In our lives we stumble upon fulcrum moments that move the whole world for us. We find them in unexpected and unplanned moments of encounter with other people, in the reading of a book, the chance conversation, a momentary glance at others in a café, bar or restaurant – or in observing an act of utter kindness that embodies all that God has called us to be and to do as His servants. The voice of God shouts to us through the whisper of the ordinary, unimportant occurrences of our lives, for it is precisely in these chance encounters that the greatest change can take place in us, and because of us, in the world.

The brilliant hues of the gospel are discovered in the ordinary colours of life. For me, 7 October 2000 was such a moment.

A Tableau of Truth

In the year 2000, I received a wonderful surprise gift for my birthday – a weekend trip to Rome with my wife Debbie. At the time, I was leading a local church on the south coast of England, and the break came at just the right moment. Commitment and enthusiasm for serving the community had brought to our congregation many blessings – but also lots of growing pains. Countless demands on our time and energy, ever-increasing needs presented to us and a sense of being tiny combatants in a much bigger battle had left us drained physically and emotionally. We knew that we needed some time to recharge our batteries and rest. For us, involvement in leading a local church and in engaging in the needs of our community was simultaneously stimulating and draining.

On top of that, our youngest child had just celebrated her first birthday. With four children under six, the idea of a few days away together just enjoying good food and wine and one another's company was about as close to perfect as we could get. So after a wonderful meal on the evening of my birthday itself we set off for a weekend of sightseeing, good restaurants and some quality time together as a couple.

On 7 October, we decided to go to hear a choir sing. We were really looking forward to the concert and together with about a thousand other people we crowded into a large and amazingly ornate church building to enjoy a mixture of classical and contemporary music. (There are churches on nearly every street in the old part of the city of Rome, although admittedly most of them would not cater for such a large crowd.) The moment the choir started, however, we realised there was a problem! Clearly the idea of harmony had quietly passed them by and their rendition of a beautiful song somehow made a cat's chorus sound more inviting! These people were making a joyful noise to the Lord, but it was more of a noise than a melody.

Leaning across to Debbie, I whispered that it might be a good idea to slip out after the first song and leave the rest of the folk to 'enjoy' the evening. I thought we might go and have something to eat and take in the sights, smells and sounds of Rome on a chilly Saturday night in October. Debbie agreed, and we slipped out of the church at what we thought was an appropriate moment. About seven hundred and fifty other people slipped out too, however, so the whole thing ended up being very embarrassing!

Escaping the departing throng, we stood in the street as we tried to decide where to go next. Red-faced and laughing, we were about to make our way to a restaurant where we had enjoyed both the food and the ambiance the evening before, when Debbie's attention was caught by the sight of a man, a woman and a child, wrapped in blankets and huddling together for warmth around a fire that they had lit on the steps of a church.

Their hands, faces and clothes were dirty and they had the eyes of those who had been forgotten. They were vacantly staring into the fire when the young woman stretched her hand into a bag full of rubbish and discarded food. I watched, deeply moved, as she fished out what looked like a piece of bread and lovingly popped it into the hand of her hungry child. This little family had nothing. We stood in silence watching a Dickensian scene unfold in front of us. I remember wondering how they had got there. What had happened to bring them to this?

Something was wrong. The kingdom of God was as real on this street, beside this fire, as it was in that ornate church with its painted ceilings and robed choir. My theology told me God was just as much on the street with this family as He was in the church building with the choir – so why wasn't anyone helping this family? Why were we the only ones still standing in the street? Where had the audience gone?

Demonstrating the Kingdom

Debbie watched the scene with me and suggested that we should do without our meal and buy this family something instead. I heartily agreed. Then, just as we were about to cross the street to explain in broken Italian what we wanted to do, it happened. A moment of sheer beauty and grace unfolded before us. Debbie and I watched as two young Catholic priests rounded the corner of the church building. They were both dressed in black, each wearing a black hat and carrying a small black medical-type bag. These two young men approached the young family, bent down and put their arms around them. Then one of the priests opened his bag and produced a small gas stove, a little pot and a jar of food. He laughed and smiled with the family as he started to cook for them. He brought out plates, forks and cups and chatted to the man and woman, ruffling the little one's hair as he set about preparing them a meal. After a little while he served them the food from his pot and nibbled at it himself – clearly what was good enough for them was good enough for him.

Then the other priest opened his little black bag. He pulled something out of it, and as I strained to see what it was I realised that he was holding a book of some sort. Perhaps it was a Bible, perhaps it was his breviary, which would have included prayers as well as biblical texts. It was too dark to tell what kind of book he held. He said something to the young family that I could not hear, and would not have understood if I did hear it because I do not speak Italian. Then he opened his book and started to read it with this family. Just as the first priest fed their bodies, now this priest seemed to be feeding their souls. Debbie and I stood watching this holy moment for some time and silently wept.

Samaritans

Here were two young men sharing what they had with a family who had nothing. The priests were not individually wealthy – few priests are. They were two servants of God choosing to share a moment of their lives with three people in need. There was no hint of power, no hint of coercion and no hint of a forced encounter. These two priests saw a need and met it. The family accepted the help they were offered. The spiritual and physical divide did not exist in this tableau of love. As heaven kissed this young family, it did so through the generosity and grace of two men who wanted to build God's kingdom. They were choosing to cooperate with God by giving their time, their resources and their lives to people that others had passed by. They were good news. They were modern-day Samaritans.

Living the Kingdom

This book is about what that means. If we are to be followers of Jesus in a broken world, how do we do it best? As I watched this scene unfold – and I have relived it thousands of times since – I realised that it was the reality of God's kingdom and its impact on the world being lived out before my very eyes. Years after the event, it continues to move me to tears. It tugs at my heart and challenges my comfort. It makes me feel uneasy with my own lack of passion and commitment and it encourages – no, *challenges* – me to give more of myself and my life to the outworking of God's reign and rule in our world.

Saturday 7 October 2000 became such a potent symbol of God's kingdom for me because it combined practical care, humbly offered, unselfconscious sharing of prayer and the word of God, and an awareness of the needs of others and respect for their choices in life.

The kingdom of God does not need a new idea – it just needs hands and hearts and lives ready to lay themselves down for others. Physical food would not have been enough for this family, nor would reading the Bible to them have sufficed. But the combination of the two was a potent symbol of what the church has always been called to do.

In serving this family, these two priests were serving Christ. This is what followers of Jesus are called to. The kingdom of God is grown through these seemingly unnoticed acts of grace and love and truth. It challenges me to look beyond business models because it perfectly demonstrates that followers of Christ are not just called to adopt a good strategy – important as strategy is – but are instead called to give our lives.

In their loving and appropriate response, the two priests became, quite literally, a Godsend. Just allow your imagination to place you as an onlooker at the scene. Can you see the hope in the eyes of the young man and woman? Can you see the little child smile because tonight she will not be hungry? Can you understand just how welcome and warm the embrace of these two servants of God dressed in black was to this family? I think they probably listened a little more carefully to the words that were read because they had tasted them in the acts of love that accompanied them. We have no idea if that young family was 'converted'. We don't know what happened the following morning. We don't know their names or the names of the priests who served them. We don't know how the family ended up destitute. We don't even know if they are alive or dead. But we know this – they experienced God's love that cold night in October. They tasted it, smelt it, felt it – and enjoyed its warmth and hope. They were immersed in care and grace and bathed in compassion – and that will have changed their lives. These priests knew what they could do and knew what they could not do. They left the mysterious work of God's Spirit to God and they dared to believe that in their simple acts of love and service the power of God to change, redeem and transform was present. They knew that their deeds were motivated by their faith. They knew that the words of Scripture brought life and light and were willing to share these words – this story of God in Christ drawing the world to Himself. They were faithful in doing what they could and trusting God to do the rest.

That night we witnessed part of the kingdom of God coming to earth, and a community of hope being born. The scene we saw represents what every local church in every neighbourhood in every country of the world is called to be and do.

Knowing and Doing

Kingdom Come has one central purpose, namely to inspire followers of Christ to cooperate with God to establish His kingdom on earth in terms of felt change in our communities and our world. This book is about recognising that good theology always leads to good practice. It is about allowing the gospel to so permeate our hearts and minds that it shines through our everyday lives in moments as full of love and hope and beauty as the encounter we witnessed in Rome. Faith that we read about, talk about, think about, but do not *live* is as much use as a person's brain when it is kept in a jar of formaldehyde on a scientist's desk. It is the living, embodied link to hands and heart and eyes and ears that make it real, empowered, of use.

Beyond Experts

The church of Jesus Christ is full of experts. Thank God for experts on church growth and church finance, on eschatology and liturgy and exposition and New

Testament Greek and Hebrew parallelism. But unless all these experts take us somewhere and help fashion our lives into the likeness of Jesus and contribute to crafting in us a genuine expression of the kingdom of God, then all expertise is pointless – all fur coat and no knickers. The greatest expert that has ever lived was Jesus Himself, and He never boasted in His own knowledge. He rarely quoted chapter and verse at people (except those who thought they were more expert on God then He was!). Instead He lived out what He believed and let His actions and words speak together. I sometimes think that a little more awareness of our own ignorance would be healthy medicine for many of us. In the words of Stephen Fry:

> People sometimes accuse me of knowing a lot. 'Stephen,' they say, accusingly, 'you know a lot.' This is a bit like telling a person who has a few grains of sand clinging to him that he owns much sand. When you consider the vast amount of sand there is in the world, such a person is, to all intents and purposes, sandless. We are all sandless. We are all ignorant. There are beaches and deserts and dunes of knowledge whose existence we have never even guessed at, let alone visited.
>
> It's the ones who think they know what there is to be known that we have to look out for. 'All is explained in this text – there is nothing else you need to know,' they tell us… What we need is a treasure house, not of knowledge, but of ignorance. Something that gives not answers but questions.

> Something that shines light, not on already garish facts, but into the dark, damp corners of ignorance...[1]

But it is not our lack of *knowing* that is a problem, it is our lack of *doing*. *Kingdom Come* is about celebrating those who *do*, the reflective practitioners who are daily making a difference in communities across the world. It is about the vital link between knowing and doing. I want to ask questions, the answers to which we will begin to explore together. Why do hospitality and holiness go hand in hand? How are kindness and character related? Why is compassion indispensible to Christians? What challenges are our communities facing? How do we answer these questions while remaining true to Christ? How can we break out of the introspective mindset that bedevils us? How do we live as kingdom people?

Journey with me in discovering the inseparable link between our identity in Christ and our mission in the world. Explore with me what the kingdom of God looks like, the principles that shape it and the part we have to play in transforming our broken world.

If you want a book with all the answers, then this isn't it! Instead, it is a modest attempt at a conversation that begins to explore what the answers might be. My prayer is that as you make this journey of exploration with me, you will discover for yourself the fulcrum with which we can move the world – just as I discovered it on that October night in Rome.

What is *Kingdom Come* All About?

Life is local and it is in the local church that life's challenges are met. *Kingdom Come* will explore how we can understand those challenges and face them confidently, yet humbly. Our lives, our ministries, our congregations and the work we share can make the difference the world needs. We have heard enough of death and demise: the future does not have to be continued decline and eventual extinction, but can be re-imagined. As we analyse the big challenges of our day and consider how we might meet them, understanding and engaging with the realities of life in our neighbourhood community with honesty and hope, this may yet prove to be the local church's finest hour.

A Time of Change and New Thinking

Albert Einstein once said that the kind of thinking that would solve the world's problems would be of a different order from the kind of thinking that created those problems in the first place. What he articulates captures perfectly one of the core assumptions in this book. It is not wishful thinking to imagine a different future for local churches, it is vital. If we in local churches do not think about the neighbourhoods in which we live, how we relate and engage with them, then local congregations have signed their own death warrant. In times of decline it is understandable to batten down the hatches and settle for dogged repetition and introspective maintenance of the familiar – but to do what we always did will result only in the situation we already face. Now is the time for a reality check.

Individual Christians and local congregations can make a deep and lasting impact on their friends, neighbours, colleagues and communities. There is a bright and wonderful future for local expressions of God's kingdom. If we are to make that difference, however, then we must think about the challenges we face and the society of which we are part. We must ask the hard and uncomfortable questions of meaning, credibility and purpose. At the same time, we must remain true to the good news that we believe, the God who loves us and the Saviour who has won our hearts. I can hold out no assurance that becoming kingdom-focused is easy, but it might change your local church beyond all recognition. It might stretch you, bend you and remold you in a way that you never imagined: but you may find new vision for your life, your loved ones and your community as a result. A future where your local church is vibrant, alive and engaged with real people, real challenges and real life. A future where you are a bringer of peace and a harbinger of hope. God's grace is able. His the vision! His the power!

Never accept and be content with unanalyzed assumptions about the work, about the people, about the church or Christianity. Never be afraid to ask questions about the work we have inherited or the work we are doing. There is no question that should not be asked or that is outlawed. The day we are completely satisfied with what we have been doing; the day we have found the perfect, unchangeable system of work, the perfect answer, never in need of being corrected again, on that day we will know that we are wrong, that we have made the greatest mistake of all.[2]

Life holds out to us many opportunities to offer ourselves as the willing instruments of God's love. Despite the fact that there are mistakes in the past, the gift of today is always new, and grace awaits us at the threshold of every beginning. The abundance of God's wisdom and power are there for us unconditionally – so now let's get down to the practicalities!

NOTES

1. Taken from the foreword to John Lloyd and John Mitchinson, *The Book of General Ignorance*, London: Faber and Faber, 2006, p. xvii.

2. Vincent Donovan, *Christianity Rediscovered*, New York: Orbis Books, 1993.

Introduction:
Big Challenges

In his poem, 'Easter 1916', W.B. Yeats uses a phrase repeatedly that perfectly sums up many people's attitude toward the way we now live. He describes the changes taking place in Ireland around the time of the Irish war of independence, and notes:

All changed, changed utterly,
A terrible beauty is born.

These words have powerful resonance for the average Christian congregation in search of a wise response to the modern world. It seems that all around us our communities have been changing and we don't quite know what to do. The way people live, the way they talk, what they do with their time, how they bring up their children, the way they think about the church, the government, the world, everything seems to be different. Not only do many of us not know what to do, we are also not quite sure of how we feel about it! Like novice sailors in a very small boat hit by a very large storm, we feel the force of the saying, 'all at sea'.

The Struggling Congregation

Anxiety aroused in us by the prospect of so much change, coupled with our sense that we are not equipped to make an adequate response, has us running for cover – seeking refuge in the security of what is familiar to us.

Sometimes as a guest preacher addressing the need for the local church to engage with the local community, I find myself the focus of this anxiety. I remember one particular church where a member of the congregation felt agitated enough to remonstrate with me at the end of the service. The community, he said, knew exactly where to find the church. If they needed our help, they should ask. His partian shot[1] to me was clear: that the church had been here for over two hundred years and hadn't changed, and they were not about to start now!

The only problem with that approach was that the church had also been in decline for thirty-five years, and the townspeople were not coming. Clearly the church was stuck, and their neighbours weren't interested in what went on behind the walls of the church building; and (if everyone in the congregation shared the view of the man who spoke with me) the congregation was not particularly concerned with what went on in the lives of their neighbours. Somehow a gulf had opened up between the local congregation and the local community, and no one really knew what to do about it. The congregation was keeping afloat, and seeing changing times as the waves crashing in on them. But what if there were people in the community that were drowning? What then?

Local Congregations

My experience of local churches is that while most struggle in connecting with their community, they do not all share the negative or defensive attitude of the example I have just given. Most people want to connect and make a difference, they just do not know how to begin. For every one antagonist I have met when I have preached or taught on the challenges facing the local church, I have had fifty people who have been keen to grapple with the hard questions of how to respond to what is happening all around them. Intriguingly, many local churches, feeling ashamed and inadequate, assume that they must be far worse than most other congregations in their inability to take on the big issues. That is just not true! Somehow local churches have been duped into thinking that everyone else's congregation is doing better than theirs. Maybe this is because of pride, maybe it has something to do with church leaders exaggerating their own 'success' or playing down their struggles, but I think it is for a different reason.

Most local churches and individual Christians are

desperate to make a difference in the lives of those around them. Most Christians feel keenly the calling of Christ on their lives, but for many of us, our personal struggles already fill up most of our time. The magnitude of the social tasks that we face are daunting. We hear stories of rehabilitation of drug addicts or work with prisoners or reconciliation agencies, and the prospect of what might be required of us is overwhelming. How could we possibly find the time or energy or passion to do such things? We have somehow lost sight of the call, modelled by people like Mother Teresa, to do small things with great love. Our reticence is an indication of our confusion and embarrassment rather than our pride and selfishness. What I am certain of, though, is that the myth that 'most churches in the UK are doing better than ours' needs to be exploded. Local congregations the length and breadth of the UK are getting to grips with the same issues.

There are almost 50,000 local Christian congregations in the United Kingdom, and the average size of those congregations is 47. Over the last three years, as I have preached across the United Kingdom and beyond, one of the questions that I have been asked most frequently is 'What can we do to connect with the people around here? How do we reach them?' Local congregations and local church leaders are desperate to connect with their communities. In the United States, the average size of a local church is just over 50 – and congregations there face the same questions. I have recently been in email conversation with a church in the Chicago area, and the pastor said this:

> Everything around us seems to be in crisis. Young people are dropping out of high school, people are hungry, healthcare is too expensive and we don't know what to do. How can my little congregation make a difference in the face of these waves of despair? I feel like this boat is sinking, and I don't know what to do.

I lead a local congregation. It is nestled between a number of villages on the border between Hampshire and Berkshire. Along with the 60 or 70 people who attend the church, I am grappling with the same issues as thousands of other local church leaders:

- What are the big issues facing my community?
- What way do people in my community think?
- How can we 'be Jesus' to the people around us?
- What can I do to equip the people in my congregation to live for God?
- What on earth is the local church here for?

These are essential questions to answer if the local congregation I am part of is to be an effective witness to Christ in the world. They are infinitely more important than other issues that so often take the time of local church leaders, such as how many communion cups we should have, whether we should paint our youth hall this year or next year and how to make sure we increase the giving in the church offerings. Often a lack of leaders and workers make these challenges worse, and those called to lead the congregation end up being forced to make decisions that the local body of believers should be releasing others to address.

There are also some very valid issues that take up the time and energy of both church members and leaders. A church leader's time is swallowed up with regular pastoral visiting of the elderly and long-term sick, or the ongoing and important demands of executive, administrative, staff or ecumenical meetings. She must commit to preparation, planning and paperwork or putting in an appearance at functions and events on behalf of the church. Whilst all of these are worthwhile, they also consume vast amounts of time for church leaders. Local churches and their leaders are faced with difficult questions and tough decisions to sacrifice or delegate a certain amount of maintenance (ministry) in favour of progress. These are not trite and inconsequential questions. How can a local church release its leaders to do the work of reaching out and loving others whilst at the same time demanding that leaders give all of their time to the current members of the church? Local congregations *will not and cannot* be effective witnesses for Christ until they begin to grapple with the challenges they are facing in their communities, and in wider society, and within their own priorities.

Individual Christians

What is true for local congregations is also true for us as individual Christians. Where we live and where we work we find people who think in a particular way and whose lives are shaped by certain assumptions. We are often very ignorant of the underlying presuppositions that have shaped the attitudes of our friends or colleagues. We must try to get to grips with the thinking that has molded their lives if we want our communication with them to be credible and helpful. Let me give you a simple example.

I often commute to London from my home. The whole journey takes about an hour and forty minutes each way, and I make the journey two or three times a week. The rest of the time I am travelling around the country or beyond or involved in local church issues. However, I only started commuting in this way around three and a half years ago. Before then, I had a huge expectation of people who were involved in the local congregation. I would accept that some folk were not involved in midweek church activities as much as I would like, but my acceptance was always a little shallow and tinged with scepticism. Deep down I thought they just needed to be more committed and motivate themselves a little more.

My prejudice and assumption was based on total ignorance of the fatigue caused by lengthy daily commutes. Had I understood just how debilitating it is after a long day at work to make a lengthy journey home on a packed train, standing with fellow commuters' elbows in your back, tired and irritated by their mobile phone calls, the way I viewed and treated others would have been much more gracious. Thankfully, I now understand the challenges of commuting and have resolved to be less demanding of others.

Now apply that same principle to your own relationships. Do you know the way your neighbours think? Do you know what experiences determine their morality or their view of the world? Do you bear in mind that the people you sit with on the train or in the office have probably only ever been to a church meeting a couple of times in their lives? Their 'frame of reference' is not just a little different to yours, it is another world entirely.

Mapping the Challenges

In the next few chapters I want to begin to look at the landscape of change that local churches are facing, and begin to consider our options in responding to so much change. I also want to ask how this might challenge us as individuals and take into account the personal transformation that must be part of the journey.

Winston Churchill once described the Soviet Union as 'a riddle wrapped in a mystery inside an enigma'. For many of us, the same is true of our society and all that makes it tick. Let's try and unwrap some of that mystery together.

NOTES

1. We often use the phrase 'parting shot' but actually the phrase should be 'Partian shot'. It comes from a particular military trick of the Partians, who were crack archers and fought on horseback. What they used to do was ride away fast, firing their arrows back over their shoulders.

1

Changing Thinking

What is truth? (John 18:38)

I am ... the truth. (John 14:6)

The worst creature in the world to ask about the temperature in a goldfish bowl is a goldfish! When it comes to trying to think about the big ideas that shape our communities and our culture, it is very difficult for those of us who are part of the culture to understand it objectively. Immersion makes comparison impossible. A white child in apartheid South Africa, devoid of the perspective of a black child, would have been incapable of understanding the evil system that offered the white child privilege at the expense of the black child. Understanding the underlying values of our community and culture does not happen by accident. It must be an intentional choice. If we are to engage coherently with our communities or with our colleagues, then we must make a choice to learn how they (and we!) think.

A good example of such short-sightedness is evident in the eighteenth- and nineteenth-century campaign against the slave trade. In the last quarter of the eighteenth century, the Christian churches of the United Kingdom rang out their bells in celebration of the fact that the early attempts to abolish the transatlantic slave trade had failed. These eighteenth-century Christians held to the conviction that slavery was upheld and endorsed in the Christian New Testament and saw the attempts to abolish slavery as sinful and wrong. Yet in 1807, when the transatlantic slave trade was abolished, most (not all) Christians in the UK saw it as a defeat of the powers of darkness. Why did such a shift take place in the intervening years? Well, largely because a group of ardent campaigners set out to *change the minds* of Christians in the last part of the eighteenth century, and went on to change the mindset of a whole culture. We are all children of our surroundings. We are fashioned by the fabric of our lives. The culture in which we live shapes how we think and the way in which we consequently live.

As an Irishman who has spent 22 years *not* living in Northern Ireland, I think I am beginning to understand this principle of being shaped by the culture in which you are nurtured. It is only since *leaving* Northern Ireland that I have become increasingly aware of the way in which that unique culture had shaped me and my view of other people. This is true not just in terms of religious persuasion,[1] but also in terms of the way I view other countries (such as England), sport (because I went to a rugby-playing school I still think football is second-rate) and music (Irish and Celtic music are so clearly the best forms of musical expression in the world that I wonder why anyone could think anything else!). In the same way that I am shaped by my culture, we all are. And at the heart of our culture lies the way we *think* about the world and our place in it.

Understanding Our Culture

If we are ever to have any hope of understanding how we can live out and speak out the good news of Jesus Christ effectively as individuals or as local congregations, then we must accept the daunting task of understanding our cultural context. Buddhists have a specialist term for this – they call it 'leaving home'. In Buddhism there is an understanding that a necessary step in growing up is to 'leave home' – to gain a clearer self-understanding and more balanced wisdom by stepping out of the culture that nurtured us. We too must learn to 'leave home'. If we fail to do this, it is like speaking Gaelic to someone who has never heard a word of that language before in their lives – we will generate some quizzical looks, but not get very far in our relationship.

The difficulty for Christians in understanding our place in the world is the fact that we have misunderstood what it means to be 'in the world but not of it'.

Many churches have taught that our communities and the wider world are to be mistrusted. The reality is that 'being in the world but not of it' means learning to do what the Buddhists call 'leaving home'. We are called to live in our culture, but to live in such a way that we demonstrate God's kingdom in our communities without losing our distinctive identity. We have that sense of 'belonging and yet not belonging' to deal with in our society. We need to work out how we remain true to Christ and live as His followers, whilst also understanding that as part of the church we are also part of the warp and weft of our society. That can be a difficult thing to manage.

We also have the additional challenge of understanding the shifting culture of our wider society, so those of us who are Christians already have a series of cultures to deal with. We have the culture of our own upbringing. On top of that we have our religious culture, and the specific 'brand' of Christianity that we find ourselves in.[2] We can often be so enmeshed and caught in a Christian subculture that the task of understanding that subculture alone is very difficult. Further to our religious cultures, then, we face the challenge that society itself is changing, and is going through accelerated changes and seismic shifts. The result is we can often feel like we are on a waltzer at a funfair! The little car that holds us is spinning and making us dizzy, but at the same time the whole platform of little cars is spinning and we are just one of many.

Remaining True but Understanding Our Communities

Somehow we need to avoid looking at the world through the filter of the prevailing assumptions, about life and where happiness can be found. Instead we must seek to understand the world in which we live from a biblical and Christian perspective and allow that perspective to shape our view of the prevailing culture. We must try to understand the nature of the world in which we live as citizens, at the same time as understanding the nature of the subculture to which we belong as Christians. We then face the responsibility of comparing the subculture of our faith to the biblical picture of a faith community, so that we can identify what is essential to Christian lifestyle and witness, and separate that from what is merely our own preference. For example, are our priorities about church buildings biblical – or may our concerns about building maintenance be overriding our true priority of loving our neighbour?

These are deep challenges. They demand serious consideration and a high level of thought, concentration and focus. They can be overwhelming. It can feel too much for us to bear. However, it is possible to think these challenges through. Let me give you an example.

Debbie and I have four children. At times, it can feel like Widow Twanky's Laundry in our home. The washing machine is constantly on a cycle to keep up with the cleaning of very dirty clothes. A couple of years ago I was about to hang out the washing, and one of my children was helping me. She saw all the washing being pulled out of the machine and put into the washing basket. As I lifted the washing basket to take it to the line, she tugged on my arm and said, 'Daddy, those clothes won't be able to hang on the line. They are too heavy. The line will break.' I knelt down and explained to her that we were not going to put all the washing on the line in a big messed up clump. Instead I showed her what we would do. I pulled a pair of jeans from the tangled pile, shook them out, and pegged them to the line. She understood! The way to dry washing is to shake it out and peg it on the line, one item at a time.

The way to address the complex issues of understanding our culture is to take each element of the culture, shake it out, and peg it on the line of our study and understanding. We can't address all the issues at once, we need to look at them consecutively. So first of all, let's examine exactly what a 'culture' is.

What is a Culture?[3]

Some people describe culture as a mental framework that holds together the way we view our lives, the world and our place in the world. Another way of looking at culture is to think of it as a sphere or a bubble within which we live and breathe. Scientifically, a culture is something that is grown, or in which something is grown. Or perhaps we could view culture as a wall that is made up of lots of different bricks – such as language, morality, political expression, accepted behaviours and passed on habits, traditions and expectations. T.S. Eliot had a deep understanding of culture:

> Culture is the way of life of a particular people living together in one place.
>
> Culture is an integrated system of beliefs, of values and of institutions that binds a society together and gives it a sense of identity, dignity, security and continuity.
>
> Culture is the effort to provide a coherent set of answers to the existentialist situations that confront all human beings in the passage of their lives.[4]

My own preferred understanding of culture is the second of Eliot's definitions. I am helped in my own considerations of culture by understanding that culture is a shared way of thinking about life, the world and my place in it. When those thoughts are translated into actions and attitudes, they shape the way I treat other people, my environment and the community of which I am part. They also deeply shape the way I think about myself, my responsibilities and belongings.

For example, my name for sand that has been heated to a very high temperature then placed in a frame in a wall to allow light to pass through it and keep the cold out is a 'window', because I have been taught to think of it this way. Had I been brought up in France, I would have called the same object 'une fenêtre'. Of course in reality it is neither 'a window' nor 'une fenêtre'. Instead, these are the names that are given to that object in my culture (where English is the language of communication and thought) and other cultures (where French is the language of communication and thought). At the same time, the object we are referring to is *both* 'a window' and 'une fenêtre' because both cultures are absolutely right in their understanding of what that object is.

Language is only one part of a culture, but is a very important part – and it is a part that changes. So when we use the word 'authority' now, it is largely looked upon with some level of suspicion and scepticism. This is because the idea behind 'authority' has changed over the last thirty or forty years quite significantly. Many words have changed their meaning in our culture.[5]

I recently spoke at a large Christian conference, and to help people understand this part of culture and change I asked them to think of words that meant something different now from the meaning of those same words when the audience were younger. Here are some of the examples – I will leave you to work out the difference in their meanings yourself. If you are not sure what the words now mean, ask someone who is not yet twenty and knows how to use a mobile phone!

- bite/byte
- book[6]
- cell
- fit

- mobile
- powerpoint
- web
- wicked

Postmodern Culture [7]

We live in a postmodern culture. That does not mean that we have gone beyond modern inventions or modern techniques, though! Instead it means that our communities and the people that we work with, or live next to, are likely to think about things in a way that is different from modernist thinking. You could call post-modern culture, post-rational culture or post-factual culture. Let me try to briefly explain how we got to postmodern culture.

Upon What is Western Culture Based?

From around the time of the Roman emperor Constantine (the end of the third and the beginning of the fourth centuries AD) until around the middle of the seventeenth century, most Western culture assumed the concept of revelation. That is to say, most people believed that God was the source of all knowledge. For that reason, the Bible and the church were at the heart of society. People believed that the only way they could understand life, one another or the world was through God revealing the truth to them. For that reason, God was to be feared, priests and monks and 'professional clergy' were the best educated people and the Christian church had a very influential and important role to play in Western nations, governments and societies.

However, huddled against a stove in a Parisian basement, a Frenchman called René Descartes was trying to work out the meaning and purpose of life. He wanted to 'prove' that he was alive! As he thought about this, he realised that if he was doubting whether or not he existed, then he knew that he was thinking. Therefore, if he was thinking then he existed. He had proved to himself that he was alive. We remember that famous discovery in the Latin phrase 'cognito ergo sum' – I think, therefore I am.[8] Thus was born the Age of Reason. This is also called the Empirical Age, or the Age of the Enlightenment, although all of these terms basically refer to the same period of time. This period is also called modernity or modernism.

From the middle of the seventeenth century until the middle of the twentieth century, Western culture was a modernist culture. In short, if it could not be proved factually then it was inherently less important. This 'discovery' of reason led to wonderful advances for which the world should always be grateful.[9] The development of modern medicine, the advances in technology, the establishment of sanitation, healthcare and the great political, economic and social institutions of much of the Western world flowed from the modern period. This period was marked by its emphasis on the logical, the practical and the 'physically provable'. In the modern period what was important was that which was visible, measurable and quantifiable.

The Drawbacks of Modernism

It was not all good news, however. In the Western world's quest for the provable, and our assertion of the rights of individuals over the rights of communities, we developed a tendency towards inherently selfish citizens and inherently selfish communities. In this modernist culture, 'what I think' or 'what I want' or 'what I need' became far more important than 'what is right' or 'what is needed' or 'what is best'. That is because the idea that something could be inherently right was lost. It was only right if it could be proved empirically to be right.

> I think, therefore I am, we mutter to ourselves as we pursue our careers, our rights and our individual freedoms, whilst simultaneously watching the fabric of society gradually break down before the wave of superficiality, drug dependency, family fragmentation and loss of community which follows the tide of individualism.[10]

The result of all of this emphasis on proof was that individuals and communities, and therefore whole societies and nations, became focused on what they could prove. In the process, many societies also lost their sense of wonder and moral centre. In the words of Max Weber:

> Our reality has become 'dreary, flat and utilitarian, leaving a great void in the souls of men which they seek to fill by furious activity and through various devices and substitutes'.[11]

It was in reaction to this sense of 'flatness' and 'emptiness' that postmodernity emerged. It is postmodernity that is the most present and powerful influence in your community, in your workplace and in your society if you live in the Western world.

The Reaction – the Birth of Postmodernity[12]

What is postmodernism? It is the rebellion against modernity with all of its assurances and emphasis on the physical, the here and the now. Postmodernity recognises that life cannot be simplified into its component parts. Instead, it celebrates the complexity of life and the fact that you cannot simply describe life, communities or society in terms of the physical, the here and now. Postmodernity recognises that there are imponderable aspects to life, that there is more to the world than the here and now and that no one has all the answers. It injects a lost sense of wonder and searching into the world and opens up the possibility of something other than that which we can see, or hear or touch. In fact, if the motto of the modern period was 'I think, therefore I am', then the motto of the postmodern period would probably be something like 'I experience, therefore I am', or, 'I encounter, therefore I am'.

It is hard to overemphasise the result of this evolution of thinking, but is important to try to understand at least a few of the consequences of living in a postmodern culture. Let me mention just three – consumption, image and journey.

What's in It for Me?

In this culture, consumption replaces production. More important than how we make things, or the need to make things for other people, is the need to consume. Hence we talk about a consumer society. Everything is consumable in postmodern culture – and everything is instant. From coffee to the internet, from instant potatoes to instant therapy, if we want it, we just have to have it.

And consumption goes beyond what we eat or drink. We consume energy at a higher rate than ever before. We go through relationships more quickly than ever before. We live in one place for shorter periods than ever before. We no longer think of jobs as lifelong commitments. We demand more technology, more gadgets, more choice, more food, more money, more leisure time, more travel. In fact we want more of everything than we ever did before.

However, it is also good to remember that consumerism also has benefits. Clothes, food and other products are relatively cheaper now than they were twenty years ago – precisely because of the power of the market. Not all consumerism is bad. As well as that, modern technology has given rise to events like Band Aid and Comic Relief – it isn't all selfishness. A good example of turning modern consumerism to positive altruistic promotion of community wellbeing is the website Freecycle that encourages the sharing of unwanted possessions at no charge with others who need just what we want to get rid of! Having benefited from this personally, it is a wonderful example of post-modernity working positively.

Bernard Levin once commented that individuals in the West had become so self-obsessed that no matter how much television, sex, drugs and alcohol they pushed into their lives they could not satisfy the hunger for more, and that they felt the search and yearning for meaning and purpose. 'What's in it for me' is the mantra of the postmodern generation.

Some time ago I was travelling to Ireland on a plane to meet with some church leaders. On the plane, I sat next to a man who came from the same part of County Antrim as I did. As we chatted he asked me what I did, and why I was going to Northern Ireland. I explained I was trying to help churches work together for their communities and that I was looking forward to a challenging few days. He then asked me what made me do what I do. As I explained my calling and my convictions to him, he became increasingly incredulous. At last, exasperated, he interrupted me and asked, 'Yeah, but what's in it for you?' I answered that I had a sense of accomplishment and that I knew that I could help in the situation I was going to address. I explained that it was worth all the effort to see communities changed and churches working together. He gave a friendly, if slightly patronising laugh and said, 'I wouldn't waste my time if I were you. The only people you should be worrying about are you and yours. I have a simple rule I live by,' he continued, 'I'm number one. I'll do what I want, when I want to. Nobody else is going to look after me, so I'm damned if I'll look after anyone else.'

What's It Look Like?

Image replaces word in postmodernity. This is true of how we view ourselves and of how we absorb data and information. The average concentration span of a child under ten is now no more than about twenty or thirty seconds. Education is through image rather than words, and reading is replaced by image surfing. Ideas are far more likely to be remembered if they are presented visually than if they are presented verbally, and self expression and self image have become the heartbeat of most people. People want their information delivered in sound bites and mini-statements. They no longer want long programmes, they want short ones. The *Guardian*, *The Times* and the *Independent* in the United Kingdom publish 'at a glance' summaries of their newspapers' contents. Headlines are more important than content and image is more important than substance.

Ideas are conveyed differently in postmodernity. Gone are lengthy tomes, long-winded lectures and detailed explanations. Postmodernity is the age of speed dating, speed learning and speed education.

I recently talked with a friend of mine about her work with a charity in the north of England. She is helping young girls who have dropped out of school and are unemployed. She told me that as part of the programme the charity delivers, they are teaching a group of young girls information technology skills. Each lesson can be no more than five minutes long, and *must* contain as many symbols and pictures as words, otherwise the girls lose interest and do not learn.

It's not the Destination, but the Journey That Matters

Lastly, postmodernity emphasises the journey over the destination. It does not matter where you are going in postmodernity, it just matters that you are going somewhere. This presents particular challenges to local churches when it comes to issues such as discipleship, spirituality and obedience. The very idea of obedience sits very uncomfortably in postmodernity. Encounter is far more important than truth. The process of discovery is more important than what you find. Hence 'spirituality' is very popular in postmodern culture, but the idea of 'religion' with its connotations of boundaries, authority, absolute requirement and obedience sits less happily with the prevailing consciousness shaping our choices.

What are the Key Principles of Postmodernity?[13]

It is important to understand why journey is more important than destination, why image is more important than words and why consumption is more important than production. It is as we understand why these things are as they are that we will be able to consider how to engage with our communities and with those around us. A book of this size does not permit a full investigation into each of the principles that I will outline, but I do want to comment on each one briefly so that we can begin to understand how we might address the wider issues associated with postmodernity

1. Self is Rejected as the Centre

Postmodern communities recognise that the answers to life's great challenges and problems do not lie within the grasp of human beings as individuals. They are summed up in the famous saying of the American programme, *The X Files*, 'the truth is out there' – somewhere. In other words, by ourselves we are not able to answer the big questions of life. Western culture is increasingly experimenting with eastern mystic techniques for meditation, reflection and centring, because individuals know they do not have all the answers to life within themselves.

2. Reason and Logic are Not Enough

This is a self-explanatory aspect of postmodernity. Being able to 'prove' something empirically is not enough. Postmodern people point to the fact that you cannot prove love between two people empirically. You cannot explain why some people like Bach and some like the Beach Boys! There are some things that are not explainable logically, and there are things that do not fit within a rationalistic worldview. There has been a huge increase in the number of programmes investigating the 'supernatural' and 'paranormal' compared with thirty or forty years ago, because our culture is now much more open to 'spiritual' or 'non-rational' explanations and phenomena.

3. The Enlightenment is Rejected

The idea that humankind is on a trajectory to perfection is now abandoned by the West. This is a marked change from the beginning of the twentieth century. At that time, there was real hope and optimism that in a hundred years the world would be free of war, hunger, poverty and most disease. As that century unrolled, bringing genocide, new epidemics, increased political tensions, development of massive armaments and fragmentation in many areas of the globe, the western world has seen its dream of a dawning Utopia crumble. We have moved from talking about the bright, shared future of humanity to a frantic discussion about how to save ourselves from absolute destruction because of our abuse of the environment.

4. There is No Objective 'World'

A key principle for postmodernity is that there is no such thing as objectivity. There is only what we experience, what we think and what we feel. Nothing else matters.

5. There is No Metanarrative

Postmodernity rejects the idea that there is any kind of 'big story'. Instead life is a series of incidences and coincidences. Nothing more, nothing less. There is no need to believe that history is linear – that is that it has a beginning and an end. It is just a forest of experiences and encounters. We don't need to make sense of the world, because the world doesn't make sense anyway – at least not in an objective way.

6. Science is Not the Full Answer

Postmodernity asserts that science cannot explain everything – indeed science itself is based on assumptions and 'faith' statements. Science cannot explain metaphysics, or the connection between two people, or the wonder of a sunset. Science cannot explain the recurrent patterns of life in its myriad forms. Science cannot explain the sense of community or purpose that many people yearn to experience.

7. The Physical World is Not Enough

Put simply, there is more to life than what we see, feel and touch.

8. Authority is To Be Suspected

Authority is dangerous and not to be trusted. Whether that authority is seen in a government, a home, a church or a workplace, authority cramps the style of postmodern people. We do not like to be told what to do, or how to do it.

9. Life is a Journey

Life is not simply an accident but is not necessarily meaningful beyond death. For most postmodern people, life is an opportunity to enjoy and experience the senses and emotions. It does not have a centred moral purpose, and its main decisions are to be based on what results in best experience or opportunity for us as individuals.

10. Truth is Relative

Lastly, there is no such thing as absolute truth. Nothing is absolutely and unequivocally right (except of course the rule that nothing is right!). All truth is relative, all truth is subjective, and all ranking of truth and morality is by personal or communal choice. Consider these words from Nietzsche, a father (or perhaps grandfather) of postmodernity, as an example of how truth is viewed:

> What then is truth? A mobile army of metaphors, metonyms and anthropomorphisms – in short a sum of human relations, which have been enhanced, transposed and embellished poetically and rhetorically and, which after long use seem firm, canonical and obligatory to a people; truths are illusions about which one has forgotten that this is what they are;

metaphors which are worn out and without sensu-
ous power; coins which have lost their pictures and
now matter only as metal, no longer as coins.[14]

How Does the Church Respond?

Faced with all of these challenges, how might Christians
respond to the challenges of postmodernism? The people in our local communities may not realise how much
their thinking has been formed by postmodernism, so
encountering their worldview without being patronising toward them is very important. If we have a handle
on why the community and society around us behaves
as it does, though, at least we can begin to frame our
responses intelligently and holistically.

It is unlikely that we will have people saying to us,
'Oh I'm not interested in God because I am a postmodernist', but we may well face statements that indicate
some of the principles I have outlined above. At the
very least, we can understand the worldview from
which they flow.

I came across a clear example of postmodern thinking while I was with a group from a church in the
Midlands of England. We had gone away for a weekend
together to explore the purpose and meaning of
Christian community. During the weekend, a member
of the group asked to speak with me. She made it clear
that whilst she knew she was a Christian, she did not
want to talk about being 'converted' as it sounded far
too definite for her – far too final when she was still

being changed. She wasn't happy sounding so perfect! I still remember one of the questions she asked me – How can I talk to other people about my faith without sounding as if I am always right and they are always wrong? As I listened to her, I realised that she was very postmodern in her thinking and attitude. So instead of quoting Bible verses and texts 'at' her, I talked about the truth of coming to Christ with her, in terms of phrases and ideas and images that Jesus had used – such as seeds, plants and journeys. We explored the significance of public confession of Christ through the image of baptism, and I explained that if she talked to other people about her journey rather than her conversion, it might help. It was as if I had switched a light on in her mind, and she went away very excited that she had discovered new tools for her own relationship with God and relating it to other people.

It is simple things such as these that will help us as local congregations or as individuals to begin to think about how we approach the challenge of postmodernity, but there are other things that we must discover too, which might be less comfortable for some of us, particularly those of us from an evangelical tradition.

Changing Our Attitudes

Much of the thinking of the Western church is modernist in character. Our presentation of the gospel is often didactic and cerebral, and our exploration of truth relies more on apologetics than intuition. This diminishes our Christian experience to a very 'left-brain' approach. Immersion in biblical teaching can lead us to a richer and fuller experience, but first we must recognise our limitations – in our preaching, our pastoral care and our style of leadership.

Preaching

If local churches are to engage with their communities more effectively, and if we are to be equipped as individuals to share our faith through words more wisely, then we must deal with the issue of preaching and how we do it. Most churches in the protestant tradition, and particularly those within the evangelical traditions, have adopted an approach to preaching and teaching which has far more to do with enlightenment and Greek philosophy than Hebrew and early Christian spirituality and community. This is not to suggest that good, strong, clear teaching and preaching should not continue, but we must learn to address our audience with more humility and less cerebral and intellectual assertion.

There is no biblical reason for forty-minute sermons, or hour-long Bible studies. They may well have their place as people mature and grow, but if we are to reach and nurture those for whom ten or fifteen minutes is a long time to concentrate, then we must learn to articulate and present truth differently. That does not mean that we change what we believe, but reminds us to present the truth in a way that is accessible, intelligible and authentic for those around us. Preachers and teachers must learn to use imagery, pictures, metaphors, parables and simple stories as the basis of our communication.

For example, Hull Community Church is committed to teaching and preaching as a dialogue. In keeping with the New Testament, they allow people to ask questions and discuss what they have heard. This form of interaction and inductive teaching may be a death knell to the age of the celebrity-driven preaching and teaching culture that has developed over the last two hundred years, but it does connect with those people who are searching and yearning.

At church.co.uk in Waterloo, London, the ministry team leader Dave Steell regularly uses dialogue and small group techniques in their gatherings to help people think through and come into contact with the truth.

As well as that, we must learn the art of being less dictatorial and proscriptive. Often we have presented teaching and preaching in a way that has elevated the preacher or the teacher, treating the listener as a merely passive recipient. Sensitive crafting of our liturgy can create a context for preaching to move beyond a one-way transmission of ideas, beyond even a dialogue between teacher and disciple, to become a beautiful three-way communication between leader, congregation and the living, moving, sanctifying Spirit of God. When we say, as we open our worship:

'The Lord is here.'
'His Spirit is with us.'

The speaker is also listening, to both the congregation and to the Spirit of God. The congregation is listening to the speaker and the Spirit of God. And God is listening to the speaker and the congregation. This three-way approach to preaching and teaching, and the use of a simple confession, ground the words away from the speaker's own intellect, into the work of God in His Spirit-presence.

This approach draws us away from the over-intellectualising of teaching and preaching and helps to connect with postmodern people on every level – emotionally, intellectually, culturally and socially. The words of the aged apostle John offer a reminder of how we should and can encounter the truth.

> That which was from the beginning, which we have heard, which we have seen with our eyes, which we have looked at and our hands have touched – this we proclaim concerning the Word of life. The life appeared; we have seen it and testify to it, and we proclaim to you the eternal life, which was with the Father and has appeared to us. We proclaim to you what we have seen and heard, so that you also may have fellowship with us. And our fellowship is with the Father and with his Son, Jesus Christ. We write this to make our joy complete.   (1 John 1:1–4)

Preaching and teaching that does not connect the heart, head and hand is not biblical preaching. Local congregations have endured philosophy lectures and personality-driven speakers long enough! A postmodern community will never be reached by pure emotionalism or by pure intellectualism.[15] Those outside of the Christian 'bubble' quickly see through the façade of preachers and teachers who fail to connect with everyday life. Genuine hermeneutics and exegesis call for humility of heart and a determination to be part of the communities in which we minister. It is only as preachers are connected to the story of their communities that they are able to grapple with the challenge of connecting the community to God's big story of life and hope. Good preaching has always been about good storytelling, not just the dissemination of facts or ideas.

Preaching as dialogue and encounter is a vital element of reaching the people of a postmodern culture. Whether we do that in a café style (like Revive in Leeds), or by living in community (like The Simple Way in Philadelphia) is not the issue, but we must find imaginative ways of inviting people into dialogue with the gospel. Our communities have never reacted well to being patronised or shouted at.

Not only that, but an interactive and inductive approach to preaching and teaching mirrors the way in which most people now learn academically outside of the church. One such approach is problem-based learning, which enables those participating to research a given problem, explore an appropriate response, discuss that response with others and utilise critical thinking and analysis. Such an approach is normally facilitated by a faculty member and practitioner, and leads to much more secure and grounded learning and changed behaviour.

Pastoring

The craft and art of the pastor has never been more needed or more relevant. A pastor is not someone who tells others how to live, but instead is a mentor, a guide, a support, a physical expression of the beautiful work of the Holy Spirit. Pastoring is not simply crisis intervention, although it involves that. Pastors are shepherds. They love and nurture and protect and walk with the flock. They shield those who are entrusted to them. They put people above programmes and are committed to the long-term development of relationships. They do not see themselves as better than others, but instead share from their own lives and weaknesses.

We have already identified that postmodern people want to think in terms of journey, rather than destination. The pastor as a spiritual mentor, support and guide acts as an aide-mémoire for the person who is journeying. This is not a new technique, but an old technique rediscovered. There is a deep and urgent need for pastors who see themselves as servants of the flock, who recognise that their calling is to be strong, but gentle. In the little church of which I am a part I have been overwhelmed by the way in which people have responded to pastoring. A conversation over a coffee can achieve more than a year of sermons. The people of the congregation and the community do not need me to tell them where their lives are going wrong. Most of them know that already. Instead they appreciate an opportunity to talk through their life situations, and with the occasional nudge and some one-to-one conversation, they are able to discover the truth and beauty of God's purposes for their own lives.

This does not mean, of course, that challenge is off-limits! Far from it, but challenge springs from relationships of trust and love and commitment, and such relationships are not built by Sunday preaching alone. They are built over time, through commitment and with a mutual understanding of the deep issues of respect, integrity and love.

As I reflect on my own Christian journey, I am not sure how often I have had a pastor. I have had leaders, teachers and preachers – many very good ones, but I am not sure I have had a pastor – someone who would commit to me not just for what I could do for the local congregation, but for who I was. Someone who saw past the mistakes and errors and bad decisions and still maintained their commitment to walk with me. This is the pastor that postmodern people need. I have seen such characteristics in the vicar of the Anglican church I attended prior to becoming part of the congregation I now lead. The leaders of the church I now lead have shown a deeply pastoral heart toward my family and me and the impact has been dramatic – deeply humbling and moving and very releasing.

Postmodern culture also needs a local church that has rediscovered the depth and beauty of the parish system. The idea that a local church exists for the spiritual and physical well-being of every living soul in the parish is a beautiful expression of God's grace, goodness and compassion. Too many local churches have erected walls of division and exist only for those who regularly attend meetings in the building, but pastoring in postmodern culture destroys that division and pulls down that wall of separation. Local congregations which welcome, love and accept those around them unconditionally will have a deep and lasting impact on the lives of those in their community. To adapt a phrase, *a pastor is for life, not just for Sundays.*

The book of Ezekiel has a whole chapter about God's vision and standards for the pastoring of the people of His flock. In this chapter His painstaking tenderness and vigilant care are contrasted with the scathing indictment of those who call themselves shepherds but in reality neglect and exploit the flock. Because of God's unconditional love, we have a responsibility in turn to care for one another:

The word of the Lord came to me: 'Son of man, prophesy against the shepherds of Israel; prophesy and say to them: "This is what the Sovereign Lord says: Woe to the shepherds of Israel who only take care of themselves! Should not shepherds take care of the flock? You eat the curds, clothe yourselves with the wool and slaughter the choice animals, but you do not take care of the flock. You have not strengthened the weak or healed the sick or bound up the injured. You have not brought back the strays or searched for the lost. You have ruled them harshly and brutally. So they were scattered because there was no shepherd and when they were scattered they became food for all the wild animals. My sheep wandered over all the mountains and on every high hill. They were scattered over the whole earth and no-one searched or looked for them...

For this is what the Sovereign Lord says: I myself will search for my sheep and look after them. As a shepherd looks after his scattered flock when he is with them, so will I look after my sheep. I will rescue them from all the places where they were scattered on a day of clouds and darkness. I will bring them out from the nations and gather them from the countries, and I will bring them into their own land. I will pasture them on the mountains of Israel, in the ravines and in all the settlements in the land. I will tend them in a good pasture, and the mountain heights of Israel will be their grazing land. There they will lie down in good grazing land, and there they will feed in a rich pasture on the mountains of Israel. I myself will tend my sheep and make them lie down, declares the Sovereign Lord. I will search for the lost and bring back the strays. I will bind up the injured and strengthen the weak, but the sleek and the strong I will destroy. I will shepherd the flock with justice.   (Ezekiel 34:1–6, 11–16)

Leadership

Leadership in a postmodern context might be a bit like packaging clouds. It is no mean feat to lead those who struggle with authority and do not like ideas such as obedience or structure. Yet, once again, a return to a biblical understanding of leadership provides a way for local congregations and individuals to lead others well and effectively. Though a biblical model of leadership incorporates an accepting of authority and personal discipline, it does not imply a relapse into modernist patterns of thought.

One of the best denominational practitioners of this approach in the United Kingdom is the New Frontiers network (although I strongly disagree with their stance on excluding women from eldership) whose local congregations are led by teams of elders with one elder operating as a *primus inter pares*, a first among equals. This model, very similar to the principle of eldership adopted by Presbyterian churches, enables collective decision-making and encourages wider consultation.

The development of leadership teams and wider congregational consultation takes seriously the inherent wariness of postmodern people in connection with authority and hierarchy. In demonstrating a higher level of accountability it ensures that congregations avoid becoming the vehicles through which an individual leader operates a personal agenda. Local congregations have sometimes become merely grist to the mill of strong and demanding leaders, who have expressed their ministry of leadership more as an autocracy than Christian care of others. Such tight and non-consultative models of leadership may sometimes enable swifter growth, but they act by an appeal to people's insecurities, undermine the priesthood of all believers, are incredibly short-term in their view and therefore create models of congregational life that are deeply unsustainable, running the risk of facilitating as swift a demise as growth.

Most autocratic leaders of local congregations love God with all of their hearts and have chosen their particular style of leadership because it is either the only one that they themselves have experienced or they view it as the most pragmatic approach to leading a local church. However, pragmatism is not always the best tool in decision-making. For local congregations to reach into their postmodern communities requires a style of leadership which is open, accountable, consultative and honest.

So preaching, pastoring and leadership are three key areas of the life of a local congregation where we need to shift our thinking if we are to engage with postmodern communities. In each area we are offering commitment and applying principles that spring from real understanding of the people with whom we wish to engage. Those principles shape and mold the way in which we live out our faith before those around us. They are true for us as individuals as much as they are true for us as members or leaders of local congregations. Let me give you an example.

Caring – the Jesus Way

Jonathan is a doctor, a general practitioner (for non-British readers, this is a doctor who specialises in general community medicine, and as such is on the front line of healthcare). He lives on the border between Wales and England and some years ago he began to feel a sense of longing to be part of a working team that demonstrated his faith more authentically to the people around him. He was becoming increasingly alarmed at the way in which general practice was moving, but knew that his calling to be a doctor was at the heart of his life and ministry for God. He knew that the surgery where he had worked was not a place of welcome and that there was a very strong sense of 'them and us' separating the doctors, the staff and the patients. The doctors were viewed with a level of suspicion because of the way in which the surgery operated – hierarchy was important, titles were particularly emphasised and things were done 'to' patients rather than treatments and therapies being discussed and consulted upon. Perhaps most importantly, Jonathan felt that such an approach to medical care was not only failing to connect with patients, it was also running against the grain of his own Christian ethos and values. So he decided to set up a new practice.

With a couple of partners (not all of whom were Christians but all of whom agreed upon the approach to patients and their care), Jonathan began to care for patients as equals. The surgery uses a system of bookings that is less cumbersome (although still very busy). Patients call doctors and nurses by their first names if they want to, and the relationship between the doctors and their patients is treated as central in the health and well-being of all those who come to see the G.P. Language is deliberately straightforward, patients are given time to ask questions about diagnosis and any treatments or therapies are discussed.

The results have been amazing. The surgery is one of the busiest in the area, and feedback and evaluation of the service they provide is consistently well above average. Not only that, but therapies and treatments themselves seem to have better effect, with faster recovery rates reported amongst patients. Some of Jonathan's commitments in his practice were as follows:

- I will treat my patients as equals and will ensure that I use language and explanations which they understand.
- I will be committed to developing a strong and trusting relationship with my patients.
- I will consult with patients about their treatment and therapy and ensure they are empowered in their own care.

Changing Our Understanding as We Engage with Postmodernity

On reflection, these commitments sound remarkably like the principles I have been discussing when it comes to the attitude and approach of a local congregation. We should not be surprised. The principles that lead to more connected and effective preaching, pastoring and leadership also lead to us being more authentic doctors or teachers or managers or neighbours! That is because the same underlying principles should shape our whole worldview, not just how we gather or practise Christian community. So, what are some of the key changes that we need to make in our own understanding of our Christian faith and how do they relate to the key principles of postmodernity? Let me outline just four:

- using different images and metaphors
- our approach to the issue of truth
- celebrating human dignity
- our commitment to justice and righteousness.

Different Images and Metaphors

The predominant language and metaphors that many local churches (particularly those with a conservative or evangelical theology and mindset) have used for coming into relationship with God have been abrupt and dramatic. So conversion as a sudden and at times unexpected experience is presented as normative. We have picked up the strong metaphors and images of salvation used by the apostle Paul, particularly in the book of Romans. We use the language of the court room, the market place and the temple. Thus, we liken conversion to things like being reprieved from punishment for a crime that we have committed because someone else has taken the punishment for us; or we speak of being bought by God, with the price being the life and blood of Jesus; we understand our freedom to be based on the sacrifice of Jesus himself for us. Whilst all of these are strong and clear metaphors for salvation and our relationship with God, they by no means exhaust the treasury of images that we could use. In fact, some of the images may well have been more effective in a different generation, for whom the stark and masculine quality of the imagery was immensely helpful.

There is a number of other metaphors and images that we can use to describe both conversion to Christian faith itself and our personal or communal development in relationship with God. The New Testament also speaks of relationship with God as belonging to a family (Corinthians); a journey from darkness into light (Colossians); being an organic part of a vine (John 15); an invitation to a banquet or a meal (Luke 14 and Revelation 22); as an act of embrace and welcome and nurture (Luke 15); as restoration in paternal relationship (in the parable of the 'prodigal son') and of course adoption (Romans). All of these images and many more reach into the thinking and attitudes of postmodern culture in a way which grabs the attention and evokes response. They are no less biblical, they are no less clear than some of the images that we have traditionally used to relate Christian faith to others, but they are more appropriate to contemporary life and thought. We should not expect those who are not yet part of our household of faith to learn our language before they feel welcome and accepted. We must learn their language and find ways of relating to them ourselves.

The core message of incarnation is that God makes Himself accessible to relationship with others, open to being really and personally known. The perfect demonstration of this accommodation is the coming of the second person of the Holy Trinity in the person of Jesus Christ. But it is worth remembering that the New Testament itself was written in slang (known as Koine Greek) and that the collection of songs, poems and prayers that we call 'Psalms' was written in earthy Hebrew. We must use language, images and metaphors that relate to and connect with the people in our communities, not just vocabulary encoded by our own tradition. In so doing, we may be surprised ourselves by the new depth of encounter that we experience with God and with one another.

In this change, we can learn much from the wider Christian tradition – the Roman Catholics, the Coptics and the Celts. All of these traditions are used to employing the language of journey and discovery. They all teach us the art of 'belonging' and 'resting' before believing and they open up new possibilities for dialogue and encounter with others. Just take as one example the idea of 'pilgrimage' which is familiar in each of these traditions. An individual is invited to make a physical journey that mirrors or imitates a parallel or similar spiritual journey. There may be moments of complete revelation on the pilgrimage, or there may not, but the journey itself helps people to discover more of both themselves and of God.

Truth as a Person, Not Just an Idea

All the endeavour of preaching, teaching and leadership of the family of faith is directed towards promoting the gospel of Jesus, which offers us an entirely new understanding of what truth might really be. For in the New Testament, knowing truth is not about acquiescing to propositions or accumulating accurate data, much less about point-scoring or being more right than someone else. In the New Testament, truth comes to us as a living, breathing person – and His name is Jesus.

As Jesus was preparing to be crucified, He explained to His disciples that he would be leaving them. He wanted them to know that the events of His betrayal, beating and death were not sudden and unexpected for Him. He also wanted them to know that He would return and that they should not fear. Having spent three and half years with the disciples, He assumed they would understand some of this, so He said to them:

> You know the way to the place where I am going.
>
> (John 14:4)

Thomas, one of the disciples was confused, however, and replied:

> Lord, we don't know where you are going, so how can we know the way? (John 14:5)

Jesus replied using a phrase that has become one of the most astounding and startling statements of self-identification and purpose in history:

> I am the way and the truth and the life. No one comes to the Father except through me. (John 14:6)

Jesus did not claim to be part of truth, He said He is *the* truth! In all of our identification of and celebration of the personhood of truth, with all of the possibilities for relationship and organic growth that this gives us, we must never lose sight of the absoluteness of this claim – Jesus is the unique and complete revelation of truth to those who are seeking God. He is the fount of all truth. We should not underestimate the power of living out this reality or the challenge that it presents. Local churches must never become embarrassed about Jesus as the truth whilst at the same time inviting people to explore a relationship with truth as a person.

So often Christianity is presented as a closed box of ideas, assertions and assumptions. Many people leave the church because they feel that they are not enabled or taught to think! I spoke with one chap I am getting to know recently who is in exactly this position. Brought up in a firm and conservative evangelical and charismatic tradition, he began to struggle with some areas of belief and doctrine. He wonders whether there is another way to view creation other than the 'six-day' model. He wonders if there is more than one way of understanding the death and resurrection of Jesus and its effect on the world. He struggles with a very closed reading of the words of the Bible and does not believe every single word in it. As a result of these genuine questions, he spoke to a series of leaders in His church. Rather than being told that there were different views and opinions on these things, he was repeatedly presented with a 'you either believe this or you don't' attitude. The result is that after much searching and yearning for a place where he can express his questions and intellectual concerns honestly, he has left the gathered church, disillusioned and hurt. There are about 16 million people like him in the UK, men and women who have left the gathered church, but not abandoned Christ, because they have felt constricted, restrained or patronised. Rather than risk a loss of emotional, intellectual or moral integrity, they have quietly withdrawn from the gathered church.

For such people, for our postmodern society in general, and our communities and friends in particular, there is an urgent need for local churches and individual Christians to rediscover the wonder and beauty of knowing truth as a person.

Statements about Him are vital, and should be robust, intellectually credible and consistent, but we are liberated by the realisation that statements can never contain all the truth. We are not invited to assent to statements alone in Christian faith, we are invited into relationship with Truth. And that relationship grows, matures and develops with time. We can never claim to understand the whole truth, there is always something that we can learn, there is always a discussion to be had, a dialogue to enter into. This does not change the certainty of assertion that Christ is the full expression of deity and that He is the perfect representation of God to the world (Hebrews 1). Instead, we are invited into a lifelong exploration of Him as truth (Ephesians 1 and 3) which will grow and deepen with the years because we cannot ever fully understand or explain away the truth (Romans 11:33–36).

Perhaps this approach explains why small group exploration of Christian faith is a much more effective model of reaching people in the twenty-first century than large event-focused evangelism is. Small groups such as Alpha and Christianity Explored work best when they are led and facilitated in a conversational and interactive (rather than a confrontational and didactic) way.

However we do it, we must learn to facilitate an encounter with the truth, rather than just falling into the rather lazy and moralistic habit of 'telling people what the truth is'.

Rediscovering Human Dignity

Postmodern society inherently understands the equality of all people. This is not a new phenomenon, however, and we must learn again that the principle of human dignity is innate to the Jewish and Christian understanding of anthropology and personhood. Deeply embedded in Jewish and Christian thinking about humanity is the belief that all people are bearers of God's image (Genesis 1:26–27). This assertion has drastic consequences for the way we treat the people with whom we live, work, and share our neighbourhoods. They are not simply pew fodder. They are not created to be the objects of our latest evangelism techniques and they are not potential notches on our conversion belt. They are people who are equal in dignity to us, and whom we are called to treat with respect, dignity and love.

Local congregations and individual followers of Christ need to rediscover the principle and challenge of human dignity and allow it to shape the way we treat others. This has deep and far-reaching consequences for the way we live and express our faith. Without grasping this principle, everything else we might do is window-dressing. One of the real joys of leading the Faithworks movement is the opportunity that I have to witness the ways in which local congregations and churches across the world are reaching out and engaging with people in need. Again and again I am amazed at the depth of kindness that is expressed by local congregations to their communities, in wonderful and innovative ways.

Open Door in Tyneside is one example. This project is firmly based in City Church, Newcastle and is led by Julian Prior. It works with destitute asylum seekers in the city of Newcastle and provides them with housing, healthcare and a safe place. The team are working with those whom many in British society have either ignored or forgotten, and they are demonstrating the love and compassion of God in amazing ways. Their work is not only serving asylum seekers, but it is also challenging the wider community in Newcastle and the surrounding areas to think again about Christian faith and the ways in which Christians engage with and serve others. Their core commitment springs from a recognition of the human dignity of all people, including those that are maligned or marginalised by others in society.

Justice and Righteousness – Rediscovering Biblical Morality

In an increasingly secularised context, the church in the Western world has developed a more personalised and narrow view of morality over the last three hundred years. Our public statements on moral issues often focus upon sexual ethics and matters that are seen as purely private – abortion, homosexuality and divorce. Whilst these are undoubtedly important issues and it is important to stand for what we believe to be right in these areas, local churches simply must cut loose from the strait-jackets we have imposed upon ourselves if we are to have a more vital and transforming presence in our communities. To do that, we must return to an authentic and deeply rooted spirituality that grows out of biblical story as organically as grain grows from the earth. Only when we have this holistic and connected approach can we follow through to a harvest that will feed the souls of the people: a faithful biblical morality acknowledging and taking seriously the contexts of both the community that waits to be fed and the sacred story that nourished this living food.

At the heart of this morality lie the commitments that I have already articulated – to human dignity, to truth and to God's intervention in the world to save it. Somehow, we have allowed our morality to be constrained to personal behaviour and sexual ethics. A cursory glance at the Bible tells us that morality includes everything we are and everything we do, and it particularly includes the way we treat the marginalised and the excluded in our communities. The call to true fasting of Isaiah 58 must once again become one of the benchmarks of our local congregations and of our individual lives.

> Is not this the kind of fasting I have chosen: to loose the chains of injustice and untie the cords of the yoke, to set the oppressed free and break every yoke?
>
> Is it not to share your food with the hungry and to provide the poor wanderer with shelter – when you see the naked, to clothe him, and not to turn away from your own flesh and blood?
>
> (Isaiah 58:6,7)

Furthermore, this is not an isolated call for justice and righteousness. Rather, justice and righteousness are the hallmarks of authentic Christian expression. If we are ever to re-imagine the place of the local church in the context of a postmodern society, then we must ask the question: how can we become advocates of justice and righteousness in this community?

God calls us to live steeped in the integrity and beauty of holiness, informed and passionately engaged in our society – he does not condemn us to a life sentence of moral tunnel vision, standing on the edge of society, hurling criticisms. How we view taxation, housing, healthcare, education, foreign policy, our careers and our responsibility to our neighbours are all moral issues. As local churches and as individual followers of Jesus we have a moral responsibility to stand with not against the excluded, the vulnerable and the poor. A local congregation that is seeking to be kingdom-focused must grasp this key principle, and speak out on behalf of those who cannot speak out for themselves.

Speak up for those who cannot speak for themselves, for the rights of all who are destitute.
Speak up and judge fairly; defend the rights of the poor and needy.   (Proverbs 31:8,9)

Integral Mission[16]

In essence, I am calling for a commitment to integral mission by local congregations and individual Christians. Integral mission is an acknowledgement that in living out and sharing Christian faith we need both works and words. It is not that one is more important than the other, rather it is a realisation that words without works are weakened and works without words have less of a moral centre.

This will require us to exercise our imagination and creativity – demonstrating our faith by not only using words when speaking the good news of God's intervention in the world through Christ, but also ensuring that our actions become part of our vocabulary. Such use of our imagination and creativity evokes a response at both a personal and a corporate level. It is not possible to separate the spoken proclamation of who Jesus is, what He taught and what He has done, from living out that reality. Local congregations must move away from the notion that when we come to faith in Christ, we are heaven-bound and nothing else matters. Instead, we must recognise that faith in Christ leads us to a completely different lifestyle.

In 2005, I was part of the Faithworks national conference, which took place in Eastbourne at the beginning of November. At that conference, the leader of World Vision in Australia, Tim Costello, said something which perfectly sums up what I am trying to articulate for you here:

In following Jesus, we follow the One who leads us to the poor.

It is as simple and as profound as that. If we are truly to see God's kingdom come through us, then we must see our actions and our words as indissolubly linked. They are not just two wings of a plane, which is a rather dichotomous illustration, nor are they just the two blades of a pair of scissors. Rather they *are* the plane and they are the scissors. Without both our commitment to justice and righteousness and our commitment to truth we are failing to live out the good news.

Summary

In postmodern culture:

- the self is rejected as the centre
- reason and logic are not enough
- the enlightenment is rejected
- there is no sense of an objective 'world'
- people do not believe that there is a 'big story'
- science is no longer seen as having the full answer
- there is far more openness to the fact that the physical world is not enough
- authority is to be suspected
- life is seen as a journey
- truth is understood as relative.

The local church can be a place where we help people learn again the story of where they came from and what lies ahead, by using metaphors and images that show them the 'big story' of life in which they have a part to play.

We can move beyond the austerity of purely logical or intellectual apologetics in the way we talk about truth and in how we disciple and mentor others, and in so doing we can tap into a much more authentic understanding of truth Himself. Lastly, we can hold out for an integrated and joined-up understanding of the good news, which sees salvation and the message of the church and of Christ as relevant at every level for every person. To do that we must ensure that words and works, worship and witness, campaigning and piety remain joined together. We must understand that often people cannot hear what we say for the noise of who we are. Integral mission holds the key to effective communication of the gospel in our day.

There is no greater example of the impact of postmodernity than that of the diversity of religious expression we have in our societies. In the next chapter we will think about the challenges and the impact of such pluralism[17] on our local congregations and individual lives.

G.K. Chesterton once entered a public debate on the state of the nation by writing a letter to *The Times*. For days arguments had been going backwards and forwards about what was wrong with British society. Correspondents were pointing to government policy, religious liberalism, selfishness, the breakdown of family, youth culture (sound familiar?). G.K. Chesterton followed the discussion with interest. Finally he entered the debate himself, and in response to the question of what was wrong with the world he wrote this:

Dear Sir, I am.

We would do well to remember that we are part of the problem in postmodern society – and must endeavour to accept that responsibility and become part of the solution.

Lord,

Help us in our weakness and inadequacy to understand the ways in which we can relate Your story to our communities in sensitive speaking, compassionate thinking and helpful action. Give us open hearts to ponder how we might help those around us understand who You are and the love You have for them. Lead us beyond angry preaching and exclusive gatherings into a demonstration of Your kingdom that is inclusive, loving and welcoming. Help us to stand up for the excluded, the forgotten and the poor. Let us be people of welcome and embrace.

Amen.

NOTES

1. I was not brought up in a Christian home. Rather, I came to faith as a teenager. In my family life, I was shaped by parents who refused absolutely to show discrimination to people who were either Catholic or Protestant, so imagine my amazement when, after coming to faith in Christ, I was taught that people who were Roman Catholics could not at the same time be Christians. This was something I had never heard before, and I am deeply grateful that my parents influence over my life caused me to immediately question this prejudicial view of people who were Roman Catholic. This is, though, an example of two cultures shaping me. One was the culture of my home, the other was the culture of the Christian church that I was introduced to in my teens.

2. It is an interesting and challenging reality that the vast majority of Christians are part of a particular denomination or theological tradition,

not because they have *chosen* to be but because they were born into that tradition, or their families are part of it. This must surely be challenged. Why are you an Anglican, or a Roman Catholic, or a Pentecostal?

3. See Richard Neibuhr, *Christ and Culture*, London: Faber and Faber, 1952.

4. See T.S. Eliot, 'Notes Towards the Definition of a Culture' in Frank Kermode (editor), *Selected Prose of T.S. Eliot*, London: Faber, 1975, p. 298.

   Also:

   John Stott and Robert Coote, *Down to Earth: Studies in Christianity and Culture*, London: Hodder and Stoughton, 1981, p. 313.

   Terry Eagleton, *The Idea of Culture*, Oxford: Blackwell, 2000.

   Ravi K. Zacharias, *Deliver us from Evil: Restoring the Soul in a Disintegrating Culture*, Dallas: Word, 1996.

   M.J. Borg, *A New Vision: Spirit, Culture and the Life of Discipleship*, New York: HarperCollins, 1987.

   Steven Connor, *Postmodernist Culture*, Oxford: Blackwell, 1989.

5. See John W. Drane, *Cultural Change and Biblical Faith*, Carlisle: Paternoster, 2000, and John W. Drane, *Faith in a Changing Culture: Creating Churches for the Next Century*, London: Marshall Pickering, 1994.

6. Okay, I have to explain this one. Apparently 'book' means 'cool' because if you are sending a text from a mobile phone, you use the same keys! It was news to me too.

7. For a good outline of postmodernity see Richard Appignanesi and Chris Garratt, *Introducing Postmodernism*, Cambridge: Icon, 1999.

8. Although interestingly and perhaps more clearly, we could argue that 'I doubt, therefore I am' is a more accurate description of his reasoning!

9. See the introductory essay edited by P. Sampson in Chris Sugden, *Faith and Modernity*, Carlisle: Paternoster 1995.

10. Alison Morgan, *The Wild Gospel*, Oxford: Monarch, 2004, p. 169.

11. Max Weber as quoted in Andrew Walker, *Telling the Story: Gospel, Mission and Culture*, Eugene, Oregon: Wipf & Stock, 2004, p. 198.

12. See the introductory essay edited by P. Sampson in Chris Sugden, *Faith and Modernity*, Carlisle: Paternoster 1995.

13. If you want to map the journey of postmodernity, then the following will be helpful. This footnote is aimed at those of you who want to explore some of the philosophy behind postmodernity a little more fully.

    Kant began to discuss questions around the 'enlightened self' and hence was a clear marking post away from Descartes. Other philosophers began to ask fundamental questions about the centrality of logic and reason. For example, Gilbert Ryle asked if we could separate thinking from existence. Martin Heidegger challenged the idea of the individual self and suggested that human beings were people enmeshed in social networks. Johann Gottlieb Fichte strongly questioned the existence of an 'objective world' and rejected the idea of the Noumenal. Friedrich Nietzche, seen by many as the father of postmodernity, discussed and developed the idea of the demise of the enlightenment idea of truth as well as rejecting the idea of 'enlightenment values'. He spoke of 'the will to power' and through the development of his thinking around 'nihilism' and the 'death of God' he developed the idea of human potential and the 'übermensch' or 'superhuman'.

    Other key contributors and ideas to explore are Friedrich Schleiermacher for his grammatical and psychological understanding of life, truth and experience; Wilhelm Dilthey for the importance of history in experience, society and humanity; Marin Heidegger (again!) for his understanding of difference; Hans Georg-Gadamer for his work and thoughts around the rediscovery of the hermeneutics of truth and method; Ludwig Wittgenstein for his emphasis of the importance and problem with language and observation and Ferdinand de Saussure for his work around language and social convention and the birth of structuralism.

    As far as Postmodernity's key thinkers themselves, I would encourage you to explore the writings of Michel Foucault; Jacques Derrida and Richard Rorty. These will give you a first-hand encounter with postmodern thinking.

14. Friedrich Nietzsche, 'On Truth and Lie in an Extra-Moral Sense' in Walter Kaufmann, *The Portable Nietzsche*, New York: Penguin, 1976, p. 46–47.

15. For an unpacking of the idea of whole life mission see David G. Burnett, *The Healing of the Nations: The Biblical Basis of the Mission of God*, Carlisle: Paternoster, 1996.

16. I return to the theme of integral mission' in chapter 6. For an accessible analysis of integral mission, see Tim Chester, *Good News to the Poor: The Gospel through Social Involvement*, Leicester: Inter-Varsity Press, 2004.

17. Lesslie Newbigin's writings on pluralism are both challenging and stimulating. See:

Lesslie Newbigin, *Truth to Tell: The Gospel as Public Truth*, London: SPCK, 1991.

Lesslie Newbigin, *The Gospel in a Pluralist Society*, London: SPCK, 1989.

Lesslie Newbigin, *Foolishness to the Greeks: The Gospel and Western Culture*, London: SPCK, 1986.

2

Changing Religious Culture

There is salvation in no one else. (Acts 4:12)

I am the way. (John 14:6)

It is reported that when Henry Ford founded the Ford Motor Company, he used to quip that when you bought a new car, you could have it in any colour you wanted, so long as you wanted black! There was a point in Western culture when you could have almost said the same thing about religious expression. You could express your religious and spiritual preference any way you liked, so long as it was Christian. Those days are gone. We cannot and should not try to rewind time to some kind of mystical and golden era when everything was wonderful and everyone went to church. I doubt such an era ever existed at all – it is more a construct of our retrospective projection than a reality. We live in a religiously and culturally plural and diverse world, and we need to work out how we live distinctively in such a world – both as faithful followers of Christ and as dependable and honourable citizens.[1]

In the United Kingdom, all of the major world religions are present and express their views and opinions freely and openly. So Buddhists, Sikhs, Jains, Baha'i, Christians, Jews, Hindus, Muslims and Zoroastrians all have communities in various places across the United Kingdom. There are very few towns in Britain, or indeed in any part of the Western world, which do not contain a variety of cultural and religious expressions. How might the local church contribute positively to such a rich social mixture whilst remaining true to Christ? We have noted that in a postmodern society it will not do for the church to hide behind closed doors, content with poking tracts through people's letterboxes; we must be alongside our neighbours as friends if we hope that they will listen to us at all. How then might we retain our distinctive character as Christians without remaining separate and aloof? To come to the heart of this question requires us first to untangle the confusion that exists in the minds of many people about the nature of faith itself.

Understanding the Confusion Around Faith, Spirituality and Religion

Faced with the trail of devastation in Northern Ireland, the Balkans and the Middle East, looking back at the

Crusades of history, and even further back to the blood-shed of Old Testament stories or more recently the rise of Islam, many people have concluded that religion is a social evil. Call it 'faith', call it 'spirituality', call it 'religion' – to the disenchanted postmodern citizen in contemporary secular society, all too often religious faith simply means 'war'.

For those who have come to this view, it seems at best irrelevant and at worst inflammatory, in a time when social problems are rife, to be expected to spend time considering the place of faith in modern life. The place of faith, they would argue, is (only) in a history book. However, spirituality and faith are not the same as religion.

The terrorist attacks in New York, Madrid, London and Jerusalem, since 2001, have brought the difficulties and the challenges of fundamentalist religion right home to us. British citizens were rocked to their core as they contemplated the reality that neighbours who seemed so ordinary had lived among them, designing and assembling explosive devices and coolly planning to blow up underground trains and a bus full of people in the heart of London. How had such dangerous fundamentalism grown to these proportions in our midst?

There is no doubt that the rise of fundamentalism with its attendant radicalisation has given power and credence to the arguments of humanists and secularists who want to see religion denied the right to a voice in the public square or have any place in delivery of services like welfare, education or housing.

We should be ashamed and embarrassed by the level of pain and hatred generated by fundamentalism across the world. Even so, spirituality, faith and religion will always have a part to play in the public life of our nation and in the local community – for we cannot help being spiritual beings.

Understanding the difference between religion, spirituality and faith is vital as we consider the place of the church in a pluralist society. I have explored that difference in my earlier book *Building a Better World*, and refer you to it if you would like to decipher and think through those issues more fully. For the purposes of our discussion now, it is enough to recognise that there are a number of competing ideas about who God is, what God does and how God expects disciples or followers to behave in their communities.

Pluralism and Multiculturalism

Britain is a diverse, multicultural and multi-faith society. The 2001 Census[2] collected information about ethnicity and religious identity in the UK. Combining these results shows that while the British population is more culturally diverse than ever before, Christians remain the largest single group by far. In Great Britain, 40 million people (nearly 70 per cent) described their religion as 'Christian'. The statistics show that the UK is a diverse and a spiritualised society, but primarily Christian in affiliation.

Majorities of black people and those from mixed

ethnic backgrounds also identified themselves as Christian (71 and 52 per cent respectively). In total there were 815,000 black Christians and 353,000 Christians from mixed ethnic backgrounds. Among other faiths, the largest groups were Pakistani Muslims (686,000) and Indian Hindus (471,000) followed by Indian Sikhs (307,000), Bangladeshi Muslims (261,000) and white Jews (259,000). The Indian group was religiously diverse: 45 per cent of Indians were Hindu, 29 per cent Sikh and a further 13 per cent Muslim. In contrast the Pakistani and Bangladeshi groups were more homogeneous, Muslims accounting for 92 per cent of each ethnic group. Some faith communities were concentrated in particular ethnic groups. For example, 91 per cent of Sikhs were Indian and 97 per cent of Jews described their ethnicity as white. Other faiths were more widely dispersed. Considerable proportions of Buddhists were found in the white, Chinese, other Asian and other ethnic groups. Interestingly, and perhaps rather amusingly, in the 2001 census returns 390,000 people recorded their religion as 'Jedi'. Apparently, the force is strong in Great Britain! Importantly, only 15 per cent of the British population reported having no religion.

These figures can mean little or nothing to us. It is easy for Christians to plod doggedly along as if nothing has really changed, but in reality the *fact* that we live in diverse and pluralistic societies means that we *must* think about our Christian faith and how we live it out in our communities, our homes and our work places.

Modern Christians must find a way to relate unique and clear allegiance to Jesus Christ to a culturally postmodern community which has predominantly lost belief in any kind of unique, authoritative or objective truth, but where other faith groups also expect their perspective on reality to be recognised, celebrated and respected.

So the Muslim claims that he is right, the Sikh that she is right and we as Christians claim that we are right. If we are not careful in our handling of these differences, we end up in a situation where we are simply shouting for our rights and demanding that we are listened to because we are right and everyone else is wrong. That is a recipe for disaster.

How Can You be Distinctive in a Pluralistic Society?

I am not a pluralist. I am a member of the Christian family and committed to the unique revelation of God in Jesus Christ. When I read that Jesus said he was *the* way, truth and life (John 14:6), I believe those words.

I have argued elsewhere[3] that we must identify and nurture the common ground of values and ideology that we share as Christians with those of other faiths and those whose integrity is secular in its profile. I remain as passionate today about this commitment to working together as I ever was.

However, the purpose of this book is to support local congregations and individual Christians in remaining distinctively Christian and finding a peaceable, authentic way to hold steady the Christ-light within them as they interact with their communities, their neighbours and their friends. We must never break faith with Christ in order to contribute to our community and our neighbour. Indeed it is our commitment to Christ that generates and sustains our commitment to our community and our neighbour and to others. Yet in order to engage in a way that fits with our Christian identity and ethos we need to form an understanding of the role of faith in the context of wider society.

Faith Motivates People to Do Something

Faith is a motivator, and faith is part of our identity. Faith motivates people to do something with their lives.

There are about 8 million Christians in the United Kingdom who are committed to local congregations in one way or another. The church in the United Kingdom provides three times as many volunteers to our society as any other organisation or group. Church networks across the United Kingdom have clearly demonstrated that they are vital contributors to the health and well-being of their communities.[4] There are countless examples of this across the UK.

The Faithworks movement was established to help churches engage with their communities unconditionally but in a distinctively Christian way. Members of Faithworks join knowing that we are not a pluralist movement but that we will and do work with people of other faiths. But the very core of our commitments, articulated in the Faithworks Charter[5] begins with the fact that we are *motivated by our Christian faith*. Therefore members of the movement across the UK and across the world are committed to making a difference in their communities.

Richmond's Hope works with bereaved young people in Edinburgh because of the Christian faith of its members. Pecan works with unemployed and disadvantaged people in London because of the Christian faith of its members. Restored Ministries in Coleraine works to provide recycled and good quality furniture to those who need it, because of the Christian faith of its members. These groups of local people do what they do *because of their Christian faith*.

But it is also true that other faith groups are committed to their communities and to doing good, because they are motivated by their faith too. As I write, I am thinking about a debate I will be hosting this evening in the Royal Commonwealth Society in London which will focus on the role of faith communities in conflict resolution. Just a week or so ago I was part of a day symposium that explored the motivation of faith in serving the poor and the excluded. Christians do not have a monopoly on doing good.

So often, as local churches or local congregations, we think that we are the only people that do any good in our communities – that is simply not true. I'll unpack the challenge of this later in the chapter, but if we are ever to understand the way in which Christian faith can be expressed in a pluralist society, then we must also recognise that any type of faith is often expressed in service of others. Faith leads to action. People of faith in your community who are not Christians may well be as committed to the good of your neighbourhood as you are. Those who have no faith at all might also be very committed to the well-being of their friends and neighbours. Local congregations need to be careful not to assume they stand alone on the moral high ground when it comes to doing good. Don't think that you are the only people who are helping make your communities better places. In a pluralist community, lots of people do good, and they do it for lots of different faith reasons.

Faith is Part of Our Identity

Faith is a significant part of what shapes our views of the world, of ourselves and of each other. The fact that our faith is part of our identity means that it plays a crucial role in forming our approach to life. We need to be careful not to over simplify this, though. Let me give you an example.

In the last twelve months in the United Kingdom, there have been several very high profile cases of people who felt their personal liberty was being threatened by the fact that they were not allowed to wear certain symbols or pieces of clothing as part of their expression of their faith. The two most notable were a teacher who wanted to wear a *niqab* (the complete physical covering that some Muslim women wear) and a Christian airline worker who wanted to wear a cross. In France, children are forbidden from wearing religious clothing or paraphernalia to school. I don't want to discuss here the rights and wrongs of these cases except to offer a word of caution to the church. Whilst the wearing of a symbol such as a cross or a dove is not an inherent part of Christian identity for many followers of Christ, for many others within other religious traditions, their garments and their symbols are as important to their expression of faith as the Christian assertion of 'Jesus is Lord' is to us. There is an inherent and qualitative difference between a Sikh being denied the right to wear a turban – a central part of his faith identity, and a Christian being denied the right to wear a cross – which is not a prescribed part of our religious practice. Christians must be careful not to trivialise the importance of garments or symbols in other faiths or to exaggerate their significance in our own.

The point I want to make is that faith-identity for Christians is about so very much more than what we wear. That does not mean that I do not recognise that in other faiths garments and symbols are a central expression of identity. Christian faith may choose to express itself in what we wear, but faith identity (at least within the protestant tradition) is not as closely related to such things as some other faiths where the central means of expression of identity can be in the use of symbols and the wearing of specific garments.

Because faith is a significant influence and plays

such an important role in our identity, it also shapes powerfully how we view life, work, relationships, possessions, spirituality and our role in the wider world. To diminish the importance of garments and symbols in some faith traditions trivialises their identity. Similarly, the assumption that Christian faith identity is expressed primarily in garments or symbols trivialises Christian faith identity. It is the equivalent of saying that you can define a British person as someone who flies the Union Jack!

Faith is a central and determining contributor to our identity. So for Jews, their faith is not just about prayer shawls, particular head coverings or circumcision, central as these outward signs are. Sikhs are not fully expressing their identity through turbans as vital and important as they are to them. In a different category altogether, Christians do not need to express their identity through the wearing of a cross, a dove or a fish! Christian practice and belief means that external symbols are reminders of a whole worldview, which is shaped by faith. In a pluralist society, however, the external symbols of faith that express distinctive identity take on exaggerated importance, and their significance increases when adherents to a faith group believe they are being marginalised or oppressed by the wider community to which they belong.

For Christians, the challenge is to recognise that just as our identity flows from our faith, so the *other* people in our community, whether they have a faith or not, have had their identities shaped by the predominant ideologies in their lives. We have no more right to ask them to give up their identities than they have to ask us to give up ours. We must grapple with the challenge of cross-cultural engagement right on our doorsteps if we are to live in a pluralist society while remaining distinctively committed to Christ. We must resist the temptation to over-simplify our relationship with people of other faiths and spiritualities. We cannot ignore the fact that identity, faith and motivation are deeply linked. If we are to engage in a pluralist society effectively and distinctively we cannot afford to make such a basic mistake.

An interesting test of whether we accept this tapestry of pluralism would be to ask whether as Christians we recognise the central importance of turban wearing to a Sikh whilst acknowledging that the wearing of a cross for a follower of Christ is actually not an inherent part of Christian identity in the same way.

Faith is a motivator and a source of identity, but these points can be hard to understand or relate to behaviour, so let me try and give you an example of what this means in real terms.

In the north-west of England John Devine, a Roman Catholic Monsignor, facilitates a regional Christian forum. This group belongs to a nationwide English forum called the Churches' Regional Network, whose task is to support and listen to local congregations as they engage with their neighbourhood communities. In some parts of the country, including the north-west, The Churches' Regional Network is itself involved in inter-faith dialogue, resulting in the establishment of the North-West of England's Regional Forum for Faiths, the launch of which I attended in 2005. In this forum, people of different faiths meet to discuss how they can work together in communities across the region and ways in which they need to remain distinctive. By so doing, they are aware of potential ideological clashes and they do not give up their identity, but they also recognise that they share a motivation to serve the poor, the excluded and the marginalised. Distinctiveness and mutuality exist side by side.

Local congregations must learn from this example and others like it. We can coexist in our local communities without retreating into a defensive and detached position. Christians do not, in fact should not, give up their commitment to the uniqueness and exclusive claims of Christ in order to work with others of different faiths.

We must also learn the art of 'decluttering' our Christianity of its cultural baggage and accessories. That is not easy, but it is possible. In the Midlands of England, a Christian charity that works alongside the Asian community is enabling a culturally relevant investigation of Christianity by those whose musical and cultural roots lie in Hinduism. At a national prayer conference called Trumpet Call in 2006, they led intercessions and prayers. Their musical style was very Asian, and some of the folk in the National Exhibition Centre Arena took some time to adjust their perception of what 'Christian' singing and prayer sounded and looked like. I was deeply moved, though, as I stood on the stage. Here was a central and sensitive expression of worship of God which was pushing over 6,000 people out of their comfort zone. As I listened, I wondered how many people around the UK in local churches would ever even think of engaging with others in such a culturally sensitive yet clearly Christian way.

The Role and Place of Faith in Our Communities[6]

There is a further challenge for local churches in engaging with other faith communities in our neighbourhoods. That is in understanding the way in which 'faith' in its general sense, but not its strictly Christian sense, has become such a topic of debate and discussion. There has been a sea of change in the attitude of governments (both in the UK and in the USA) towards the role of faith in community renewal. George Bush's 'faith-based and community initatives' programme has seen billions of dollars pumped into the work of charities that have a faith basis. Here in the UK, there are more faith-based organisations and initiatives working across communities than there have been for fifty years. Since 1997, the role and contribution of faith groups in the UK, and the profile they have been given, have mushroomed. You would think that this is all good news, but it isn't. Very often government language and attitudes betray both a deep ignorance of faith as a motivation and faith as identity. If local churches are confused about these things, the government and statutory agencies are even more confused. The UK does not have a distinct recognition of 'faith-based organisations' yet. Rather, faith groups that engage in their community are primarily categorised as 'voluntary groups' or as part of 'the third sector'. We have yet to have as clear a recognition of the distinctive contribution of faith groups to social renewal as the US faith-based and community initiatives programme has sought to provide. The conversation has begun, but much more understanding of faith as a motivator, not just a service provider, is required if we are to progress more effectively.

Having said that, public figures seem to be coming out of the woodwork to acknowledge the role of faith in the lives of citizens. Back in the mid 1980s[7] Margaret Thatcher, then the UK Prime Minister, told the Bishop of Liverpool, David Sheppard, that he should leave politics to the politicians and get on with religion. She did not welcome comment from the church in areas where they were not invited to express a view, yet she sought the guidance of the church in issues more traditionally understood to fall within the context of morality.

Margaret Thatcher rarely commented on the role of faith. Yet it is striking to note that she adapted the prayer of St Francis when she came to office in 1977 – expressing a desire to bring peace where there was discord and hope where there was despair. She also had a very clear view of how to address the real problems of poverty in terms of international development. She argued for help in practical terms because, in her view, people could not be taught principles of a religion unless it meant something practically and enabled them to do things for themselves.

As Prime Minister, she argued that you replace poverty with a better standard of living through people's own efforts, recognising that everyone has talent and ability, suggesting that in teaching what is necessary to life, you would teach religion as well. She ultimately recognised that if poverty, ignorance and disease are relieved, individuals and communities are still confronted with the real religious problem in the choice between good and evil, which is a choice of ethics and belief.

She argued that Christianity was about more than doing good works. In Mrs Thatcher's view, Christianity is a deep faith that expresses itself in your relationship with God. For her, it was sanctity, and no politician was entitled to take that away from you or to have what she referred to as corporate state activities that only look at interests as a whole.

Interestingly, Mrs Thatcher ultimately believed that it was vital for individuals of faith to ensure they really know their own faith and to live it out in everyday life. That would then shape the whole of a community. She argued that faith and practice, religion and lifestyle could not be separated. For her, good works were not enough because without conviction and faith, good works would be like flowers cut from their roots; the flowers would soon die because there would be nothing to revive them.

Yet somehow these personal convictions did not result in frequent public comments on the role of faith communities in Britain. Like Tony Blair in the late 1990s and early part of this century, Mrs Thatcher sought to keep faith private and personal. Unlike the last ten years in the United Kingdom, however, the late 1980s and early 1990s were times of relative silence on the part of government on the role of faith in a healthy society. The ground has shifted significantly since then. Britain is seeking to find a more open and inclusive place for people of faith and their contribution to the public good. In fact, in May of 2006 the Church of England published a report entitled *Faithful Cities: A call to celebration, vision, and justice* from the Commission on Urban Life and Faith that articulates some of the differences between the Britain of the late 1980s and the Britain of the twenty-first century.

That being said, there is still a long way to go! Faithworks hosted a series of lectures in March 2005 with the leaders of the three main national political parties in the run-up to the general election. The central theme was the role of faith in public life. Tony Blair, Michael Howard and Charles Kennedy (all of whom have now left office) stated that they thought there was an important role for faith communities in the life of Britain. Early in 2007, the Christian Socialist Movement, sponsored by Faithworks, hosted a hustings event for the six prospective candidates for the deputy leadership of the Labour Party. All of the candidates expressed the view that faith communities had a vital contribution to make to healthy communities, even if they were a little vague about what that actually meant.

Tony Blair and other politicians in the last decade have been much more open about the role of faith in their own lives and the contribution that faith has to make in British life. Too often, we are negative about politicians when it comes to the way they handle faith. For example, if instead of looking at Tony Blair as a Prime Minister who went to church, we looked at him as a Christian whose faith was expressed in being Prime Minister, then we would recognise his contribution in terms of the role and place of faith in the public arena as massive. Tony and Cherie Blair throughout their time in Downing Street maintained regular commitment to attendance of church services and regularly received the Eucharist. Not only that, but Mr Blair also regularly consulted with people of faith, including Jim Wallis, around issues of policy and poverty alleviation both domestically and internationally. All the indications are that Gordon Brown and a number of prominent politicians in the United Kingdom are increasingly recognising the contribution of local churches and other faith groups to social renewal. Faith is increasingly recognised as having a very public set of consequences, even when it is privately held.

While politicians increasingly celebrate and acknowledge the importance of local churches and faith groups in building healthy communities, those same politicians are also looking to people of faith to help work out what healthy communities look like.

This puts the onus upon local people of faith to learn the art of reconciliation and communication. It is unrealistic to rely upon either the political institution or the institution of the church to understand and manage our interaction as we work together in the community. Harmony, courtesy, diplomacy, peace, respect – these qualities can be expressed only locally and immediately, though they should certainly be hallowed at an institutional level as well. Local congregations like yours and mine have to deal with issues of pluralism every day. We are on the cutting edge of what the government calls 'community cohesion'. If churches and other faith groups are not able to relate to one another peaceably and safely, then how can we expect our wider communities to be cohesive? Furthermore, if we cannot work out how we remain distinctively Christian and at the same time faithful, loyal and good citizens, then we have no defence when we are accused of bringing division and breakdown in our communities. Ultimately, if local churches are not working to build up and strengthen their communities, then they are not simply being passive – instead they are directly contributing to the breakdown of their communities and to growing distrust and suspicion.

So how do Christians engage in their communities without losing their identity? How do local churches work with others without losing their commitment to the exclusive claims of Christ? Can your local church work with other faith groups and yet at the same time

remain distinctively Christian? These are the fundamental questions to which we now must turn.

The Role of Christian Congregations in Local Communities and the Challenge to Distinctive Christian Faith

Joy Madeiros, my colleague at Faithworks, has worked
for many years on the distinctive contribution
Christians can offer in their community. I so appreciate
her work in this area, and the ways in which she has
helped not just me, but hundreds of Christians understand how they operate distinctively in a very diverse
world.

Joy is not just a theorist. Her work is infomed by
membership of her local church in Essex, as well as
chairing her local branch of the YMCA and having been
a director of that movement nationally for many years.
She is a passionate follower of Christ, deeply committed to living out her faith before others. In her conversations with government, with local authorities and
with other faith groups, she epitomises what it is to be
distinctively Christian. Like hundreds of thousands of
other people across the UK, she refuses to take the easy
road of either separation or assimilation. Each local
congregation and individual Christian must learn to do
the same.

What Are the Options?

There are five fundamental options from which a congregation might choose:

- separation
- assimilation
- multi-faith
- interfaith
- distinctive faith

Separation

Local churches can choose not to work with anyone of a different faith. Many choose this approach. They fundamentally believe that they would be compromising their allegiance to Christ if they worked with other faiths, and they have decided that it is better to remain respectfully separate from other faith groups than compromise their own beliefs and convictions. This attitude is particularly prevalent amongst conservative evangelical churches. Their argument would normally be that you cannot mix light with darkness. The biblical texts they would identify in support of their view are, for example:

> Do not be teamed with those who do not love the Lord, for what do the people of God have in common with the people of sin? How can light live with darkness?   (1 Corinthians 6:14, *Living Bible*)

> Who is the liar? It is the man who denies that Jesus is the Christ. Such a man is the antichrist – he denies the Father and the Son. No one who denies the Son has the Father; whoever acknowledges the Son has the Father also.   (1 John 2:22–23)

I think this view is fundamentally flawed because it ignores the call of Christians to serve others. It assumes that there is nothing to learn from other people and it makes the mistake of believing that by working with another faith group on an issue of social or community focus, you somehow dilute your own identity. Such a view ultimately leads to separation not just from people of different faiths, but from everyone who does not agree with you, including the community itself, statutory bodies, voluntary agencies and even other Christian churches. It also ultimately leads to legalism, judgmentalism, pride and death. It may arise from going to the Bible for proof texts rather than reading Scripture holistically and in context.

Assimilation

The second option is assimilation. Here a local church decides that there is nothing that is distinctive about what it does and why it does it, and therefore it is not overly concerned about its identity. Thus, in an effort to work with everyone, this local congregation becomes no more Christian or distinctive in their work and ethos than a non-Christian agency. This results in a loss of identity. The scriptural motivation for this approach may lie in the command of Jesus to be 'salt', 'light' and 'yeast' in the world:

> You are the salt of the earth. But if the salt loses its saltiness, how can it be made salty again? It is no longer good for anything, except to be thrown out and trampled by men.
>
> You are the light of the world. A city on a hill cannot be hidden. Neither do people light a lamp and put it under a bowl. Instead they put it on its stand, and it gives light to everyone in the house. In the same way, let your light shine before men, that they may see your good deeds and praise your Father in heaven.   (Matthew 5:13–16)
>
> The kingdom of heaven is like yeast that a woman took and mixed into a large amount of flour until it worked all through the dough. (Matthew 13:33)

Assimilation may lead to short-term partnership, but ultimately it will also dissipate commitment, passion and energy, because in giving away its distinctive faith-motivation this local church has also given away its lifeblood. A Christian congregation can no more give up its identity than a petrol engine can give up petrol and still run. One example of this approach is a local church in the Midlands that decided that their building was actually to be used for the worship of the God of any faith group in the town and that there was no partnership that they could not engage in. The result was that the building was used for any religious group or non-religious group for any purpose. In fact, the minister of the church recently conducted a Muslim wedding, mixing Islamic texts and commitments with Christian songs and hymns and prayers to God from both traditions. Asked on a Radio 2 programme whether he saw any theological conflict in what his church was doing, he set out a thorough defence of assimilation, stating that all faiths served the same God and that there was nothing too distinctive about the Christian faith. His Christian faith had led him to believe that Christ was an entry point to faith, but that Jesus was only one entry point of many.

Multi-faith

This approach developed in the years after the Second World War and is similar in some ways to assimilation. With this outlook, people in different faith communities assent to the idea that they all believe in the same God and that their various expressions ultimately lead to the same reality.

> For whoever is not against us is for us.
>
> (Mark 9:40)

> God is love. Whoever lives in love lives in God, and God in him.   (1 John 4:16)

While it appears appealing at first, any experience of multi-faith expression quickly leads to quite a high level of frustration. Muslims do not want to become Christians and vice versa. How can someone simultaneously believe that part of their religious conviction is the desire to see other people embrace the God they serve and that the members of different faiths all believe in the same God and that their various expressions ultimately lead to the same reality? It is illogical to suggest that two competing truth claims are both true. Let me give you an example.

As a Christian, I believe that Jesus is the second person of the Trinity, that He is God in human form and that He is the only avenue to a true and right relationship with God for all humanity. No other faith holds that view. Furthermore, all other faiths disagree with that assertion. It seems relatively straightforward to me, but it is important to recognise that intellectually and philosophically I cannot be right at the same time as all those other faiths are right when it comes to the person and work of Jesus Christ. I do not feel that I can compromise this fundamental conviction, and therefore the multi-faith model ultimately breaks down for me. But it also breaks down for conservative Muslims, Jews, Hindus, Sikhs and so on. Those for whom it does not break down in each of the faith traditions are those who would view themselves as either progressive or liberal. They would argue that they do not set such store by being right and would suggest that their convictions, whilst strong, are inherently different in nature and priority from those who are more conservative.

Interfaith

The interfaith approach acknowledges that there are differences between faiths but argues that what is needed is increasing dialogue. From a scriptural perspective they might argue, in the words of John:

> Perfect love drives out fear. (1 John 4:18)

In the interfaith movement, discussion and listening is vitally important. In the United Kingdom, the Inter Faith Network leads a large number of local networks in towns and cities across the country. They have not taken the route of the multi-faith movement, because they have recognised that there are real and significant differences between faiths. There is no doubt that the interfaith movement has achieved a huge amount. It has promoted better understanding of one another and it has led to a rich and diverse dialogue between faith groups. I am convinced that there is less tension between faith groups in many cities and towns in the UK because of the sterling work undertaken by this group.

I have a great deal of sympathy for the interfaith movement. It believes that greater dialogue will lead to greater understanding and that greater understanding in turn leads to a promotion of peace, social harmony and goodwill. Ultimately understanding one another should, in the interfaith movement, lead to greater cooperation and action together. However, because it often is stuck at the intellectual and cerebral understanding of each other's faith traditions, the interfaith movement can become static. It is undoubtedly true that by talking and listening to one another differences can be overcome and harmony can be reached, but there is a strong need for a unity of purpose and action alongside unity of thought and discussion. Furthermore, whilst many people in different faith communities will find the interfaith approach the one that works best for them, this method does not meet the needs of those who are conservative in their faith expression and are still suspicious of interfaith activity, despite the clear differences between interfaith dialogue and multi-faith groups. There are some differences between faith traditions that cannot be removed, particularly between those in faiths who seek to convert others, such as Christianity and Islam. Dialogue will not remove such distinctiveness and for many people the differences lie at the heart of their faith and are too important to ignore. They limit the extent to which you can act in partnership, and they are not issues simply of preference or style. Once again, I give you my own personal example.

My own expression of Christian faith means that I cannot lay down the exclusive and unique claims of the church around the person and the work of Christ. This means that my partnerships must be established with that clear commitment on my part understood. But I also recognise that there are those in other faith traditions who also have distinctive perspectives and views. So how do we work out ways of working together that will not compromise our beliefs and convictions?

Distinctive Faith

The core purpose of this book is to try to ask how a local congregation can face the big challenges of society without losing its distinctive commitment to Christ. There is no more urgent area for this discussion than in the arena of how we work with other faith traditions. We need a distinctive approach that is theologically grounded, externally accountable and measurably pragmatic.

Faithworks has developed such an approach and we now employ it in everything we do. It not only forms and shapes our relationships with other faith groups; it also shapes the way we talk about other faiths to government and statutory agencies. This approach owes much to the interfaith dialogue and is a development from that approach rather than an approach to be viewed in opposition to the interfaith movement.

Faithworks is a Christian movement and we neither hide that nor apologise for it. I cannot depart from that position, not least because there are 25,000 partners, members and affiliates who have trusted both Faithworks as their movement and me as the leader of Faithworks to remain true to Christ. But at the same time as being unashamedly Christian, I understand, accept and respect the fact that others hold their own unique views of life and spirituality. Therefore, in the distinctive faith approach, we explore the common values that we share, we set out agreed commitments and aims and we acknowledge the areas where our partnership will not or cannot work because of a clash of ideologies. This means that we are free to be who we are, others are free to be who they are and we know what we expect of one another. Let me give you an example.

I was invited to discuss the possibility of a joint piece of work with a national agency based in the east of London. The idea was that we could work together to establish training centres. The initial meeting went well, and at the end I felt positive about the possibilities of working together. There was also quite a lot of money associated with the project, which would have helped immensely with the development of the Faithworks movement. As I was leaving the meeting, the chief executive of the other organisation pointed out to me that they were a multi-faith agency and that they could only work with agencies that were happy to acknowledge that there were many ways to knowing God. This was a requirement for working together, and it was a requirement I was not able to meet with integrity of conviction or purpose. So I explained our position and left the meeting, leaving with it the chance to gain access to a great deal of money. For the reality is that Christ has never been ashamed of me, and I will not apologise for Him. Distinctive faith allows me to work with other faith groups on issues of social welfare, healthcare, community transformation, delivery of goods and services and a whole host of other important issues. It also enables me to be clear about who I am, what my faith-motivation is, and my Christian identity.

This is the approach that thousands of local congregations are looking for in the UK – a way of working with others who are committed to their communities without sacrificing their allegiance to their creeds. For that to happen though, there must be shared values and commitments. These values will probably include issues like the dignity of all people, a commitment to eradicate poverty, a desire to stand up for the marginalised and excluded and a humble and gracious understanding of power. There may be other values and commitments that you think are important for your local church as you seek to work with others in your pluralistic community. Before you embark on such partnerships in shared community projects, it may be helpful for your church to take time to establish what, for you, will be the common ground you hope to share with others, and the non-negotiable areas of distinctive Christian faith that you must publicly uphold.

These are the core theological values that I have identified in the exercise of setting my own boundaries for working with those whose worldview is at variance with my own.[8]

1. Human dignity matters and creation is God's gift – therefore we must respect other people, even when we disagree with them. We must understand our responsibility for the world – both human institutions within it, and the environment as a whole.
2. Justice should be a priority – therefore we must commit to serving the poor and excluded in our partnerships and speaking out on their behalf with others who will stand up for them.

3. We must be committed to servant-heartedness – therefore we must adopt an attitude of humility and not use power in a way which is contrary to the example of Jesus Christ.

4. Community is vital – therefore we need to work with others and we can learn from others. Working with others is not just an option, it is the best way to achieve sustainable change in our communities.

5. Inclusion and diversity are fundamental principles – therefore other people have a vital role to play and we can learn from them. We must be committed not only to working with others, but to learning from them and to working with those who are different from us.

6. A holistic and integrated approach is the only one that works – therefore we will ensure that our work is integrated and joined up. We will seek to address the whole needs of our communities, not just parts of those needs.

7. Participation is empowerment – therefore we will seek to release other people rather than hold them back. We will be committed to fair and equitable partnership.

8. Involvement means sacrifice – therefore we must be ready to act sacrificially. We will not always get our own way, nor should we expect to in our partnerships with people of other faiths.

9. God is intrinsically involved in the world he has made – therefore He is already at work in others, whether we choose to work with them or not.

10. There is always hope – therefore we will never approach our partnerships in an attitude of cynicism.

The Faithworks Charter

The ten core values I have set out above are just an example of how you can set about considering what it is that you believe enables you to work with other faith groups in your community. But in your rush to establish links and partnerships with other faith groups, be careful to ensure that you take the time to work out what you believe and why you believe it. This is important whether you are involved in social action in your community or you want to be a good neighbour or work colleague. This is why it is so important to think about what the kingdom of God looks like and how you live it out in your community.

Taking a distinctive faith approach enables us to both remain true to Christ and work with other faith groups. It demands of us that we will be clear about who we are, what we believe, and where we can and cannot work together. Choosing distinctive faith is not the easiest option, but it is an approach of absolute integrity, openness and honesty.

As Christians we believe that all people, however different they may be, are made in God's image. We believe that their differences tell us about God's character and we praise Him for his gloriously diverse creation. At the same time we believe that because we are all made in

God's image, we are all equally valuable. Without appreciating diversity, there can be no equality!

When it comes to our society, equality between the faiths is only possible when the distinct identity of each faith is recognised. We will never build healthy and sustainable communities without recognizing both what we share and what we hold as distinct convictions. 'Harmony between the faiths' does not require us to renege on creeds we believe, but to remember that just as Christians may wish to proclaim salvation through Jesus Christ alone, so our society should afford Sikhs or Muslims the freedom to express their own passionately held beliefs.

Distinctive faith recognises that people from different faith traditions often share the same concerns about society as a whole or about their particular local community. But this approach maintains that all religious traditions are not the same and should be treated in a way that respects and affirms their differences.

As the leader of a Christian social action movement, I want to promote the distinctiveness of Christian social action. We need to be clear that we are motivated by our faith in Jesus, at the same time as we assert the right of those from other faith traditions to articulate what makes their work distinctive and to use language and religious ideas that resonate with their own religious tradition. However that does *not* mean that I affirm their convictions – I still hold to my belief and conviction that Christ is the unique revelation of God. It is in holding the principles of partnership and distinctive identity in tension that local churches can help build strong and healthy communities. Any approach that tries to make all faith groups the same, or tries to cut them out completely, will ultimately fail – and both approaches will fracture communities. Nothing is a greater threat to good community relations than misconstruing people's identity or homogenising different faith-identities.

One way of local churches ensuring that they remain distinctively Christian and that they work with other faith groups is the use of the Faithworks charter. This fifteen-point plan helps Christians to clarify their identity, their motivation and their contribution. It helps us work through issues of postmodernity (which we explored in the last chapter), pluralism and professionalism. It is a tool that has been used by thousands of churches, projects and individuals. Hundreds of local councils across the UK recognise it as an important set of commitments, and in recent years national government has welcomed it.[9]

In the charter, we as Christians commit to providing an inclusive service to our communities by:

1. Serving and respecting all people regardless of their gender, marital status, race, ethnic origin, religion, age, sexual orientation or physical and mental capability.
2. Acknowledging the freedom of people of all faiths or none both to hold and to express their beliefs and

convictions respectfully and freely, within the limits
of the UK law.

3. Never imposing our Christian faith or belief on
others.

4. Developing partnerships with other churches,
voluntary groups, statutory agencies and local government wherever appropriate in order to create an
effective, integrated service for our clients avoiding
unnecessary duplication of resources.

5. Providing and publicising regular consultation and
reporting forums to client groups and the wider
community regarding the effective development and
delivery of our work and our responsiveness to their
actual needs.

Secondly, we commit to valuing all individuals in a way
that is consistent with our distinctive Christian ethos
by:

1. Creating an environment where clients, volunteers
and employees are encouraged and enabled to
realise their potential.

2. Assisting our clients, volunteers and employees to
take responsibility for their own learning and development, both through formal and informal training
opportunities and ongoing assessment.

3. Developing an organisational culture in which individuals learn from any mistakes made and where
excellence and innovation are encouraged and
rewarded.

4. Promoting the value of a balanced, holistic lifestyle as part of each individual's overall personal development.
5. Abiding by the requirements of employment law in the UK and implementing best employment practices and procedures designed to maintain our distinctive ethos and values.

Thirdly, we commit to developing a professional approach to management, practice and funding by:

1. Implementing a management structure which fosters and encourages participation by staff at all levels in order to facilitate the fulfilment of the project's goals and visions.
2. Setting and reviewing measurable and timed outcomes annually and regularly, to evaluate and monitor our management structure and output, recognizing the need for ongoing organisational flexibility, development and good stewardship of resources.
3. Doing all we can to ensure that we are not over-dependent on any one source of funding.
4. Implementing best practice procedures in terms of Health and Safety and Child Protection in order to protect our staff, volunteers and clients.
5. Handling our funding in a transparent and accountable way and to give relevant people from outside our organisation/project reasonable access to our accounts.

Simple Tests

When it comes to working out how we relate to people of other faiths, or how as a local church we work with other faith groups, there may be a tendency toward suspicion or fear. To allay these fears and promote confidence in the process, we may like to apply a checklist of ground rules in working alongside those of a different perspective. For example:

1. DO NOT become involved with a project or service provider that asks you to deny or keep secret your faith in Jesus.
2. DO NOT prioritise funding above matters of Christian principle or freedom to make it known that you are Christian.
3. BE CAUTIOUS when asked to participate in a project where you may not be free to express your faith in Christ by your words, choices or actions – do not be embarrassed to withdraw if necessary.
4. DO go ahead with projects arising from shared values and convictions that also respect the participants' distinctive beliefs and practices.
5. DO ask yourself 'What would Jesus do?'

Summary

As Christians, we do not have to give away our allegiance in order to work with others. In many ways, the pluralist society around us is one that is similar to the first-century context into which the apostle Paul spoke.

He reminded the early church of their allegiance and their commitment to God through Christ, but he also reminded them of God's expectation of them – that they would love their enemies (Romans 12) and that they would do good to all people, especially (but not only) those in the church (Galatians 6).

Jesus himself encouraged the church to let the light of our good deeds shine out before the world and to be salt that flavours our communities (Matthew 5). He also reminded his followers that they should feed the hungry, clothe the naked and care for the vulnerable because in so doing, they would be serving and touching Christ Himself (Matthew 25).

The apostle James reminded the early church that every good gift came from God (James 1). Wariness of pluralism is not an excuse for local churches to turn their backs on people of other faiths. Rather, we must live as Jesus intended – serving others and working with others to build a better world.

However, we must also be true to the heart of God's commands to us. We must have no other gods and we must *never* compromise our faithfulness and allegiance to God (for example, the first two of the ten great commandments, recorded in Exodus 20). It may be popular and easy to deny the unique revelation of God in Christ, but the price is too high and the consequences too great. A local church without allegiance to Christ is nothing more than a social service – and we are called to be so much more than that. The local church is called to be at the heart of its community, serving and living as Jesus called us to. Only then can we see the world changed and the kingdom of God advance.

Let us pray:

Lord,

Help us to see the good in others. Forgive us for making assumptions about those in our communities whose faith is different from ours. Help us to pause and look for Your image in them when we talk with them or meet them. Give us the grace to choose the work we can wholeheartedly share with others and leave the tasks that are not ours to do. Enable us, at all times, to stand clearly for You, Your Son and Your kingdom.

Amen

NOTES

1. If you are interested in exploring more of the religious diversity of the UK beyond this book take a look at:

    David Wells, *Losing Our Virtue: Why the Church Must Recover Its Moral Vision*, Leicester: Inter-Varsity Press, 1988, chapter 6.

    Malcolm Duncan, *Building a Better World: Faith at Work for Change in Society*, London: Continuum, 2006, chapters 2 and 3.

2. Source: Office for National Statistics & Census, April 2001, General Register Office for Scotland. The census question about religion was optional.

3. Malcolm Duncan, *Building a Better World: Faith at Work for Change in Society*, London: Continuum, 2006.

4. See reports such as *Angels and Advocates; Beyond Belief; Faith in England's North-West; Acting in Good Faith; the Norwich Church/ City Dialogue and the Faith Audit of Stoke-on-Trent* produced by Saltbox.

5. See www.faithworks.info for more information.

6. For a good discussion of the role of faith in contemporary society see Alan Aldridge, *Religion in the Contemporary World*, Oxford: Blackwell, 2000.

7. This was in 1988, at the launch of the Church of England's crucial report 'Faith and the City' which examined the issue of deprivation and poverty and how Christians could engage in addressing the needs of society. The Commission on Urban Life and Faith's *Faithful Cities: A call to celebration, vision and justice* is a report published in May 2006 that details the view twenty years on. The findings are striking. Copies are available from www.mph.org.uk.

8. I have explored the question of shared values and core commitments shared across faiths and beyond in *Building a Better World*, particularly in chapters 3 and 4.

9. For more information on the Faithworks Charter see www.faith-works.info/standard.

3

Changing World

God created the heavens and the earth

(Genesis 1:1)

I am ... the life   (John 14:6)

The Son is ... sustaining all things by his powerful
word   (Hebrews 1:3)

From the suites of Davos to the streets of Seattle,
there is a growing consensus that globalization must
now be reshaped to reflect values broader than simply the freedom of capital.[1]

(John Sweeney, President of the American
Federation of Labour and Congress of
Industrial Organisations)

What is Globalisation?

One of the greatest challenges facing the world today is globalisation.[2] It is almost impossible to pick up a newspaper, surf news sites on the web or watch a television news bulletin without discovering at least one story about the impact of globalisation. What is globalisation and how does it affect a local church? Why should such a big idea even be considered when we are thinking about how our local congregations connect with our communities or how we go about our daily lives?

An Economic Phenomenon

Globalisation is certainly an economic phenomenon. We only have to take a glance at high streets across much of the 'One Third World'[3] to realise that – brands such as Gap, Nike, IBM, Coca-Cola, McDonalds and Starbucks are a clear indication of both globalised markets and globalised brands. In fact, globalisation is often seen as a purely economic phenomenon. That perception could be reinforced by riots at events such as the World Trade Organisation conference in Seattle in 1999 or demonstrations at the various G8 conferences[4] or from the sheer volume of reporting, discussion and dialogue around the impact of a globalised economy and a globalised market in much political discussion in the UK and the USA. In the Trades Union Congress report on globalisation in the UK published in August 2006,[5] the general secretary of the TUC, Brendan Barber, commented:

> Globalization has made a real difference to the quality of life of working people in the UK and across the world but there are victims as well as winners. Too many British workers are losing their jobs when companies move abroad or fail to compete. Cheap DVD players and clothes are scant compensation if you are being downgraded to poor quality, insecure, low-paid work.
>
> Of course we cannot say 'stop the world I want to get off' and turn back the tide of globalization by erecting barriers to try and protect industries and jobs. But that does not mean we are powerless in shaping its impact. The government must provide support to older and unskilled individuals to help them adapt to the opening up of world markets and ensure that all UK workers benefit.[6]

With the rapidly growing markets and economies of countries such as India and China, it is no surprise that the economic impact of globalisation is often at the top of the agenda for discussion, debate and action. China's economy is now the fourth largest in the world, reporting a 10.6 per cent growth in 2006,[7] and India's is the second fastest-growing economy in the world, reporting growth of 9.2 per cent in the years 2006 to 2007.[8]

These facts and figures make interesting and challenging reading for economists and politicians, but in local communities they are the facts behind the loss of jobs as call centres are relocated and production bases are shifted from the UK to other parts of the world. They are also the facts that explain why manufactured goods are available at such inexpensive prices.

For many individuals and communities in the United Kingdom, everything else about globalisation is viewed through the lens of economics, because it is with reference to economics that globalisation is usually encountered or discussed. Colin Hines, the author of *Localisation – A Global Manifesto*, quoted in a report for the Christian relief and development agency Tearfund, described globalisation as 'the ever-increasing integration of national economies into the global economy through trade and investment rules and privatisation, aided by technological advances'.[9]

Yet globalisation is so much more than this, and it is because it is so much more than economics that it is vital for individuals and local churches to understand it and respond to it appropriately.

More Than Economics

Globalisation also affects sport, communication, electronics, cultural and religious trends, terrorism and security measures, to name but a few areas. The United Kingdom has repeatedly experienced attempts by terrorists to wreak havoc, such as those on the streets of Glasgow and London. Terrorist attacks in recent years demonstrate that what happens in the mountains of Afghanistan and the deserts and cities of Iraq, Israel and the Palestinian territories deeply affect the lives of ordinary people not only in those countries, but also in Europe and the USA.

Globalisation is not just about what is exported 'from the West to the rest'. It is a highway upon which ideologies, religions, spiritualities and worldviews travel at breakneck speed. Globalisation is complex, and cannot be defined by one single set of ideas, exchanges or processes. Like postmodernity, globalisation is multifaceted and changes quickly, encompassing a wide range of phenomena. In fact, trying to define it is like trying to categorise snowflakes.

A Working Definition – Big and Small

> Globalisation as a concept refers to both the compression of the world and the intensification of consciousness of the world as a whole ... both concrete global interdependence and consciousness of the global whole.[10]

Living in a globalised world makes us aware, paradoxically, of how very big, and how very small, the world is. This paradox is experienced across a spectrum of events. The collapse of the Asian financial markets in 1997, for example, triggered an economic downturn across the world. Within days of the crisis hitting the markets in Asia, the markets in New York and London were reacting strongly. The range and fluctuation of commodities markets such as wheat, coffee, grain,

cocoa and oil also highlight the extent of the connections between nation states. What this means in real
terms is that a war in the Middle East or a rise in cocoa
prices in the Côte d'Ivoire will result in rapidly
increased prices for petrol or chocolate in the northern
hemisphere, and what is true in the markets is also true
in terms of security.

The attacks on the World Trade Center on 11
September 2001 quickly triggered a series of events
across the world that have led to a completely different
view of national security and have reshaped the landscape of international relations. The attacks, together
with those on the Pentagon and in Pennsylvania on the
same day, destroyed forever the idea that the United
States was beyond vulnerability to terrorism. Because
these attacks were the first on 'home soil' in the US,
they changed the perception the United States had of
itself, and of the world, for ever. They also changed the
way the rest of the world viewed the United States. But
whether it be the collapse of the twin towers in
September 2001, the Bali nightclub bombs of October
2002, the train bombings in Madrid in March 2004 or
the London bombings of July 2005, each incident highlights the globalised nature of both security and terror.

Debbie and I were in New York one month after the
twin towers were destroyed. I was also in my office in
London on the day of the attacks on the tubes and the
bus in July 2007. There was, in each situation, a sense
of unspoken realisation that our view of the world
could no longer be the same. It had become dangerous.

The impact of a global terror threat was the sense that nowhere is safe. While in New York, we met a lady who had worked in the twin towers and escaped, deeply traumatised. As I talked with her, she repeatedly said to me, 'I never thought it would happen to us.'

About a month after the London bombings, I was preaching in a church in Enfield, North London. At the end of the meeting a lady spoke with me who had been on the tube train at King's Cross station. She was deeply traumatised too and as we finished our conversation, she used exactly the same phrase: 'I never thought it would happen to us.'

Perhaps it is because I spent my first twenty years living with a constant terror threat in Northern Ireland that I have been surprised by the depth of change wrought by the terrorist attacks of the last six years. The sense that anything could happen on a train, a bus, a plane or an underground station is present and very real. It is a direct consequence of a globalised world, where what happens in a distant country like Iraq or Afghanistan has a direct impact on how we live in our own communities. The effects of globalisation reach beyond economics and security and have a deep impact on our own neighbourhoods.

Social Situations and Relationships are Connected

The people who live in our streets and our communities bring with them colliding worldviews and ideas that we would not have been exposed to thirty years ago. I would even suggest that globalisation is nurtured and nourished in local communities. The social consequences of globalisation are worked out in the relationships and awareness we have of our neighbours. It is in the local school, in our office, that globalisation forms and then reforms our relationships and our sense of identity and belonging.

From the proliferation of religious expression and lifestyles that we touched on in the last chapter to the very food that we eat, our communities are deeply impacted by the globalised world. Our communities are diverse as a direct result of ease of travel, communication, employment and the sharing of ideas, convictions and worldviews.

We now find ourselves directly connected to the remotest parts of the world. Whereas the islands of Indonesia would have been a remote and mysterious place thirty or forty years ago, they were popular holiday destinations when the tsunami rushed across the Indian Ocean on Boxing Day 2004. There are few places in the world that we would now consider isolated: tourism has also gone global.

How Do We Deal With Communities that are a Hotchpotch of Ideas?

Social, political and economic activities now take place across borders and as a result the ideas around 'citizenship' and 'nationality' are themselves changing. Hence there is now a huge debate raging in many nations in the one-third world around citizenship. In the United Kingdom, this subject may become one of the most significant political and social debates of the next few years with a focus on both the rights and the responsibilities of citizens.

At a local level, we must address the multitude of questions we face in this evolving situation. What does it mean to be black, Muslim and British? How do we sustain a healthy community in the context of such diversity? How do we reach out in acceptance and love without losing our own identity?

How Do We Manage Greater Connectedness?

From moving between places to sharing of ideas, our connectedness is greater than it has ever been. The increase in ease, access and speed of connectedness has led to a deeper connection between the local and the global.[11] More people now live and act locally in the full knowledge that they are connected globally. For example, a friend of mine runs a cottage industry in Peru making greeting cards. The cards are marketed via the internet and are shipped all around the world, producing a wider market than would have been remotely possible just fifteen years ago and all at a minimum cost, but with maximum benefit to the women who make the cards.[12] Another example is Jacob's Well – an innovative social enterprise set up in India to produce goods that are sold around the world.[13] Our interconnected global society can be a great benefit, as well as a threat, to life at local level.

Advances in electronic communication have combined with other changes in modern life (the increase of car travel, for example) to create a society whose members may be frequently and regularly in touch with people on the other side of the planet yet never get to know their neighbours in the same street. The challenge this offers local churches is to find ways of creating local community for people who are connected globally but feel isolated and alone in their own home town.

Climate Change and Globalisation

Climate change is the most severe problem that we are facing today, more serious even than the threat of terrorism.[14]

(David King, Chief Scientific Adviser
to the UK Government)

There is no doubt that the greatest and most pressing issue of this century is that of environmental responsibility – the issue of climate change.

At current trends and without drastic intervention, we are facing something of a doomsday scenario.

At the current rate of carbon emissions, global average temperatures will rise by 2 per cent by 2050 according to research by the Intergovernmental Panel on Climate Change. Most experts agree that this increase is unavoidable. The consequences of this sort of change in temperature are nothing short of catastrophic. It would lead to the creation of 150 million environmental refugees, the majority of them in poor countries. Between 1 and 3 billion people (that is just under half the world's population) would face water shortages. As the production of food goes into decline around 30 million people would go hungry.

By the end of the twenty-first century, at current trends, sea levels will have risen by an average of 95cm – this would submerge 18 per cent of Bangladesh, creating 35 million environmental refugees. A rise in sea levels of one metre would displace 10 million people in Vietnam and another 8 to 10 million in Egypt. The UK's Department for International Development predicts that the number of Africans at risk of coastal flooding will rise from 1 million in 1990 to 70 million by 2080.

However, at the same time as a rise in sea levels, reduced rainfall will lead to widespread water shortages. This is not new to many areas of Africa – particularly in the sub-Saharan region. The Sahel region of Africa has experienced drought-like conditions stretching back to the 1960s with no prospect of change. In East Africa, 11 million people are at risk of hunger because of drought. Meanwhile, in Asia and South America, millions of people depend on melting glaciers for drinking water. Since 1995, 90 per cent of the glaciers upon which they depend have been shrinking – they cannot be replaced. The last tropical glacier in Africa, on Mt Kilimanjaro, will have disappeared by 2015.

It is expected that the world faces a 1 per cent

increase in temperature by 2020. This would result in 240 million people facing the reality that water supply cannot meet demand – already in Australia there are widespread plans to use water recycled from the waste system for drinking because of water shortages. Temperatures are predicted to rise by 1.3 per cent by 2025 which would lead to tens of millions of people going hungry because of the impact of crop production and increased prices for food.

There is no doubt that global climate change will reverse the impact of campaigns such as Make Poverty History or Live 8 because it will make poverty permanent. The European Commission in 2003 stated that climate change was one of the most significant issues facing the world.[15]

Globalised climate change also leads to extreme weather conditions. From the tsunami of Boxing Day 2004 and Hurricane Katrina[16] in August 2005, to repeated and increased flooding faced by the United Kingdom over the last decade, extreme weather patterns are becoming more established and more severe. It is one thing to cope with such extreme weather in an economically rich country. It is quite another in the poorer countries, where 90 per cent of the victims of weather-related natural disasters live. Over the past thirty-five years, storms of the force of Hurricane Katrina have almost doubled. Weather experts say that rises in the temperature of the sea surface are the most likely cause. A global hotspot for flooding is Bangladesh, which could experience 15 per cent more rainfall by 2030, putting 20 to 40 per cent more of its land at risk of flooding.

These problems are not localised and easily solvable, instead they demand a global response – and there is a sense in which industrialised nations must lead the way. Pollution of the planet has led to the oppression of the poor, and we must accept responsibility and do something about it. This is an issue which affects every citizen of the world, and which we must tackle. One person flying in an aeroplane for one hour is responsible for the same greenhouse gas emissions as a typical Bangladeshi in a whole year.[17]

Warming and Warning – a Long Time in Coming

Since the mid-nineteenth century, the time when most of the one-third world began to industrialise more rapidly, levels of the 'greenhouse gas' carbon dioxide in our atmosphere have risen by 28 per cent and methane levels have risen by 112 per cent. This has meant that the world's surface temperature has risen more quickly than at any time in the last 10,000 years. The 1990s were the hottest decade since records began – and the rate at which the temperature is rising is increasing. The World Health Organisation estimates that at least 150,000 people die every year from diseases which are more prevalent due to the warming planet. As a result of global warming, malaria (which currently kills around 3 million people a year) will spread to new territories. It is already moving into the highland areas of

Rwanda and Tanzania. So climate change is nothing new. It has not happened overnight and it will certainly not be tackled overnight.

Discussions about how to address the issue are also not new. The United Nations produced *The Report of The United Nations Conference on the Human Environment*[18] as a result of talks in Stockholm in 1972. At the Rio Earth Summit in 1992, 172 representatives of national governments and 2,400 representatives of non-governmental organisations met in separate tracks to discuss and debate the issues of climate change. The summit called for a change in the way we engage with and use the environment and warned of the consequences of not addressing the issue of environmental sustainability. It called for changes in production methods, use of renewable energy sources, an urgent attempt to address carbon emissions from vehicles and a greater awareness of the scarcity of drinking water.

In 1997, the Kyoto Protocol called for a drastic commitment to the reduction of carbon emissions around the world by nation states. The United States have still not ratified the protocol and the reluctance to do so is a major stumbling block in addressing the issues of climate change, although there have been significant changes in tone as the scale of the consequences has begun to emerge beyond denying. In Al Gore's words, 'climate change is not so much a political issue as it is a moral issue'.[19]

Ten years after the Rio Earth Summit, the United Nations summit in Johannesburg in 2002 (named

Rio+10) sought to strengthen commitments to tackle sustainable development. Although many meaningful conversations and discussions took place, action was once again weak. In February 2007, the Citizens of the Earth Summit which took place in Paris set out strong evidence for the link between human activity and climate change and called for a worldwide organisation to be established to deal with the issue globally.[20] The last G8 summit at Heiligendamm in June 2007 seems to have produced more of a consensus on global responsibility for climate change than anything thus far – the proof will be in the action that flows from it.[21]

Clearly climate change is now a major conversation, not just amongst scientists but on political agendas both nationally and locally. It leads to discussions about recycling on a local level, carbon footprints and sustainable energy sources. It is discussed by our children in their schools, and increasingly it is being recognised as an issue upon which the church should both say and do something.[22] Christians and local churches have an opportunity to set an example and to engage in shaping our community's response to the issue of global climate change, by encouraging an approach to our planet that highlights our responsibility as stewards of the created order.

Good?

Whether its challenge is experienced economically, socially, technologically, culturally, religiously, or in terms of climate threat or security threat, the reality is that globalisation is all around us. There are those who would argue in favour of globalisation and those who are wholly against it, but with all its benefits and challenges, globalisation cannot be reversed. On the positive side, globalisation leads to increased trade, reduced protectionism and the opening up of new markets, which leads to increased prosperity and greater affluence. This is not only true nationally, it is also true locally and regionally. There are new markets and new opportunities for small businesses and cottage industries to flourish in today's world.

The same positive consequences exist for individual followers of Christ and for local churches. Globalisation means we can now develop direct links with other local churches in different parts of the world. We can engage in directly linked mission and prayer and support of one another across the globe. On more than one occasion in the last year, thanks to the globalised communications networks we now enjoy, I have been able to support work overseas, speak directly to people in India and elsewhere, and link with Christians in other parts of the world via a live video feed in a conference where I was speaking, all at no cost to Faithworks or Oasis, the movement and organisation of which I am proud to be a part, and without the contribution to environmental damage that travelling there by air would have implied. My local church in Hampshire is also now able to explore links with sister churches in Sierra Leone or other parts of the world in a way which would have been unimaginable ten years ago.

As well as that, we have the wonderful privilege of having the world community on our doorstep, with the opportunities to learn from other traditions and cultures and to share with them our own worldview and ideas – all without having to travel beyond the end of our road! Many local churches are now able to engage in cross-cultural and global mission without travelling more than a few miles geographically. This is a wonderful privilege and one that presents many opportunities for the local church to build the kingdom of God and be shaped by the way in which God is moving in other parts of the world.

Bad?

Globalisation has been used to transfer resources into the one-third world and away from the two-thirds world and enhanced interconnection could exacerbate this trend. Those whose voice is perceived as quieter or weaker could be vanquished by the powerful. Those who are deemed less influential do not always have the resources to defend themselves.

The greatest challenge of globalisation is that it can breed a competitive voracity that will exploit the poor still further for the benefit of the wealthy, widening the gap between rich and poor – not just between the two hemispheres of the world, but between nations, between regions and even between groups in our community. We can become exploiters rather than partners.

The church can be as guilty of exploitation and manipulation of the southern hemisphere as the secular world. We often forget that Christianity was birthed in the Middle East, and that we have westernised our faith. It is a salutary thing to remember that from Jesus Himself, through the apostles, Paul and all the way to such people as Augustine, the church owes much to the continent of Africa and the countries of Iraq, Iran and Israel.

Mapping a Way Ahead

Globalisation contains the seeds of both good and ill. How we realise that inherent potential will be determined by the way we participate in our global society, whether in the choices we make as local churches and individual Christians, or in our institutional responses and attitudes as the church of the northern hemisphere.

Globalisation is not only the recognition that the extraordinary diversity of cultures in the world exists ... but that each culture has as much right to speak and be heard as ours does and that this shapes the way we do things. Moreover, in the urgency with which they need to sift out truth from local culture, Christians in the Two-Thirds World are recapitulating early church history; while the church in the

West wrestles again with what it means to articulate
the gospel in an age of complex, cosmopolitan characteristics.[23]

(Don Carson)

Globalisation has the ability to help sustain those who
are poor, and to enable the local church to rediscover
our commitment to the whole gospel for the whole
person. To do that, we must first understand the importance of integral mission itself. Without an integrated
understanding of the good news, we will always fall
into one of two traps – either running away from the
opportunities of globalisation because we consider it to
be a threat, or becoming exploitative of the opportunities of globalisation for our own gain.

To map a way ahead, we must have the humility to
be willing to learn something from our engagement
with this phenomenon as well as imparting our own
point of view. Humility will help us to avoid what
George Ritzer calls the McDonaldisation Effect,
whereby the cultural norms of the Western world are
globally imposed. We must recognise that neither the
success nor the effectiveness of a local church is based
solely on the one-third world's evaluations of efficiency,
calculability, predictability and control,[24] and we must
learn from the southern hemisphere new ways of
expressing and being church. Alongside that, we need a
ready willingness to analyse our own understandings of
what is meant by 'good news' and 'Christian living' to
ensure that we have not so westernised our faith that

we consequently turn the immense opportunity global-isation presents into an imperialist and paternalistic cru-sade.

Challenges

It remains to be seen whether local churches can rise to the three broad areas of challenge that globalisation holds out to us – theological, cultural and social.

Theologically, we must establish a principle of using biblical theology as the foundation for our faith, rather than the preferred approach of systematic theology prevalent in the West. Will we live out of a revealed faith that has at its centre the life and example of Christ as portrayed in Scripture, or will we continue to west-ernise him, and therefore our faith?

At the local level, the church must rise to the chal-lenge of addressing the extent to which we have become culturally submerged rather than culturally alternative. Will we seek to be authentic Christian com-munities in the light of our history and breadth across the world or will we allow ourselves to become simply a reflection of the cultural mores of our day?

Socially, will we rise to the challenge of being a peo-ple of hospitality, welcome and dialogue as we embrace the world on our doorstep, or will we retreat into the known, the safe and the comfortable, pulling up the drawbridge as we go? To paraphrase Martin Luther King Jnr's comments on the early church, we must decide whether we are merely a thermometer that records the ideas and opinions around us or a thermo-stat that actually transforms the mores of society.

To rise to these challenges, as local churches across the UK, we must be humble enough to be led by the wisdom and perspectives of churches in the southern hemisphere when they are right and we are wrong. Their experiences of poverty, civil unrest, environmental change and even persecution have led to a deeper grasp of the whole-life nature of Christian faith and we would do well to learn from them. Is it possible that in the one-third world we have narrowed the good news over the last three hundred years, only to have it opened out again by the churches of the two-thirds world? Do we realise the immense advantage we have in being part of a faith that has been global for almost two thousand years?

Before communications, technology, economics and politics were global, the Christian faith was already stretching from Jerusalem to London. As Christians we belong to a global family, and we have networks, resources, support and experience across every continent of the world. A holistic embrace of these resources is undoubtedly a challenge – but it is also the most amazing opportunity.

What do Christian Communities in Britain Face as a Result of Globalisation?

The churches in the United Kingdom face many unanswered questions as a result of the growing impact of globalisation. How can we celebrate and respond to the reality that we have the world in a nation? How might we interpret what it now means to be British? Is our Christian spirituality formed by our relationship with American churches, European churches or those of Africa, Asia or Australasia? In Britain, where there is still a nationally established church, how might Christian citizens communicate to the wider world that there is so very much more to British Christianity than Anglicanism? How will local churches support and encourage Christians at work in business and commerce, in the environmental sciences or within the political arenas? Can churches model excellence in the ethical aspects of environmental responsibility, citizenship, and national or international trade?

No local church can afford to ignore the issue of globalisation, because every town and village in the world faces its challenges. We engage with people who have different social, cultural, linguistic and spiritual perspectives from our own. We must do the necessary work to understand truly what our own identity is, and to confidently and clearly articulate it while remaining compassionate, open and Christ-like in our engagement with others.

The immense changes of the times in which we live push us into the vortex of actually working out what we believe, and differentiating between what is central to our faith and what is simply an idiosyncrasy of our culture. We will find ourselves at times not only grappling with current difference as a result of globalisation and its multicultural impact on our communities, we will also find ourselves confronted with the memory, the social legacy and the contemporary implications we have inherited from both a British imperialist history and a Christian imperialist history.

For these reasons, the language that we use, the assumptions that we make and the example that we set as individuals and as local congregations will become even more important than they are now. In the same way, as every community in the United Kingdom has to come to grips with what it means to be British, we as followers of Christ have to grapple with the even larger issue of what it means to be both a follower of Christ *and* British. How do these formative aspects of our characters, personalities and identities work themselves out in the way we deal with people who are different from ourselves?

We must also interweave biblical theology with informed good practice in making our contribution to the healing of environmental damage. For us, this must be about far more than climate change. It is also about what it means to be part of a created order and a community, about accepting our responsibility as stewards of the earth that we believe has been entrusted to us by God Himself – and this reaches into areas where we have previously not held a strong track record.

Postmodernity confronts us with the challenges of how contemporary society perceives things like truth, authority, society and individualism. Pluralism confronts us with the challenges of how those around us understand community, spirituality and religious practice in a society as diverse as ours. Globalisation confronts us with a rapidly changing but deeply connected world and sets us the challenge of loyalty to the abiding truths of our tradition in a world that can be travelled in less than a day and where conversations can take place more readily with someone on the other side of the globe than with our neighbours.

Postmodernity and globalisation are the history and geography of the ideological challenges facing everyone alive today. Contemporary Christians, even should we wish to do so, cannot avoid the challenge of re-evaluating our identity, our sources of truth and authority, and the way forward for a biblical faith in a world which is postmodern, pluralistic, globalised, and still God's.

Impact on the Local Church

Local churches are more exposed to theology now than at any other time in history. The massive growth of black Pentecostal churches in London alone, where they now make up around half of the Christian population, is just one example. The assumptions of theologians in the one-third world are challenged by the experience and perspectives of Christian communities in other parts of the world; especially concerning such matters as healing, demonology and the nature of evil, power structures, and persecution from political authorities. The passion and commitment to prayer demonstrated by the churches in South Korea, with the attendant revival of Christian faith in that nation, is one such challenge, obliging us to confront the apparent lack of emphasis placed on prayer in many of our local churches.

Alongside the impact of theological convictions from across the world, local churches are grappling with an ever-increasing awareness of their responsibilities to the rest of the world. From supporting those who are poor in other parts of the globe, to taking seriously our responsibilities for the planet, local churches are finding themselves more engaged in a whole-life approach to mission than ever before. This often leads to a greater awareness of the cultural strait-jackets that constricted and inhibited us in expressing the fullness of the gospel. This realisation then leads to an acknowledgement of the need for a clear articulation of what we believe the good news of our faith to be. What is its impact spiritually, physically, socially, psychologically, emotionally? Paradoxically, it is as globalisation extends our horizons that we are compelled to contextualise the personal reality of our faith.

Recognising the Power of God in the World

At the heart of our response to globalisation lies a recognition that God is the creator of the whole world. Whether or not we believe in a seven-day creation is not the vital issue for the church. Rather, we must take responsibility for living out the global nature of our faith and its impact on the world. Gandhi's maxim 'think globally, act locally' suggests the shape of mission for each local congregation.

From the potential devastation of climate change, to the injustice of human trafficking,[25] to the global need for justice in international trade agreements, there is much that needs our contribution on a micro scale to influence the macro change we wish to see. We can encourage our churches to engage in fair trade initiatives;[26] we can ensure that we campaign on issues of justice and poverty alleviation through such global campaigns as the Micah Challenge,[27] aimed at halving world poverty, or the Stop the Traffik anti-human-trafficking campaign.[28] Local churches can be at the forefront of recycling and environmentally friendly initiatives too.[29]

The church I pastor has recently held a week-long holiday Bible club for children entitled 'Waste Watchers' that combines teaching about environmental responsibility with personal spirituality – all in a fun-filled way that helps children understand that God is creator of this planet and that we as human beings made in God's image are responsible for stewarding creation.[30] There are countless opportunities for local churches to make a start in addressing global issues that affect our own communities. Here are just ten:

1. Why not explore what people groups (any category of people defined by common characteristics) live in your community through contacting the local

council? Find out what services they need and see if there is any way that you can help.

2. Ask your church to become a Fair Trade Church and commit to not only serving fairly traded produce, but selling it.

3. Consider becoming a carbon neutral church. Work out your carbon footprint and ensure that you 'neutralise' it.

4. Become a local church that is committed to the poor – both at home and abroad. Get behind campaigns that aim to tackle global poverty.

5. If you have the grounds and space, consider allowing some of it to be used for allotments for the local community and set up a food cooperative.

6. Consider the banking arrangements of the church – and switch to ethical accounts and investment.

7. Partner with a church in the southern hemisphere somewhere and share resources with them.

8. Encourage global awareness in the church by starting a 24-7 global prayer group.

9. Live simply.

10. Enable teaching on issues of politics, campaigning and economics.

If we are to make a lasting difference in our world then it is not enough merely to ponder and debate the challenges that we face because of issues such as postmodernity, pluralism and globalisation. It is vital that we rise to those challenges in planned, informed, inspired action. That action flourishes when saturated in faithful prayer, forming a response that is vibrant, engaged and connected with our communities. The kingdom of God depends upon it.

Let us pray.

Father,

You are the God who made the whole world. You have fashioned, from nothing, the created order. You gave us responsibility to look after this planet and to care for it. We are sorry that we have failed in this task. Not only environmentally, but in our nations and our communities, we have not served You as we should. Please help us.

Help us to understand our purpose in the world. Help us to see the challenges of globalisation as opportunities to rediscover our role and place not only in the wider world, but in our communities. To take advantage of a globalised world without abusing anyone. To put You above economics, politics and our own preferences. To live from the revealed centre of our faith as we have seen it in Christ. To be willing to learn from others, particularly our brothers and sisters in the southern hemisphere. Help our churches to be communities of welcome, embrace and humility. Give us the grace to listen, the courage to acknowledge our need of change and the strength to step out of our comfort and into Your plans and purposes for us.

And in all of this, we thank You that you lead the way, and that You are the God of the whole earth.

We thank You that there is not one part of this world where you are not present and that you do not love. We thank You that You are already at work in us and in our communities. Give us the vision to accept Your invitation to join You in that work of healing love.

Amen.

NOTES

1. Quote taken from http://thinkexist.com/quotes/john_j._sweeney/ on 22 August 2007. John Sweeney is the President of the American Federation of Labour and Congress of Industrial Organisations.

2. For helpful summaries and guides to globalisation and its impact, I suggest:

    Richard Tiplady, *World of Difference: Global Mission at the pic 'n' mix Counter*, Paternoster, 2003, chapter 1.

    David Greenlee, *Global Passion: Marking George Verwer's Contribution to World Mission*, Milton Keynes: Authentic, 2003, section 3.

    Don Carson, *The Gagging of God: Christianity Confronts Pluralism*, Grand Rapids: Zondervan, 2002, chapter 14.

3. For the purposes of this chapter, I want to avoid using phrases like the 'developed world' or 'the first world' because I believe they unconsciously assert some kind of moral or political superiority simply in their tone. Instead I will refer to the 'northern hemisphere' and the 'southern hemisphere' or to the 'one-third world' and the 'two-thirds world'.

4. For example in Lyon in 1996, Cologne in 1999, Genoa in 2001, Evian-les-bains in 2003 or in Heiligendamm in 2007. Perhaps it is not surprising that economics take centre stage in protests at G8 summits, since the population of G8 countries make up 14 per cent of the world's population, but a staggering 66 per cent of economic output when measured in terms of Gross Domestic Product. For more details see http://www.g7.utoronto.ca.

5. See 'UK Business Vulnerable to Globalisation' at http://www.hrmguide.co.uk/general/globalisation.htm, highlighting the TUC's report which was published on 29 August 2006.

6. As above.

7. Figures from http://www.chinadaily.com.cn/china/2007-01/26/content_793128.htm, published on 26 January 2007.

8. Figures taken from 'India's Economic Growth Unexpectedly Quickens to 9.2% (Update7)' at http://bloomberg.com/apps/news?pid=20601087&sid=ayAK98NMbmCA&refer=home on 30 September 2006.

9. See *Globalisation and the Poor: Tearfund Policy Paper*, available at www.globalconnections.co.uk/pdfs/globalisation.pdf.

10. Malcolm Waters, *Globalization*, London: Routledge, 2001, p. 4. Also, for a wider and deeper view of globalisation see:

    Craig Bartholemew and Thorsten Moritz, *Christ and Consumerism: A Critical Analysis of the Spirit of the Age*, Exeter: Paternoster, 2000.

    John Benton, *Christians in a Consumer Culture*, Fearn: Christian Focus, 1999.

11. See David Held, Anthony McGrew, David Goldblatt and Jonathan Perraton, *Global Transformations: Politics, Economics and Culture*, Cambridge: Polity, 1999.

12. The project is called Esperanza Cards and more information can be obtained from www.cardsfromperu.com.

13. For more information see www.oasisindia.org.

14. David King, Chief Scientific Adviser to the UK Government, quoted at http://environment.newscientist.com/channel/earth/dn9911-quotes-climate-change.html.

15. See www.christianaid.org.uk/stoppoverty/climatechange for more details.

16. This was the sixth strongest Atlantic storm ever recorded, and the third strongest to hit the land mass of the United States of America. It killed almost 2000 people and was responsible for over $80 billion worth of damage.

17. Beatrice Schell, European Federation for Transport and Environment, November 2001.

18. Downloadable from www.unep.org.

19. From the film *An Inconvenient Truth*. The DVD is available from www.climatecrisis.net.

20. http://www.terradaily.com/reports/Call_For_Climate_Summit_As_Scientists_Ponder_Grim_Report_999.html.

21. For official information on the summit see http://www.g-8.de/Webs/ G8/EN/Homepage/home.html.

22. One of the leading Christian voices on the issue is James Jones, the Bishop of Liverpool, whose book *Jesus and the Earth* (SPCK, 2003) is a clarion call to engagement with this issue.

23. Don Carson, *The Gagging of God: Christianity Confronts Pluralism*, Grand Rapids: Zondervan, 2002, p. 539.

24. See George Ritzer, *The McDonaldization of Society*, Thousand Oaks, CA: Pine Forge Press, 1991.

25. For a moving account of the impact of human trafficking from victims, see Caroline Cox and John Marks, *This Immoral Trade: Slavery in the 21st Century*, Oxford: Monarch, 2006.

26. For more information see www.fairtrade.org.uk.

27. See www.micahchallenge.org.uk, and George Grant, *The Micah Mandate*, Chicago: Moody Press, 1995.

28. See www.stopthetraffik.org.

29. See www.christianaid.org for a whole range of ideas.

30. See www.scriptureunion.org.uk/holidayclubs for more details.

4

Great Expectations?

What do people around us think of Christianity? What do they expect of the church? These are crucial questions to answer if we are to work out how we engage in our local communities. As we explore the general understanding of the church held by people in our country we shall be better placed to engage in constructive dialogue with them, and to identify areas where change is overdue in our own lives.[1] Dr Alison Elliot, the first female Moderator of the General Assembly of the Church of Scotland, addressed their General Assembly in May 2004 and challenged the Church of Scotland to continue to change in order to be credible and relevant to society. She clearly felt that the church was perceived as intolerant of change:

> The assumption that change is somehow alien to our faith is a terrible criticism, I believe, of the Church.[2]

Rowan Williams (as Archbishop of Canterbury, the most senior churchman in the Anglican Communion) said in the general synod on 27 February 2007:

> The public perception ... is that we are a church obsessed with sex. [And] this is what many in the church feel as well. It feels as though we are caught in a battle very few really want to be fighting.[3]

Consider this thought from Callum Brown (Professor of Religious and Cultural History at the University of Dundee):

> It took several centuries to convert Britain to Christianity, but it has taken less than forty years for the country to forsake it ... religious decline as a long-term process ... has left today's Britons with a residual Christian belief but no church-going habit... Christian decay in Britain has been perceived as a decline without an imagined end...[4]

Given that communication is as much about what others hear as it is what we say, it is important that we do not react against sentiments like those I have quoted above. It might be an uncomfortable process for us, but it is important that we try to be as open as possible to hearing how we are perceived by people outside our Christian communities without rushing to point out why those perceptions might be wrong. We have to learn to listen if we are to be effective. Listening does not mean we agree with the perception – but perception itself is a very subjective and deeply personal thing and we must therefore ensure that we listen to others properly. I do not necessarily endorse or criticise the perceptions and expectations that we will explore here. Instead, I am building a picture that may help to define how the general public and others view the life of the church and evaluate its role in our communities and wider society.

Perceptions and Preconceptions: Running Away From a God 'Delusion'?

Richard Dawkins' book *The God Delusion*[5] sold 180,000 copies in hardback, demonstrating clearly that people are hungry to discuss the relevance and credibility of belief in God for rational modern people, and the place faith might find in their lives. *The God Delusion* has won widespread support in the intelligentsia and deserves both our intellectual and spiritual response.[6] The chapter headings of the book summarise its approach for us:

- A deeply religious non-believer
- The God hypothesis
- Arguments for God's existence
- Why there almost certainly is no God
- The roots of religion
- The roots of morality: why are we good?

- The 'Good Book' and the changing moral Zeitgeist
- What's wrong with religion: Why be so hostile?
- Childhood abuse and the escape from religion
- A much needed gap

In the appendix, Dawkins gives a list of contact addresses for individuals needing support in 'escaping from religion'. He seeks to dismantle the centrality and relevance to society of Christian faith, brick by brick. From arguing that God is no more than a construct or an idea through to advising people how to 'escape' the clutches of religious institutions, his intent is to help remove the myth of God from the minds of people everywhere. He dismisses criticism of the book from the church and other religious groups, which is hardly surprising, but we must be careful not to exhibit the same attitude.

The number of Christians who have simply dismissed Dawkins' book and refused to read it has staggered me. When we consider that the average Christian book in the United Kingdom only sells around 2,000 copies and compare that to the sheer volume of sales of Dawkins book, we should perhaps realise just how important it is that we are able to think through the ideas, convictions and statements that he has made. It is unwise to maintain wilful ignorance of how others think about us.

Richard Dawkins is only one example of a writer who has critiqued religious convictions in the UK.

Christopher Hitchens, author of *God Is Not Great: the Case Against Religion*, concludes his first chapter, 'Putting it Mildly', with the words:

> As I write these words and as you read them, people of faith are in their different ways planning your and my destruction, and the destruction of all the hard-won human attainments that I have touched upon. Religion poisons everything.[7]

The National Secular Society offers a downloadable certificate of 'de-baptism'. The society encourages those considering leaving a religious group, particularly the church to 'Liberate yourself from the Original Mumbo-Jumbo that liberated you from the Original Sin you never had'.[8] We would be forgiven for thinking that this is the common sentiment of people in the United Kingdom toward the church, but that is not the case. There are millions of people who have a very different view of the church and of other expressions of religious faith. That very fact underlines the importance of ordinary Christians (not just theologians and academics) taking responsibility to inform themselves about the magnitude and development of the debate around this issue.

If we are to contribute credibly to this discussion as it may arise among our friends and neighbours, some of whom will certainly have seen one of the 180,000 copies of *The God Delusion*, it is of vital importance that we acquaint ourselves with the facts about the profile of religious faith in modern times.

Voting with Their Feet - What is Happening Statistically?[9]

A quarter of British churches grew in the 1990s. In the 1980s and 1990s 1.6 million people joined the church, but in the same period 2.8 million people left.

Since 2000, the Anglican Church alone has planted 5,000 'fresh expressions' of church. These are attempts to create Christian communities that explore faith and community differently and are one of the most exciting initiatives to have sprung from the Christian church in the United Kingdom in the last ten years. The church in the UK records a loss of around 2,000 people every week, 1,500 of whom are lost through ceasing to attend any form of church that keeps records, rather than transferring membership to another denomination, or through death.[10] Within growth statistics and strategies in the Christian church in the UK, there is a heavy reliance on church transfer.[11] It is likely that the fastest-growing part of the Christian community is the 1 million or so people who have left the church but are still alive and well.[12]

A survey of English churches in 2005 gives us even more details to consider.[13] Between 1998 and 2005 half a million people in England stopped going to church services on a Sunday. On an average Sunday in 2005, 6.3 per cent of the population went to church, compared to 7.5 per cent in 1998. The age profile of regular church attendees is rising, with 29 per cent of churchgoers aged 65 or over, though only 16 per cent of the population are in this age bracket. Sunday church-going is declining at 2.3 per cent per year, a trend that seems to be slightly slower than in the 1990s when it was 2.7 per cent per year. It appears that almost all church growth recorded in England is as a result of immigration.

The Roman Catholic Church has seen its numbers of regular attendees halve in the last sixteen years, with a 29 per cent drop in the age bracket 20–29. It appears that the fastest decline in the church outside of Roman Catholicism is in Methodism, with the Methodist Church falling into fourth place behind Pentecostalism in the United Kingdom, which is one area of the church that is seeing marked growth. London has 11 per cent of all churches in England, and 20 per cent of all churchgoers. It has 53 per cent of all English Pentecostals, and 27 per cent of all Charismatic Evangelicals. The London churches account for a full 57 per cent of all Christian worshippers in their 20s.

What do People Believe?

A Mori poll in 2003 yielded some surprising results when it came to belief in various religious and spiritual things.[14] Of those polled, 18 per cent said they were a practising member of an organised religion, with 25 per cent stating they were *members* of a world religion.

At the same time, one fifth of self-declared members did not want to describe themselves as practising that religion. Presumably they remain members for traditional reasons or due to social pressure.

When it comes to personalised belief, the findings are even more interesting:

- 24 per cent said they were spiritual but do not belong to an organised religion.
- 12 per cent said they were sure there was no god whereas 14 per cent said they were unconvinced that one exists.
- 26 per cent claimed to be agnostics or atheists, and in a similar question (phrased differently) 29 per cent said that they did not believe in God.
- 60 per cent said they did believe in God, though only 52 per cent believe in heaven and 32 per cent believe in hell.
- While 60 per cent said they believed in God, 68 per cent believed in souls, highlighting the fact that there are many people practising a spiritual faith who are not theists.
- When asked what they considered to be spiritually inspiring, 46 per cent said close friends, 41 per cent said a walk in the country, 24 per cent said Jesus, 20 per cent said Nelson Mandela and 13 per cent said Princess Diana. Only 6 per cent said that they found inspiration in a 'sacred text'.

What Does That Mean?

Statistics can be used to prove almost anything! Working through them can be both cumbersome and complicated, but the challenge for us as members of local congregations is to consider carefully the consequences of some of the statistics that I have just cited. The reality is that the church is largely seen as irrelevant and that Jesus is less popular than a walk in the country! The Bible is largely seen as uninspiring and irrelevant and more people are leaving the church than joining it.

Alan Jamieson has suggested that there is a four-stage process to leaving the church. Firstly, individuals grapple with doubts, often privately struggling and finding it difficult to confide in fellow believers because of a fear of being judged or criticised. They then begin seeking and weighing alternatives to the convictions that they have held, working out what would happen if they believed something different. Thirdly, they begin negotiating turning points and developing exit strategies from the believing community and finally they begin developing a new sense of identity.[15] Surely being armed with such information means that local churches can begin to develop discipleship material, teaching and support that can address these issues in people's lives, in order to help them to think through their questions, doubts and concerns in a safe environment?

Trends of decline and departure encourage an understanding of church and Christian faith as increasingly anachronistic and irrelevant, and the cold reality is that the general trends have not yet been reversed. Nor will they be, unlesss we can imagine a different future and do something about it!

General Expectations and Perceptions of the Church in the UK [16]

There are deep challenges confronting us in assessing the general view of the church. The figures themselves show that the relevance and connection to everyday life of church membership and attendance are widely called into question. But beyond that, there are concepts about the church, held in the minds of those outside the Christian family, that may surprise us – and certainly deserve our attention. Having examined these perceptions, we may conclude that they are inaccurate. But as they are ideas held by large numbers of people, they cannot be entirely unfounded; and we have a responsibility to address them.

Because of the demographics of church attendance set out above, churches are seen as largely middle-class institutions. They are also considered to be predominantly the domain of women. Furthermore, there is a strong assumption that churches are more interested in money and fundraising than in general issues of life and supporting people. The language and liturgy of churches can appear archaic and irrelevant to those outside the congregation, and this gives rise to the conclusion that churches are both boring and disconnected from life. It is also usually assumed that the local church is for those who are already religious, and will have nothing of interest to say to those not already persuaded of the Christian worldview.

Scandals and skirmishes about sex and sexuality in the church have screamed from newspaper headlines in recent years: this has done little to recommend the Christian faith community to wider society. Acrimonious debates about Christianity and homosexuality have torn one denomination after another: most recently focusing on attitudes to the ordination of gay priests in the worldwide Anglican communion. The passion, indeed ferocity, characterising this debate has heightened public perception that churches are obsessed with issues of sexuality and are guilty of discrimination. When stories of failure to prosecute those who have abused children in their congregations are added to the stories of a church that will allow itself to be torn asunder over attitudes to homosexuality, it is little wonder onlookers evaluate the church as intrinsically hypocritical and guilty of double standards.[17]

The result of all of this is a commonly held perception of the church as internally divided, inherently quarrelsome, and thoroughly confused about its own identity and purpose in the world. We may contribute valuable work and wisdom enhancing the health and well being of our communities, our wider society or our world; but public attention is distracted by the extreme stridency and bitterness of the sexuality debate, and by the scandal of child sexual abuse – one of the most damaging and shameful betrayals of the gospel in the entire history of the Christian church.

We Know a Different Side of the Story

It is easy to think, when we read such damning statistics and such depressing perceptions, that they tell us all we need to know. The reality, however, is that those of us who are part of local churches know that there is another story to tell. We may not pretend that the church we are part of is perfect, and we may even recognise many of the traits that have been articulated by those outside the church, but we also *know* that God is at work in His church.

There are just over 48,000 Christian churches in the United Kingdom, and we are engaged at every level of society. In the past ten years, churches have been at the forefront of campaigns for debt cancellation in the two-thirds world through coalitions such as the Jubilee Debt Campaign, and calls for a more radical and effective approach to poverty eradication such as the Make Poverty History campaign.

Christian agencies such as Christian Aid, Tearfund and World Vision take their place alongside other non-Christian agencies in the delivery of development and relief support across the world. The Micah Challenge is a global campaign, driven by evangelical Christians, aimed at seeing the eight millennium development goals of the United Nations honoured by 2015.[18]

The Stop the Traffik coalition, with Christians at its

heart, is working across the globe to challenge the practice of human trafficking and eradicate this modern day form of slavery.[19] There are dozens of city academies being opened and run by Christian churches or charities in the United Kingdom. Oasis Community Learning will run and support inclusive community schools based upon the commitments of the Faithworks Charter in a number of locations across the UK,[20] providing focused and invaluable education for children. Everywhere Christians are involved in their communities through acts of kindness, service and the forging of new partnerships.

The Faithworks movement itself works with almost 25,000 churches and other Christian partners, supporting them in their delivery of services to their communities. These services are inclusive, compassionate and engaged in making a real difference in their neighbourhood.[21] From St Andrew's Memory Club in Great Yarmouth, which supports those dealing with memory loss, to Maghera Parish Caring Association in Northern Ireland, which works with the whole community of the town in County Londonderry, Christian initiatives are transforming communities throughout Great Britain.

Across the regions of the United Kingdom, report after report has highlighted the impact of Christian social action in the health and well-being of communities.[22] Each one makes evident the massive contribution that the church offers the community, not only in terms of presence, but in terms of economic contribution, volunteering and use of buildings, resources and experience.

There is also, despite the scepticism of atheist critique, widespread hunger for truth, as truth is in Jesus. Ordinary people want to hear and explore the gospel, as well as receive the benefits of its compassion and option for the poor, as can be seen in the 2007 update on the work of Alpha across the world.[23] In 1992, five Alpha courses were run. By 2007 that figure will have grown to 33,500, with an estimated cumulative attendance of over 10 million people – and that is only those courses that have registered. The church from which Alpha originated, Holy Trinity Brompton, now reports that since it made its Sunday sermons available for free download in September 2005, there have been more than half a million downloads from their website. Jonathan Aitken's[24] presentation alone (entitled 'I want to break free') has been downloaded 18,000 times. There are some 71,520 downloads taking place from this site.[25]

I travel extensively, preaching and teaching and meeting with local Christian leaders, encouraging them in the work of community-engaged practical faith. In my travels, I have been delighted and encouraged beyond measure to see the amount of good work that local churches are engaged in. Quietly, and often without government funding, local churches are working for, with and in their communities, providing goods and services and compassionate action because of their faith. Reports of the church's demise do not correlate with the vitality and passion and vibrancy that is experienced and seen on the ground by many local congregations. Indeed, of the last twenty churches in which I have preached, eighteen are reporting growth in their engagement with the community – an indicator of health and life even where it does not so far register statistically as numerical growth in the congregation.

There is no clearer example of Christians providing a meaningful service to the wider community than The Salvation Army. It is the largest provider of social and welfare services in the United Kingdom after the government, and in the last twenty years has gone through a significant rediscovery of its spiritual life and purpose. In the UK and Republic of Ireland, The Salvation Army has approximately 50,000 members, 4,000 employees and 1,500 Salvation Army officers (who work full-time for The Salvation Army). They run 776 local church and community centres, including outreach centres and outposts, 59 residential centres for homeless men, women and families, 17 residential centres for elderly people, 6 centres for families, a community home for children, 6 substance misuse centres and 2 centres for people with special needs. The Army's mission statement reads thus:

> The Salvation Army is a worldwide evangelical Christian Church and human service agency.
>
> Its message is based on the Bible; its motivation is the love of God as revealed in Jesus Christ.
>
> Its mission is to proclaim his gospel, to persuade people of all ages to become his disciples and to

engage in a programme of practical concern for the needs of humanity.

Its ministry is offered to all persons, regardless of race, creed, colour or gender.[26]

The Connecting Journey – Linking Who We Are With Our Communities

The challenge[27] for us as Christians and members of local churches is to understand exactly who we are and what we can offer, and then to connect that with the perceptions and views of those outside our church in our communities. The voluntary action and practical engagement of churches across the United Kingdom are the lifeblood of many of our communities, but unless we find a way of connecting the good news that we believe, and the good news that we are, with the perceptions and lives of those around us, we will remain the best kept secret that the UK has. We must identify and undertake the vital steps of connection that will enable us to realise our potential as beacons of light and hope to the communities around us, and bridges of discovery across which people can walk to experience the love and truth found uniquely in Christ.

Step One: What Do We Believe?

In the process of connecting with our local communities, the first essential step is to make sure that we know what we believe. In exploring the three predominant themes of postmodernity, pluralism and globalisation in section one, I have identified some of the big concepts that shape the way people around us think.[28] We live in the same world and are subject to the same influences and cultural trends as our neighbours, but we as Christians are open and eager to being shaped by our convictions about God and the world in which He has placed us, at least as much as by the Zeitgeist of our cultural context. Understanding and identifying the tenets of our faith are therefore of central importance to us in preparing the ground for engagement as the church with the local community. This preparational reflection is not a sideline for local churches; it is a fundamental building block for establishing the basis on which we may proceed. It is absolutely vital that local churches understand what they themselves are built upon. As we create the vision of engagement with our local communities, we must first reconnect with the vision of the community of faith that stretches back 2,000 years to Christ Himself – and beyond even that to the calls and the commitments articulated in the Hebrew Bible.

Step Two: What Do We Do?

Having consolidated our understanding of what we believe, our next area of reflection focuses on the implications of that faith. How might we ensure that our convictions and our commitments shape what we do with our buildings and our resources and our times?

How do we as local churches authentically uphold the connection between our convictions and our actions? We have seen that the good work being done by local churches across the United Kingdom is not always successfully communicated to promote an informed understanding in the way our neighbours view us. This may be because considerable numbers of Christians still regard church membership as essentially private and personal – akin to membership of a club or pursuit of a hobby. If we are to connect with our communities then we must discover the big picture of the kingdom, and understand that we are part of it, called to it, essential to it – we must discover our mission in the world.[29]

Step Three: How Do We Behave?

Having made the fundamental first step of establishing what we believe and taken the second step of envisioning how that might inform our choices of practical action, we progress to the equally essential matter of how we behave towards one another in our local expression of the Christian family of faith. This is vital because it will shape our relationships not only with each other within the church family, but also our relationships with other churches, neighbours, work colleagues, friends, our communities and potential partners. When we understand what we believe and what we should do, we are in a better place to make decisions about how we should behave – and this in turn will mean that we are both more engaged and more effective in our actions and relationships. Understanding how we should behave also deeply impacts the way in which we serve our local communities.

Conclusion

Our reading of the New Testament is our entry to the amazing vision that God has called His people in the church to change the world. Although we began this chapter with the depressing and alarming statistics around church attendance and affiliation in the UK, and we were further challenged by the perceptions held of the church by many people, it is important to remember that God Himself has chosen His church to be a powerful and transformative force for good in local neighbourhoods, nation states and the global community. We must be honest about the challenges that we face – but that means that we must also celebrate the things that we do well and recognise that God is with us.

In the story of Christ's exchange with Peter, told in Matthew 16:13–21, Jesus asks His disciple what people are saying about Him. Peter reports that some think He is a prophet – but the moment of challenge at the heart of the story is in Christ's next question: 'And you? Who do you say I am?' The confession upon which the Christian church is built is Peter's response: 'You are the Messiah, the Son of the living God' (verse 16, TNIV). Jesus replies, 'This was not revealed to you by flesh and blood, but by my Father in heaven. And I tell you that you are Peter, and on this rock I will build my church, and the gates of death will not overcome it. I will give you the keys of the kingdom of heaven; whatever you bind on earth will be bound in heaven, and whatever you loose on earth will be loosed in heaven' (TNIV).

In the gospel stories, Peter is the archetypal disciple; he is the one who represents us all, in our insight, our struggle, our dogged love of Christ that persists despite all our failures. This means that Christ's reply is not just for Peter the individual; it is the word of empowerment for every disciple of Christ. It means that the church can never be reduced to the sum of its parts or adequately measured by statistics; for it is the instrument and the vessel of the Holy Spirit.

The foundational rocks of any local church are the confession of Christ as 'the Messiah, the Son of the living God', and the personal commitment to living and articulating that by the members of that local Christian community. As we explore together what we believe, what we do and how we behave, there will be many uncomfortable moments for each of us. We may see ourselves and our actions in the light of the convicting presence of God's Holy Spirit. We may be challenged by our own cynicism or lack of faith. Perhaps we will realise that for our local church to be engaged, *we* must be engaged and therefore our own lifestyles will need to change.

We may also be encouraged to keep going, to keep

believing and to keep trusting that the good news we have been given still works – and it surely does. As we examine what we believe, what we do and how we behave, perhaps it is helpful to remind ourselves that we stand on the shoulders of a generation of followers of Christ who themselves stand on the shoulders of a generation, all the way back to the early church and the apostles themselves. Every generation has faced challenges concerning the future and the relevance and the life of the local church; the challenge is not new in our day, though the details will be specific to our times. What is perhaps new is the extent to which we face such challenges. If ever it was true that the church is only a generation away from extinction, then it is true for us today.

But if we can touch the live reality of the genuinely good news of Christ, then even in our own mistakes, frailties and failure, we can be channels of the hope that it brings to the communities around us. We may even be surprised ourselves by the depth and vibrancy and wonder of this gospel all over again. We might become excited, impassioned and enlivened again as we discover the mystery of God's power and work again in our lives together – because God's wonderful plan and rich variety is made known through the church to the world. There is life in the local church yet – let's share the secret![30]

My prayer for each of us echoes Paul's prayers for the followers of Christ in Ephesus. In the first, he prays that followers of Christ might know who they are, who it is that they worship and follow and the power of hope in their lives (Ephesians 1). In the second prayer, Paul prays that they might be strengthened in their resolve and determination and passion as a result of what they know (Ephesians 3).

> I pray that the God of our Lord Jesus Christ, the Father of glory, may give you a spirit of wisdom and revelation as you come to know him, so that, with the eyes of your heart enlightened, you may know what is the hope to which he has called you, what are the riches of his glorious inheritance among the saints, and what is the immeasurable greatness of his power for us who believe, according to the working of his great power. God put this power to work in the church when he raised him from the dead and seated him at his right hand in the heavenly places, far above all rule and authority and power and dominion, and above every name that is named, not only in this age but also in the age to come. And he has put all things under his feet and has made him the head over all things for the church, which is his body, the fullness of him who fills all in all.
>
> (Ephesians 1:17–23, NRSV)

> I pray that, according to the riches of his glory, he may grant that you may be strengthened in your inner being with power through his Spirit, and that Christ may dwell in your hearts through faith, as you are being rooted and grounded in love. I pray

that you may have the power to comprehend, with all the saints, what is the breadth and length and height and depth, and to know the love of Christ that surpasses knowledge, so that you may be filled with the fullness of God.

(Ephesians 3:16–20, NRSV)

Let us pray:

Father,

Help us to take seriously the reasons why people leave the church. Help us also to recognise in humility that we get it wrong. Forgive us when we have been the cause of someone leaving the local community of faith or when we have been an obstacle to people discovering Your love and grace for them.

Help us also to think about the way in which we are perceived by those around us. Give us the wisdom and the power to challenge the stereotypical images that people have of Your church. We pray that you would encourage Your people in our local congregation, and in every congregation that owns Your name. Remind us of who we are and give us the confidence that comes from the discovery of Your wonderful love and purposes for us as Your people. As we consider what we believe, what we do and how we behave, enable us to change to become more like You and to better represent what You have called us to be.

Thank You that You have called the church to be Your bride. Thank You that we are Your temple, both individually and collectively, and thank You that You have given us the wonderful promise that You will build Your church to stand strong against all opposition, even against the gates of Hades.

Please give us, in the daily reality of our ordinary lives, confidence and expectancy of great things flowing from Your promise to us.

Amen.

NOTES

1. One of the best attempts to understand the church in modern society is Stuart Murray, *Church After Christendom*, Paternoster, 2005.

2. See http://news.bbc.co.uk/1/hi/scotland/3737105.stm.

3. For more details see http://www.guardian.co.uk/religion/Story/0,,2022229,00.html

4. Callum Brown, *The Death of Christian Britain*, London: Routledge, 2001, p. 1.

5. Richard Dawkins, *The God Delusion*, London: Bantam Press, 2006.

6. Alistair McGrath has written a response entitled *The Dawkins Delusion*.

7. Christopher Hitchens, *God is Not Great: The Case Against Religion*, London: Atlantic Books, 2007, chapter 1.

8. See www.securalism.org.uk.

9. For a helpful overview of some of these facts and figures, see Stuart Murray, *Church After Christendom*, Paternoster, 2005, chapter 2.

The following works begin to pick up the way the church might handle its decline, and are worth looking at:

John Finney, *Finding Faith Today*, Swindon: Bible Society, 1992, records findings from interviews with around 500 people who made some kind of public commitment to church and Christian faith in 1991. His findings are worth exploring.

Robert Warren, *Signs of Life: How Goes the Decade of Evangelism*, London: Church House, 1996 examines the progress of the 'decade of evangelism'.

Mike Booker and Mark Ireland, *Evangelism – Which Way Now? An evaluation of Alpha, Emmaus, Cell Church and other Contemporary Strategies for Evangelism*, London: Church House, 2003.

http://www.vexen.co.uk/religion/rib.html examines the issues in more detail.

10. Philip Richter and Leslie Francis, *Gone But Not Forgotten: Church Leaving and Returning*, London: Darton, Longmann and Todd, 1998, p. 2.

11. Martin Robinson and Dwight Smith, *Invading Secular Space: Strategies for Tomorrow's Church*, London: Monarch, 2003, from p. 30.

12. Stuart Murray, *Church After Christendom*, Paternoster, 2005, p. 45.

13. See http://www.christian-research.org.uk for more details. See also www.secularism.org.uk.

14. For more information see www.ipsos-mori.com/polls/2003/bbc-heavenandearth-top.shtml, and a summary: www.ipsos-mori.com/polls/2003/bbc-heavenandearth.shtml.

15. See Alan Jamieson, *A Churchless Faith*, London, SPCK, 2002 or William D. Hendricks, *Exit Interviews*, Chicago: Moody Press, 1993.

16. See Rob Warner, *21st Century Church*, Kingsway, 1999, particularly chapters 2 and 3.

17. Points 7-16 are added

18. For more information see www.micahchallenge.org,uk.

19. See www.stopthetraffik.org.

20. For example the Oasis Academies that are opening across the UK between 2007 – 2010 will provide educational places at city academies. This flows from a Christian commitment to inclusion and individualised support. They will admit people based on geography, not based on religious convictions and they will teach fully within the National Curriculum. For more information see www.oasiscommunitylearning.org.

21. For information on the work of Faithworks see www.faithworks.info.

22. Just a few examples are 'Angels and Advocates' produced by the Churches Regional Commission in Yorkshire and Humber (www.crc-online.org.uk); 'Beyond Belief' produced by the South East of England Faith Forum (www.hitc.org.uk/cms/downloads/publications/beyond_belief.pdf) and 'Faith in England's North West' produced by the North West Development Agency (www.faithnorthwest.org.uk).

23. *Alpha News*, May–October 2007, published by Holy Trinity Brompton, London SW7 1JA

24. Jonathan Aitken is a former cabinet minister who was jailed for perjury and came to faith in Christ.

25. For more information on downloading from HTB see www.htb.org.uk.

26. For more information see www.salvationarmy.org.uk.

27. See licc.org.uk/imagine for more details.

28. Michael Moynagh, *emergingchurch.intro*, Oxford: Monarch, 2004, from p. 237.

29. Walter Brueggermann's thinking has been highly infulential in farming my understanding of the role and purpose of the church. See:

    Walter Brueggermann and Patrick D Miller, *The Word That Redescribes the World: The Bible and Discipleship*, Minneapolis: Fortress, 2006.

    Walter Brueggermann, *Texts that Linger, Words that Explode*, Minneapolis: Fortress, 2000.

    Walter Brueggermann, *Hopeful Imagination: Prophetic Voices in Exile*, London: SCM, 1996.

    Walter Brueggermann, *Biblical Perspectives on Evangelism: Living in a Three-Storied Universe*, Nashville: Abingdon Press, 1993.

    Walter Brueggermann, *Texts Under Negotiation: The Bible and the Postmodern Imagination*, Minneapolis: Fortress, 1993.

    Walter Brueggermann, *Finally Comes the Poet: Daring Speech for Proclamation*, Minneapolis: Fortress, 1989.

    Walter Brueggermann, *The Prophetic Imagination*, Philadelphia: Fortress, 1978.

30. See Ephesians 3:7–13, upon which I have based this paragraph.

5

What Do We Believe?

Your kingdom come   (Luke 11:2, NRSV)

Only, live your life in a manner worthy of the gospel
of Christ.   (Philippians 1:27, NRSV)

'What do we believe?' must be our
central, basic, foundational
question, because how we
answer that will determine everything we are and do.
As we consider what we believe, it is important to dif-
ferentiate what is central and non-negotiable for us
from what is peripheral and negotiable. There are some
things that we *must* change if we are to connect with
the world around us, and there are some things that we
must *not* change.

For example, our language has changed over the
centuries. The church must always ensure that it communicates with people in the language and the parl-
ance of the day. Hence the Psalms were recorded in

vernacular – some might even say vulgar – Hebrew. The New Testament was recorded in colloquial or Koine Greek, and the greatest translations of the Bible have been those in the common tongue of the day. The authorised version was a fit and appropriate version for the seventeenth century and whilst many people still enjoy its language and flow today, the New International Version or the New Revised Standard Version are examples of versions of Scripture which connect with people in the twenty-first century. Our understanding is enriched and expanded by para-phrases of translations such as *The Message*, though we must recognise that paraphrasing takes us one step further away from the original meanings of the text, and ensure that we study with direct translations.

We are not free to change the 'good news'. It has been entrusted to us from the generations that have gone before and we ourselves are only stewards of it. It is our responsibility to understand and remain true to the gospel as laid out for us in Scripture. It is from this rich source of inspiration and story and example that we find the threads of truth that are tested by time, and woven by the hands of tradition and experience into the very fabric of our faith. If we are to engage with con-temporary society, then we must know what we believe in a changing world. *Crux stat dum orbis volvitur* (the motto of the Carthusian monastic order – 'the cross stands while the world revolves'). Through the creeds and confessions[1] of the church, as they have been passed down to us, we are given a bedrock upon which to stand and from which it is both foolhardy and dangerous to depart. The church must also recognise, however, that the task of reforming and reshaping never ends.[2]

You Shall Know the Truth, and the Truth Shall Set You Free[3]

Though local churches should take full advantage of the latest ideas, techniques and approaches to our communities, we must never make the naïve assumption that technique alone is enough to make a lasting impact. While we should, and must, be committed to the best practices and standards possible in our social action faith proclamation, we must first ensure that we know who we are and what motivates us.

Without this strength of conviction we will end up being people who buy into the latest ideas and fads and techniques, with the result that we put more emphasis on our 'sales pitch' than we do on our character and commitments as local churches. We are not called to be a sales force promoting a product; we are called to be witnesses to the truth. The hard work of engaging in our local communities or in our work places begins with the even harder task of asking ourselves some very fundamental questions, the first of which is 'what do we believe?'

Kingdom People – Living out Integral Mission

The fundamental purpose of the Christian church, and therefore of every local Christian congregation, is to realise God's kingdom. It is the kingdom of God that lies at the heart of the teaching, life and action of the Lord Jesus and it is this kingdom that pervades His parables, His miracles and His passion.

> There is, however, one area in the testimony of the gospels to Jesus, the authenticity of which is agreed on by virtually all New Testament scholars – namely the teaching of Jesus on the kingdom of God. It pervades the entire proclamation of Jesus recorded in the gospels and appears largely to have determined the course of His ministry. While this has been acknowledged, its significance ... has been strangely ignored.
>
> (G.R. Beasley-Murray)[4]

In the books of Matthew, Mark and Luke, the phrases 'kingdom of heaven' and 'kingdom of God' are interchangeable.[5] In fact, the phrase 'kingdom of heaven' is itself a translation of a Jewish replacement for the name of God (which Judaism regards as too holy to utter or write down).[6] If we read Matthew, Mark and Luke, 'kingdom' expressions are found more than one hundred times, yet the phrase is only used twice in John's Gospel – in John 3:3,5 and in John 18:36.

The opening cry of John the Baptist's ministry was, 'Repent, for the kingdom of heaven has come near'

(Matthew 3:2, TNIV), and in that cry all of the longing of the Hebrew Bible[7] for the Messianic age, both its dawn and its establishment, are fulfilled. Immediately after John the Baptist was arrested, Jesus took up the same message – on arriving in Galilee after his cousin's arrest we are told Jesus was 'proclaiming the good news of God and saying, "The time is fulfilled, and the kingdom of God has come near; repent and believe in the good news"' (Mark 1:15, NRSV).

Jesus spent the forty days between his resurrection and His ascension speaking 'about the kingdom of God' (Acts 1:3). In His healing of the sick, Jesus explained that He was signifying the coming of the kingdom of God (Matthew 11:2–6); in His casting out of demons He explained that His actions signified that the kingdom was coming through Him (Matthew 12:28 and Luke 11:20). It was the kingdom of God that lay behind the public inauguration of His ministry when He read from the scroll of Isaiah (chapter 61) in the synagogue in Nazareth:

> 'The Spirit of the Lord is upon me,
> because he has anointed me
> to bring good news to the poor.
> He has sent me to proclaim release to the
>   captives
> and recovery of sight to the blind,
> to let the oppressed go free,
> to proclaim the year of the Lord's favour'

> And he rolled up the scroll, gave it back to the atten-
> dant, and sat down. The eyes of all in the synagogue
> were fixed on him. Then he began to say to them,
> 'Today this scripture has been fulfilled in your hear-
> ing.'   (Luke 4:18–21, NRSV)

The present coming of the kingdom lies at the heart of
many of the parables, such as the binding of the strong
man[8]; the treasure, and the pearl of great price[9]; the
lost coin, sheep and son[10]; the story of the harsh servant[11]; the cruelty of the labourers in the vineyard[12]; the
story of the great banquet[13]; the stories of the mustard
seed and the leaven[14]; the hidden growing seed[15] and
the parable of the sower[16]. Jesus goes even further
though, when speaking of the future coming of the
kingdom in his telling of the parables of the wheat and
the tares[17]; the dragnet[18]; the unjust steward[19]; the judge
and the widow[20]; the burglar[21]; the wise and foolish vir-
gins[22] and the parable of the talents and the pounds[23]. If
we add to these Jesus' teaching and sayings on the coming of the kingdom of God[24], on the Son of Man and the
kingdom of God[25], and his teaching on the final establishment of the kingdom of God when he returns[26], we
have a vast array of gospel material that shows just how
important the kingdom of God was in the life, work and
ministry of Christ.

As Christians we are 'kingdom people', but I wonder
how many of us have come to a clear understanding of
its meaning. Preachers may have exhorted us to be
'kingdom-minded' or 'kingdom-focused', but if I were to

give you a pen and paper right now and ask you to write down what you identify as the key elements of the kingdom of God, would you be able to do it? In fact, if I were to ask you to describe, without using religious words, what your street would look like if God's kingdom were to come to life in it tomorrow, what would you write down? It is impossible to understand the purpose of the local church without understanding the purpose and characteristics of the kingdom of God. Not only that, but it is also impossible to fulfil the great commission of Matthew 28 (or Mark 16) if we do not first get to grips with what the kingdom of God means. In the great commission we read:

> All authority in heaven and on earth has been given to me. Therefore *go* and make *disciples* of all nations, baptising them in the name of the Father and of the Son and of the Holy Spirit, and teaching them to obey everything I have commanded you. And surely I am with you always, to the very end of the age.
>
> (Matthew 28:18–20, emphasis mine)

The two key points of the great commission that I want to highlight are italicised. First, although most translations have an active and commanding 'go' at the beginning of the great commission, the verb in the original Greek actually reads as something more like 'as you go' or 'in your going'. In other words, the great commission is less about going somewhere else with the specific intention of making disciples than it is about living our lives on a day by day basis with the specific intention of placing God's plans and purposes at the centre. It is in day-to-day living that we are to work out the purposes and mission of God. In other words, we do not only 'go' somewhere else to make disciples, instead we are called to 'make disciples as we live'. This is a much more holistic, and frankly difficult task. *Everything* we do has a missional impact.

Secondly, we are not called to make converts, we are called to make disciples. Only God, through the power of His Spirit, converts. We are called to grow disciples – to help those who are journeying toward God to become more and more like Christ. In this task, we are not 'experts' but fellow travellers. In the words of the nineteenth-century preacher and pastor, C.H. Spurgeon, we are beggars telling other beggars where to find bread. The task of disciple-making is more akin to the role of a craftsman and an apprentice than it is to an academic teacher and a student. Again, this is a far more holistic understanding of mission and the purpose of the great commission. We are commissioned for everyday life, to grow and make disciples all the time, not just some of the time. The kingdom of God affects everything we say and everything we do. Indeed, we cannot understand the church, the gospel or discipleship without first addressing the issue of the kingdom of God.

Getting to Grips with what 'the Kingdom of God' Means

The gospel writers do not systematically unpack the nature and understanding of the kingdom of God in their writings. Perhaps because the writers chose not to mention it, or perhaps because Jesus and John did not further explain it, there is little explanation in the gospels of what the phrase 'kingdom of God' actually meant. For whatever reason, the modern reader is left with a phrase that needs to be contextualised in order to be understood, so it is important to define what I mean when I suggest that followers of Christ are 'kingdom people'. Fundamentally, the kingdom of God is the rule and authority of God Himself being worked out on earth. In this rule and authority, God intervenes to rescue, preserve and save His people, puts right the wrongs in the world and manifestly establishes justice and righteousness.[27] Hence, in the Hebrew Bible, the idea of God's kingdom is 'good news' synonymous with God's own coming and reign.

A voice cries out:
'In the wilderness prepare the way of the Lord,
make straight in the desert a highway for our God.
Every valley shall be lifted up,
and every mountain and hill be made low;
the uneven ground shall become level,
and the rough places a plain.
Then the glory of the Lord shall be revealed,
and all people shall see it together,

for the mouth of the Lord has spoken.
...
Get you up to a high mountain,
O Zion, herald of good tidings;
lift up your voice with strength,
O Jerusalem, herald of good tidings,
lift it up, do not fear;
say to the cities of Judah
'Here is your God!'   (Isaiah 40:3–7,9, NRSV)[28]

The Jewish people then developed and expanded the idea of God's kingdom, associating it with their longing for a political Messiah who would remove foreign domination and oppressors and replace them with God's rule. Other strands of Jewish thought began to speak of a dramatic intervention by God through the Messiah that would usher in a perfect age of God's rule and power.[29] In Jesus' healing and exorcism ministries, in His nature miracles,[30] in His forgiveness of sins, in His ministry amongst the poor and the marginalised and in the way in which He held 'open tables' for eating and drinking particularly, He proclaimed that the kingdom rule of God had begun in Him. But at the same time, He also pointed forward in his teaching, demonstrating that although the kingdom had been 'inaugurated' in Him, it would not be fully established until His return. So in Jesus' teaching and example of the kingdom there is an important tension between the 'here and now' and the 'yet to come'. Ultimate justice and righteousness will only be established by His return.

Avoiding Two Dangers

The two greatest dangers to Christian teaching and practice lie in the two extremes of teaching on the kingdom of God. One is that it will only come at the end of time when Christ returns. The other is that it is entirely about the here and now. Both are flawed, because they need one another to be held in tension. If we adopt the former view, we end up with a theology and practice which does not adequately address the current pain and need of the world. If we adopt the latter, we end up thinking that the return and triumphant rule of Christ will just be the crowning to the efforts of our own social gospel.

A brief reading of the list of New Testament references, teaching and parables cited earlier will show that the tension between the 'already' and the 'not yet' is vital if we are to strike the right balance in becoming kingdom people.[31] In the birth, life, death, resurrection, and ascension of Jesus and in the giving of the Holy Spirit to the church in Acts 2, the reclaiming of the earth and everything in it back to God's original plans and purposes has been inaugurated. In the return of Christ to rule in power, the consummation of the kingdom will take place, never to be undone.

Jesus, God's righteousness revealed,
The Son of Man, the Son of God, His kingdom
    comes.
Jesus, redemption's sacrifice,

Now glorified, now justified, His kingdom comes.

And His kingdom will know no end,
And its glory shall know no bounds,
For the majesty and power
Of this kingdom's King has come
And this kingdom's reign,
And this kingdom's rule,
And this kingdom's power and authority,
Jesus, God's righteousness revealed.

Jesus, the expression of God's love,
The grace of God, the word of God, revealed to us;
Jesus, God's holiness displayed,
Now glorified, now justified, His kingdom comes.[32]

Whole-Life

Jesus' teaching and ministry demonstrate that the extent and nature of the kingdom and the rule of God is all-encompassing – affecting every level and arena of human life and existence. His inaugural reading of Isaiah 61 is so powerful because it announces the integral and holistic nature of the coming kingdom. The integral nature of the kingdom means that it will only be fully established when the whole of the created order, so deeply affected in the fall, is healed by God's renewal and re-creation.

In Jesus' calling of His followers, He makes it clear that the holistic compass of the kingdom determines their commission. His disciples are not only to preach; they are also to embrace lives of simplicity, to exorcise and to heal:

> Then he [Jesus] went about among the villages teaching. He called the twelve and began to send them out two by two, and gave them authority over the unclean spirits. He ordered them to take nothing for their journey except a staff; no bread, no bag, no money in their belts; but to wear sandals and not to put on two tunics. He said to them; 'Wherever you enter a house, stay there until you leave the place. If any place will not welcome you and they refuse to hear you, as you leave, shake off the dust that is on your feet as a testimony against them.' So they went out and proclaimed that all should repent. They cast out many demons, and anointed with oil many who were sick and cured them. (Mark 6:6–13, NRSV)

Mark's summary of Jesus' entire ministry is important to remember:

> The time is fulfilled and the kingdom of God has come near; repent, and believe in the good news.
> (Mark 1:15, NRSV)

The relevance for our lives of the New Testament story is that the church is called by the same God to live out the same kingdom principles today as the first disciples two millennia ago. We pick up that age-old call to be bringers of God's rule and reign in our own communities today.

The work of the kingdom is not an exercise in proselytising. We must avoid focusing our mission on notching up converts, or using acts of kindness and compassion in our communities as a means to an end. We stand with the poor, the excluded and the marginalised because that is where God is standing; because it is intrinsically right. We are not called to have hidden agendas and secret plans. Of course we must proclaim the message of repentance and turning to God, and the complete reorientation of lives to God, which is the message of the early church, not to pump up our statistical profile but because that is what will bring healing and peace to people as individuals, as local communities, and as nations. We live out the principles and example of Christ and the kingdom not to showcase our ideology but because it is the right thing to do. We do all of this, not *in order* to bring the kingdom near, but because the kingdom is *already* near through the work of Christ in the church and in the world. This is the fundamental difference between thinking that we must somehow spin the world's straw into gold, and realising that the mystery of God's touch at work in and through our lives is already creating the alchemy through which transformation can come. It is the Spirit energy of God's kingdom already inaugurated in the ministry of Jesus and continued through the life of the church that pushes us out into our neighbourhood and wider society. The kingdom shapes the mission of the church. It is because we, as followers of Christ, have had our lives reorientated around the message and mission of God – which is the establishment of His kingdom – that our local churches will also be orientated around that same message and mission: and God's mission is the transformation of the world. It is because of the depth of change wrought by the kingdom's inauguration that the Sermon on the Mount makes sense.

Isaiah's moving and inspirational portrayal of the fully established kingdom has filled the faithful with hope for centuries. As we allow ourselves to be filled with their hope and passion, we find ourselves motivated to engage in healing and blessing of our neighbourhood community.

> For I am about to create new heavens and a new
>   earth;
> the former things shall not be remembered or
>   come to mind.
> But be glad and rejoice forever in what I am
>   creating;
> for I am about to create Jerusalem as a joy,
> and its people as a delight.
> I will rejoice in Jerusalem,
> and delight in my people;
> no more shall the sound of weeping be heard in it,
> or the cry of distress.
> No more shall there be in it
> an infant that lives but a few days,
> or an old person who does not live out a lifetime;

for one who dies at a hundred years will be
    considered a youth,
and one who falls short of a hundred will be
    considered accursed.
They shall build houses and inhabit them;
they shall plant vineyards and eat their fruit.
They shall not build and another inhabit;
they shall not plant and another eat;
For like the days of a tree shall the days of my
    people be,
and my chosen shall long enjoy the work of their
    hands.
They shall not labour in vain,
or bear children for calamity;
for they shall be offspring blessed by the Lord –
and their descendants as well.
Before they call I will answer,
while they are yet speaking I will hear.
The wolf and the lamb shall feed together,
the lion shall eat straw like the ox;
but the serpent – its food shall be dust!
They shall not hurt or destroy
on all my holy mountain,
says the Lord.   (Isaiah 65:17–25, NRSV)

Living out Integral Mission – Being, Doing, Saying

Another way of understanding the impact of being
'kingdom people' is to understand the importance of

'integral mission'. There is a number of phrases that we could use to describe 'kingdom people', or 'kingdom communities', or 'kingdom mission'. We could describe it as 'whole-life mission' or 'holistic mission' or even 'whole-life transformation'. I prefer to use the phrase 'integral mission' because it connects all the aspects of kingdom thinking and immediately communicates the sense of a joined-up approach to Christian work and service. It is a phrase that has been gaining ground across the world in describing a holistic approach embracing social action and gospel proclamation.[33]

Integral mission is about both announcing and demonstrating the good news. It is more than recommending that evangelism and social involvement are to be undertaken in tandem. In integral mission our proclamation has social consequences as we call people to love and repentance in all areas of life, and our social involvement has evangelistic consequences as we bear witness to the transforming grace of Jesus Christ. If we ignore our communities and the pain of the world around us then we betray the Word of God which sends us out to serve the world. If we ignore the Word of God we have nothing to bring to our communities or the wider world.

The Life and Example of Jesus

In integral mission, justice and justification by faith, worship and political action, the spiritual and the material, personal change and structural change remain and belong together. As in the life of Jesus, being, doing and saying are at the heart of the task of the local church and our own individual lives and we must hold them in balance together. If one strand is weakened, the whole fabric is weakened.

At the heart of integral mission stands Jesus Christ, His life of sacrificial service the pattern for our discipleship. In His life and through His death, Jesus modelled identification with the poor and inclusion of the alien and the stranger. On the cross, God shows us how seriously He takes justice, reconciling both rich and poor to Himself as He meets the demands of His justice. Local churches must learn to serve by the power of the risen Lord through the Spirit as we journey with the poor, finding our hope in the ultimate Lordship of Christ and the ultimate transformation of the world.

We also learn to confess that often we have failed to live a life worthy of this wonderful good news. That being said, too often the 'victory' of Christ has been interpreted in terms of militaristic language, domination, aggression and power. Such interpretation flies in the face of Christ's life of grace, peace and devotion and seems to turn on its head the ultimate power and transformational purpose of God's kingdom and His Spirit at work within His people. Christians and local churches do not 'battle' other human beings. We are not called to aggressive posturing either in our behaviour or our language – the kingdom comes in quite a different way.

Local churches learn to serve 'not by might, not by

power, but by My Spirit' as they journey with the poor, learning to trust the provision and protection of God. God has sometimes been portrayed as the weaver of a web or cloth, patiently mending the threads wherever they are torn or broken, the One who designed and therefore understands the beauty and inherent logic of life's pattern. On this journey we too learn to see the unfolding pattern, and appreciate that wherever we touch a thread, the whole web trembles.

In the making of books, 'justifying' the page of type achieves the pleasing effect of creating straight edges to the margins from the many ragged endings of the lines with their uneven lengths – a business of the artful management of spacing. The work of integral mission is about understanding the relationship that all things in the world – including the spaces – have to each other, because all of them are justified as they are reconciled to God in the atoning death of Christ, all the ragged edges brought into alignment. Our task (a necessary contribution that God waits for because we too are part of the pattern) is simply to open our every moment to the reign of the 'peaceable kingdom'.

The grace of God is the heartbeat of integral mission. As recipients of undeserved love we are in turn to show grace, generosity and inclusiveness. Grace redefines justice as not merely honouring a contract, but helping the disadvantaged, standing up for those who cannot stand up for themselves.

This means that local churches are called by God to engage with their communities at every level, recognising that our words and our actions must go hand in hand, that we must connect our preaching with our lifestyles if we are to be authentic followers of Christ. Commitment to integral mission enables us to see that the gospel is more than a message of spiritual change, it is good news at every level for every person.

Integral mission tries to move away from the language of evangelism at one end of the spectrum and social action on the other, to a holistic and joined up approach which inseparably links actions and words in the lives of both individual Christians and local churches. It springs from the mega-commandment of Matthew 22:37–40:[34]

'You shall love the Lord your God with all your heart, and with all your soul, and with all your mind.' This is the greatest and first commandment. And a second is like it: 'You shall love your neighbour as yourself.' On these two commandments hang all the law and the prophets.   (NRSV)

Jesus did not separate love of God from love of our neighbour – and we are not free to create such a separation. Indeed, much of the division and dichotomy of churches in the northern hemisphere has arisen because we have separated these two principles, which are inextricably linked. We cannot claim to love God if we do not love our neighbour and we cannot truly and authentically love our neighbours if we do not love God. Indeed, we cannot even become reconciled to *ourselves* until we know who and what we are in the light of God's healing and redeeming love. Local churches are called by God to love Him, to love their communities and other human beings, and to love one another. This simple, profound, transforming truth is at the heart of Christian engagement in discipleship, worship, mission and proclamation.

For too long churches have divided these things. We have seen social action as a means to an end – so that we can preach at those whom we serve – or we have seen preaching as a means of getting more people into our projects, programmes and meetings. This false dichotomy is both biblically incorrect and relationally damaging. But here and there we have got it wonderfully right.

The Bridge Bond Scheme is run by the Jesus Centre in Coventry, issuing bond guarantees and building relationships with private landlords on behalf of homeless people. In a city with a shrinking social housing base, the initiative provides a way for local private landlords to take on the high risk of housing people who have been sleeping rough or living in temporary accommodation. The project is run in conjunction with a church drop-in centre, and succeeded in housing and providing ongoing support for forty people in its first ten months of operation. Not only that, the project has a remarkably high repayment rate for the bond.[35]

The group that runs the project is passionately committed both to the proclamation of the gospel and to living it out in practical terms. Without the intervention of the Bridge Bond Scheme, most if not all of the forty people they have helped would still be on the streets. In this work the needs of the whole person are met. There is no attempt to separate out love for God from love for the people they serve. Their words and their actions go hand in hand. The same motivation that leads them to provide the bond scheme is the motivation that leads them to share their faith and their lives with the people that they help. To try and separate out these two aspects of their work is like separating life and breath – you cannot have one without the other.

Key Building Blocks of Belief

If local churches are to understand what it means to be kingdom people and a kingdom community again, then we must learn a new vocabulary to help us rediscover our theology and beliefs. In so doing, we will also come to terms with the implications of being 'kingdom people' and 'kingdom communities'. We will join together phrases, actions and commitments that should never have been separated from one another in the first place.

Moving forward in this process of rediscovery, as we fashion a new vocabulary to express our theological motivation and practical commitment, we can identify some basic building blocks of belief to underpin our understanding of integral mission. These are:

- human dignity
- the gospel

- incarnation
- neighbourliness
- justice

These terms are nuclei of conviction, around which will grow practical action, social outreach and what John Wesley used to call 'personal holiness' – the inner roots of the life of faith.

Human Dignity

The Bible makes it clear that all people share human dignity.

> Then God said, "Let us make humankind in our image, according to our likeness; and let them have dominion over the fish of the sea, and over the birds of the air, and over the cattle, and over all the wild animals of the earth, and over every creeping thing that creeps upon the earth".
> So God created humankind in his image,
> in the image of God he created them;
> male and female he created them.'
> (Genesis 1:26–27, NRSV)

The image of God is shared by every human being that has ever lived. This means that all human beings deserve to have us treat them with the same respect and dignity as we have been treated by God. How might we translate this principle into action in our local church?

We might evaluate our thinking about the needs of disabled people in the light of the principle of human dignity: whether to regard them as an inconvenience, or as an opportunity to demonstrate grace and inclusion and love. Local churches across the length and breadth of the country have an opportunity to put their belief in human dignity into practice every day.

EXAMPLES OF ACTION

Torch Trust for the Blind and Churches for All

Torch Trust for the Blind, an organisation for people who are blind or partially sighted, ensures that the Christian ethos of the trust is reflected in all that they do. Their chief executive, Gordon Temple, is a champion not only for people who are blind, but also for people living with any disability. As the facilitator of a network of Christian agencies called Churches for All, which works on disability issues, he is a tireless advocate. He has given up a lucrative career in engineering and business to pursue this passion and commitment, and the organisations in which he is involved are making a difference every day in the lives of people whose concerns are often neglected or ignored.[36]

Open Doors, Plymouth

Sometimes our commitment to the principle of human dignity presents us with dilemmas we must resolve if we are to maintain the integrity of our response. How do we ensure that we respond to and respect the image of God in people who hold a different religion, or those whose lifestyles we cannot condone? When faced with these challenges, we return to the process of thinking through what we believe and allowing it to shape what we do.

Open Doors in Plymouth, Devon, is an international English language school that works with asylum seekers. In 2004, a gang of forty youths were shouting abuse at a group of twenty asylum seekers in a school, and seventeen-year-old Ramazan Mohamed had a football thrown in his face. A local congregation in the town, the Waterfront Church, decided to do something. Under the leadership of a tenacious lady called Cassie Roberts, Open Doors began. It works with dozens of agencies across the town and is committed not just to providing English language classes, but also a whole range of social and spiritual support groups for those who are viewed with suspicion by many. One local church is not just making a difference in lives of asylum seekers, but is helping to change a town's view of people who are seeking refuge.

A key question for you to consider might be: in your community, who are the most marginalised people, and how could you help them?

The Gospel

Far too often, we have understood the 'good news' as something like this: 'Jesus Christ died for your sins to save you. You must repent or you will go to hell, but if you confess your sin and repent you will go to heaven. So repent, so you can go to heaven when you die.'

This is so far from being the whole gospel that we can hardly call it 'the gospel' at all. At best it is a consequence of the gospel. The good news, as we touched on earlier, is that God has intervened in human history through the person and the work of Jesus Christ. In a nutshell, the good news is that Jesus is Lord (Romans 10:9 – perhaps the earliest creed of the church)! He has inaugurated His kingdom and He calls all people everywhere to become part of his family.

God is putting right the consequences of the fall and He has given His Holy Spirit to His children to empower them to point to Christ, to speak truthfully about the purposes of God and to enable them to be catalysts of hope and transformation in the world – His kingdom coming.[37] The call to repentance is the call to a lifestyle of service and devotion to others in the awareness of the transforming power of God at work in the world. The good news is that God is at work in the world, that ultimately all things will be put right, and that He invites us to work with Him, believing that He is working through us to be catalysts for change and hope in our communities. The transformation and renewal of our communities is an expression of God's coming kingdom. Followers of Christ, whatever our theological differences and preferences, are each part of His church and we have been given the privilege and power to live as people of this kingdom, demonstrating its power and purpose in our lives, in our communities and indeed throughout our world. The kingdom of God is not labelled with terms such as evangelical or liberal. We must not alienate our brothers and sisters in our efforts to be servants of God. How can we proclaim a message of the kingdom in our communities if we do not also acknowledge our love of those within the family of God and our devotion to one another? Every Christian in the world, and every local church is called to an orientation around this one simple reality – 'Jesus is Lord'; and to demonstrate His lordship in our personal lives, in our commitments to one another and in our service of the world.

EXAMPLES OF ACTION

Glamis Adventure Playground

Glamis adventure playground is an open access playground in East London that provides a community hub and free supervised activities to children aged 8–15 years old. The playground, situated in the middle of Shadwell, provides physical recreation for young people in an overcrowded inner city housing estate which has little outside public space and few gardens, where the only alternative is sedentary indoor entertainment. The disused playground had been decaying for ten years before being resurrected by a local church group and turned into a focal point for the community. It is staffed by three full-time workers with a Quality In Play accreditation. The project employs 'Best Play' theory and practice, consulting young people about the playground.

The staff oversee a packed programme of activities, which include an opportunity to grow vegetables and attend to the on-site gardening plots. The project is living out the good news in the community by offering young people and their families a safe place where they can encounter an integrated expression of Christianity that touches their hearts, their bodies and their spirits.[39]

Nightstop, Banbury

Roger and Margaret Verrall are involved in the Nightstop scheme in Banbury, Oxfordshire. When neighbours awoke at 2.00am to find a young man trying to get into Roger and Margaret's house, they inevitably feared the worst. 'We were going to call the police,' the neighbours told the couple the following morning, 'But then we remembered what goes on in your house and decided against it!'

The Nightstop scheme provides temporary accommodation to homeless young men in the area. Since volunteering to take part in the scheme over two years ago, they have had the pleasure of welcoming more than twenty homeless young people into their home. 'The experience has brought us so many joys,' says Roger. 'We have been a small part of the recovery process for many of these young people.'

It all started when a young man who was homeless turned up at Margaret and Roger's church one Sunday night and asked for help. Roger and Margaret embarked on a journey which led them from a typical reaction of wariness and suspicion to enrolling as volunteers in the Nightstop scheme. They also helped Luke.

Like many of the young people who find themselves looking for emergency accommodation through Nightstop, Luke had been made homeless through a sudden domestic crisis. After the death of his brother in 1998, things started to go seriously wrong for Luke and his family. Several months later, his already strained relationship with his parents deteriorated further as they underwent a painful separation. When Luke arrived home one day to an empty flat and no sign of his father, he knew that he had been made homeless. The only item of furniture left in the apartment was his mattress lying on the floor.

In the summer of 2003, Luke signed up to the Nightstop scheme and found himself at the door of Roger and Margaret Verrall. 'It wasn't the easiest thing to do, staying in the house of total strangers,' Luke recalls. 'They were easy to talk to though, and I also liked the fact that they took a real interest in me.'

Over the course of several weeks, Luke became accustomed to staying at the Verrall house, with Roger actively encouraging Luke to apply for the position of assistant at a local pie shop. Since his initial appointment, Luke has progressed to shop manager, a move that also helped him secure permanent housing in the Banbury area.

In effect, by providing a safe place for children to play in East London or by providing a bed in Banbury, the people involved in Glamis Playground and in Nightstop are being and demonstrating the good news of the kingdom. They are putting their faith and their belief into practice.

Key questions for you to consider might be: how does your local congregation live out the good news that the kingdom has arrived? What opportunities are there for you personally to show by the way you live and act that you really believe Jesus is Lord?

Incarnation

The Christian belief in the incarnation beholds and adores the humility of God in coming to find us where we are. Those who met Jesus, from his friend and disciple Peter confessing, 'You are the Christ, the Son of the Living God', to the man born blind saying, 'I don't know who He is – all I know is I was blind and now I can see', testified to having encountered something utterly unique.

The early church in evaluating the transformative power of encounter with Jesus (whether in the days of His ministry in Palestine or in the power of His risen presence) came to the view that the one God has three persona: God is with us as Father (who gives us life, provides for us, whose word is law, whose judgement is absolute but whose love is unconditional); as Son (with us as one of us, bone of our bone, flesh of our flesh, child of Mary, God who is our brother); and as Holy Spirit (free as the wind yet indwelling our hearts).

Without this gift of God's grace, we could never quite reach Him. All paths may well lead up the mountain, but none of them quite make it to the top. God in Christ understands human weakness, comes down to find us, understands that the responsibility lies with power and abundance to bridge the gap. So the Christian doctrine of the incarnation teaches not just about the divine response to humanity, but the divine response to the 'anawim' (a Hebrew word meaning 'little ones') – all the poor and forgotten, the helpless, the children; the ones who never count. God in Christ is among us not like a Greek god bypassing the indignity of the nappy stage, but as a baby too young to pray, to reason, to work, to speak; too small to do anything but need the shelter of strangers and the mother love of Mary and the protection of Joseph. When we think of incarnation we are not contemplating an abstract theological proposition; that would be to miss the point entirely. When we think of incarnation we are adoring (and then as incarnation catches hold, following) Jesus.

It is seen in the whole of the life of Christ, from the fact that a young virgin became pregnant and bore the Son of God, right through to the fact that Jesus was subjected to the brutal and horrific death of a criminal through whipping and crucifixion. The incarnation takes seriously the whole of the life of Christ, from His conception right through to His resurrection and His ascension, and His continuing ministry of intercession for us at this moment in time. God was in Christ, reconciling the world to Himself (2 Corinthians 5:19).

God did not look on at the pain of the world from a distance. He endured and felt and entered into that pain. He is not a detached observer of the challenges of being a human being, He became a human being and endured those challenges personally. He chose to walk the path of humanity, and to endure hunger, thirst, pain, loneliness, rejection and temptation. As Christians we believe that God not only acknowledges our challenges and our pain, He feels it, because He became one of us.

> For we do not have a high priest who is unable to sympathise with our weaknesses, but we have one who in every respect has been tested as we are, yet without sin. Let us therefore approach the throne of grace with boldness, so that we may receive mercy and find grace to help in time of need.
>
> (Hebrews 4:15–16, NRSV)

We also believe that Christ, though He is Lord, became a servant. He chose not to exert power through demands, but instead through washing the feet of his disciples, including Judas Iscariot, who would betray him (John 13). Jesus said:

> You know that among the Gentiles those whom they recognise as their rulers lord it over them, and their

great ones are tyrants over them. But it is not so among you; but whoever wishes to become great among you must become your servant, and whoever wishes to be first among you must be slave of all. For the Son of Man came not to be served but to serve, and to give his life a ransom for many. (Mark 10:42–45, NRSV)

The challenge for local congregations, then, is to consider how encountering God as a first century Jew shapes how we engage with the pain of our community and the needs we see around us. The incarnation smashes into a thousand pieces any arguments of 'detachment' or separation from the pain of the world. God is *not* watching us from a distance, and therefore we are never justified in merely 'watching' our communities. We are called to serve them.

EXAMPLE OF ACTION

Newport Credit Union [40]

Tales of irresponsible, high-interest moneylenders preying on those struggling with their financial circumstances are all too common in Britain today. Like so many others around the country, the residents of Newport in Wales are susceptible to the 'black hole' of spiralling debt and unrealistic payments to moneylending companies. However, many of these residents have now found an alternative, thanks to the determination of several local churches to provide hope for the financially downtrodden.

When local churchgoer Val Delayahe heard that several members of local churches had begun to raise concerns over the effect that money lending companies were having on the welfare of families on the deprived Bettws estate, she was immediately interested. 'Having been the victim of legal moneylending companies in the past, I wanted to help members of my community avoid having to suffer in the same way,' says Val.

She began supporting a group set up by individuals from three local churches (URC, Anglican and Catholic) along with the Bettws Community Development Officer, which hosted several open meetings on the estate. It was at these meetings, attended by residents of the estate, that the extent of the problem of high-interest lenders became apparent to the church-founded group. 'We saw the need for access to affordable credit for those who were not presently able to obtain it,' recalls Val.

After gathering support and the necessary financial start-up costs from local churches and Newport City Council, the group of dedicated volunteers saw their vision of relieving the financial difficulties of Bettws residents become a reality. In May 1999, Newport Credit Union began providing residents of four wards in Newport with access to a low-cost savings and loan scheme. Local residents were invited to become members of the Credit Union whereby they contributed a certain amount of their savings, and were then allowed to borrow up to twice the amount of those savings, making repayments at an affordable rate with low interest. The project, which began operating out of the Bettws estate shopping centre, serves five wards of the city with membership of over 900. Staff at the Credit Union are eager to express their delight at the many members who now claim that they are better off financially than they were before joining the Union.

One member accessed a loan from the Union in order to purchase a set of ladders, which he then used to set up what is now a thriving window-cleaning business. In its first few months of existence, the Credit Union gave one mother, struggling to keep up with high-interest loan repayments, a £100 loan that allowed her to buy much-needed school uniforms for her children.

'Although it's not a "quick fix",' explains Val, 'the Union does offer an answer to those who have fallen into the hands of loan sharks and other high-interest lenders.'

As well as benefiting residents of deprived wards in the Newport area, the Credit Union has also offered local churches a unique opportunity to work together to meet a priority need within the community. By effectively tackling financial hopelessness in Newport, the project has received the support of differing elements of the community. 'Our project has been greeted with great enthusiasm by local churches, schools and business,' says Val. 'We have also received a fair amount of support from Newport City Council.'

The Credit Union has a base in the centre of Newport, giving it a central point from which to help residents from all wards of the city. With the ongoing support of dedicated volunteers, churches and other community groups and statutory agencies, Newport Credit Union is able to offer more local residents hope in the face of financial adversity.

The Credit Union in Newport began because one woman understood the pain and the challenge of financial collapse and was determined to help other people avoid the same mistakes that she had made. Her empathy led to her doing something about it. The project grew out of one person's commitment to do something, which itself sprung out of understanding of the problem. Val was determined to serve others because of what she had been through.

A key question for you to consider might be: how do the two truths of the incarnation – identifying closely with people and serving them – affect your day-to-day life, or the day-to-day engagement of your local church with your community?

Neighbourliness

Jesus' teaching on neighbourliness and how we treat others is simple, yet profound. All people are our neighbours. This is most profoundly illustrated in the parable of the good Samaritan. In the story, those who had most in common with a man who had been attacked chose to pass him by rather than help. The man who came to his rescue would have been a hated foreigner in the eyes of the victim of violence – and in the eyes of those listening to the story as well. Jesus finished His parable by putting them on the spot with these words:

> 'Which of these three, do you think, was a neighbour to the man who fell into the hands of the robbers?' He [the lawyer] said, 'The one who showed him mercy.' Jesus said to him, 'Go and do likewise.'
> (Luke 10:36–37, NRSV)

Christians believe that we have a responsibility to show care and compassion to our neighbours. Not only that, our neighbours are those around us, whatever their background, colour or creed. Even those who attack us are to be loved and cared for when they are in need. This is the illustration of the mega-commandment – that we are to love our neighbours as we love ourselves.

EXAMPLES OF ACTION

One 25 Limited

One 25 Limited was founded by several Christian churches and is recognised as the lead agency in Bristol for dealing with the multifaceted problems of prostitution. Through street outreach and drop-in sessions, they offer practical support and care to women trapped in street prostitution. The majority of women prostitutes are addicted to drugs and alcohol and many are homeless. The team assist with immediate needs e.g. food, health and housing, as well as advocac; and provide support when the women move towards a new way of life.

By developing a mutual referral system and working in close partnership with several agencies offering help in issues relating to drugs, health, homelessness and educational agencies, One 25 Limited have built up an excellent reputation with social services and Barnados. In offering practical help to women caught in prostitution in Bristol, they are displaying the neighbourliness that Jesus described in the parable of the Good Samaritan.

The Terminus Initiative

The Terminus Initiative is serving the Lowedges community in Sheffield. It is a church-based project that functions as a community hub, comprising a low-priced community café selling second-hand clothes and goods, a youth café, a drop-in centre for elderly people and a befriending scheme for asylum seekers and refugees. They also offer opportunities for volunteering. The initiative is a place for social networking, relieving stress and reducing isolation.

To improve services, they are in ongoing consultation with other agencies working alongside; the aim being to complement the services of these existing agencies. Reviews of standards occur annually with help from the Faithworks Charter. The project was awarded the Duke of York Community Initiative Award in 2006.

The Terminus Initiative is run on a low budget, with

few volunteers, but is having a massive impact on the community spirit of the surrounding estate, and is a wonderful 'good news' story of neighbourliness, love and support.[41]

A key question you might consider is: is your local congregation considered a 'good neighbour' by those who live around you? Could you name the neighbours who live in the six houses on either side of your own home?

Justice

Justice is a vital element of the call and commission of the local church, and of the church world-wide.

> Speak out for those who cannot speak,
> for the rights of all the destitute.
> Speak out, judge righteously,
> defend the rights of the poor and needy.
>   (Proverbs 31:8–9, NRSV)

Throughout the Hebrew Scriptures, whether in the infrastructures created by the Torah, or in the word of God to contemporary society by the prophets, social justice and true worship were seen to be twin strands of every faithful life and community.[42] What the prophets denounce is invariably either apostasy or social oppression. The biblical ideas of God's righteousness and justice are closely linked and the Christian church is called to be a prophetic voice for justice in our communities and in our world.

EXAMPLES OF ACTION

West Croydon Refugee Day Centre

The West Croydon Refugee Day Centre[43] is a project of West Croydon Baptist Church. In March 1998, Jwan arrived in Britain, frightened and desperate, with her three children and a fourth child only a few months from birth. As a Kurd living in Northern Iraq, Jwan's husband had been imprisoned for speaking out against the Baathist Regime. Jwan had also found herself pursued by the brutal regime that wanted to drive her family out of her hometown and imprison her too. Forced to flee to Britain without her husband, she soon found herself standing amongst a throng of refugees who regularly gather outside the Home Office building in Croydon, eager to proceed with an asylum application that will grant them the right to stay in the country.

While her application for asylum was being processed, Jwan heard about a refugee day centre in West Croydon where her family could receive basic assistance and meet with fellow Iraqi refugees. 'I didn't know anyone, I had no one to talk to and I wasn't sure how I was going to look after my children,' says Jwan. 'The West Croydon Refugee Day Centre gave me what I needed – food, clothes for my children and a chance to learn English with other Iraqis.'

The West Croydon Refugee Day Centre opened in

1996 and currently provides Croydon's asylum seekers with cooked food, second-hand clothing, household goods, a crèche, access to bilingual advice, and a non-threatening environment in which to meet. Twice-weekly English language classes also provide them with a much-needed way in to a country that can sometimes appear intimidating and confusing.

'The centre looks for practical ways to help individuals find their way in a new and sometimes hostile environment,' says Beryl Telman, manager of the day centre. 'Asylum seekers are often referred to us because we are considered people's "last port of call" for basic amenities such as food and clothing.'

The catalyst for Croydon's churches to begin meeting the needs of asylum seekers and refugees was provided in the form of the 1996 Asylum and Immigration Act. Changes in the law affecting asylum seekers resulted in financial benefits which were previously available to them being replaced by a system of vouchers that left many people lacking the provision of basic amenities. Following a meeting of Churches Together in Croydon (CTC), West Croydon Baptist Church was chosen as the most appropriate venue to house a facility for refugees and asylum seekers. The West Croydon Refugee Day Centre began operating from its church hall in October 1996, later expanding into other rooms within the church complex.

Since then, the centre has seen hundreds of refugees and asylum seekers, some referred from the Home Office and other local statutory agencies such as

National Asylum Support Service (NASS), and others hearing of the centre by word of mouth. Although checks are performed on each visitor to screen out people who are not asylum seekers or refugees, the centre has been regularly full to capacity. As Beryl Telman explains, 'Over the last two years we have not had a promotional exercise and still we have over 100 people visit our Tuesday drop-in service each week.'

When asked what she thinks the Christian response to the issue of refugees and asylum seekers should be, Beryl answers, 'What would Jesus do? Jesus would have helped people in need. He didn't question their motives, he just helped them.' While Beryl is clear that we should not be gullible or uninformed about those we are seeking to help, she believes that above all we should not judge them. With such direct, non-judgemental and compassionate response to a politically complex and volatile issue, the West Croydon Refugee Day Centre has developed an excellent reputation amongst the refugee community and beyond. Alongside the support work that they provide for asylum seekers, they are also committed to challenging government policy on asylum, working towards a fairer deal for those who are victimised and marginalised by both the community and the law.

Jwan is one of the Centre's success stories. Miraculously, her husband, who was left disabled from the torture he endured, managed to escape from prison and rejoin his family in Croydon six months after they had arrived. In August 2002 Jwan received an award from the Mayor of Croydon for persevering to complete an Access to Teaching course and moving on to study for a Bachelor of Education degree. Her family joined her as she was presented with the award during a ceremony held in Croydon's Town Hall. Both Jwan and her husband are now actively involved in the running of the refugee day centre.

There are countless opportunities for local churches to engage in issues of justice and advocacy – from campaigning for the rights of asylum seekers to taking a stand against human trafficking or the abusive use of women and children in the sex industry.

CHASTE

CHASTE (Churches Alert to Sex Trafficking Across Europe)[44] was founded in 2004, and since that time has been working with women who are escaping the clutches of the traffickers, opening up some new possibilities for life as they recover from the deep and lasting trauma which this form of sex slavery entails.

CHASTE was developed from the experience of working with those victims of trafficking who were awaiting deportation from the United Kingdom in our immigration and removal centres. The young women concerned were from Angola, China, Romania and South Africa. Some were found refuge through the intervention of detention centre chaplains, human rights lawyers, voluntary visitors, local ministers, asylum adjudicators, asylum and refugee workers and the cooperation of Operation Reflex team members. Others were returned to their countries of source.

The CHASTE round table on safe housing first met in the offices of Churches Together in Britain and Ireland in the spring of 2005. The vision was set to match the Government funded provision of UK safe bed space, which was then solely represented by the Poppy Project – a pioneering London-based housing provider for vulnerable women, which provided a total of 27 safe beds for recovery and recuperation. The Salvation Army and the Conference of Religious offered capital resources and personnel, providing independently financed safe houses to enhance what was available at the time.

The CHASTE network's first safe house was opened early in the spring of 2006 by The Salvation Army. At Michaelmas in the same year a safe house was commissioned by the Medaille Trust, who have taken forward the commitment of the Conference of Religious in this area.

Since CHASTE's inception there have been over 87 young women referred through their pastoral network. CHASTE has enlarged the understanding and participation of all the major denominations in the UK through its work in training, conferences, educational campaigns, networking and lobbying.

From humble beginnings in a small study in Cambridgeshire to a movement which is working its way through the churches of Britain and beyond, CHASTE has been entirely funded from voluntary contributions and trust funds. Its small but dedicated team work tirelessly, developing the network's capacity to respond to the outrage of trafficking for sexual exploitation, and providing a safe place for those who escape and survive their ordeal. Supporting its work are hundreds of praying men and women determined to overthrow the contemporary evil of trafficking and see its victims find justice and security.

A key question you might consider: in which social justice campaigns is your local church involved? What campaigns are you personally backing?

Conclusions

The anthropologist Margaret Mead once commented that we should never doubt that a small handful of individuals could change the world. Indeed, she argued that this was the only thing that ever had. In this chapter, we have considered the theology and doctrine underpinning practical action. We have reconnected with the call to be kingdom people committed to integral mission. We have explored briefly the key building blocks of social principles – human dignity, the gospel, the incarnation, neighbourliness, and justice; and we have rejoiced in contemporary examples of lived Christian theology and commitment. We have considered key questions for our own local churches and for our own lifestyles and choices.

We can be part of the work of the kingdom as we ensure that the beliefs we have discussed and the ideas we have explored take root and bear fruit in our own lives and attitudes and in our churches. That in turn will result in a more effective and distinctive engagement in our communities. Ultimately if our lives contribute nothing to the advancement of the kingdom of God in all of its implications, then we must reconsider what we believe, what we are doing and why.

Let us pray, remembering the words of Jesus:

Strive first for the kingdom of God and His righteousness.   (Matthew 6:33, NRSV)

Father,

Thank You for the breadth and the height and the depth of Your plan to rescue and renew the world. Thank You that You have won the victory over evil in all its manifestations through the life and death of your Son. Thank You for the good news that Jesus is Lord! Thank You that You love us and have showered us with Your grace and blessing. Thank You for Your commitment to Your church.

We pray that You will empower us to be kingdom people. Help us to be Your agents in our communities and in the world, living out the reality of Your lordship and Your power. Help us to bring the good news to people at every level. Help us to sustain commitment and balance in word and action, engagement and dialogue. Help us to remain true to You.

We pray for our local churches and for communities where we live. Help us to serve the broken, the excluded and downcast. Help us to see Your image in all people. Help us to be willing to meet people where they are and help us to serve them as equals. Translate the things that we have discovered here into real and lasting commitments. We pray for the individuals and projects in the stories we have read; bless and strengthen them. We ask that you will enable us to live the gospel with the same resolve, passion and commitment to You.

So fill us with Your generosity and love that we just can't help it spilling over into our communities and our world.

Amen.

NOTES

1. Please note that from my point of view, the classic creeds and confessions of the church articulate the doctrinal stances from which we must not depart. So, for example, the confessions found in the Apostles' Creed, the Nicean Creed, the Chalcedonian Creed, etc., are central to the convictions that we hold. I do not intend to investigate these here, rather to acknowledge that the traditional confessions of the church are part of the bedrock of who we are.

2. See:

   Michael Moynagh, *Changing World, Changing Church*, Oxford:Monarch, 2001, chapter 7.

   Alison Morgan, *The Wild Gospel: Bringing Truth to Life*, Oxford: Monarch, 2004, chapter 6.

3. John 8:32, NRSV

4. G.R. Beasley-Murray, *Jesus and the Kingdom of God*, Grand Rapids: William B. Eerdmans, 1996. This is a magisterial outline of the teaching and importance of the kingdom of God and well worth reading.

5. See also Matthew 13:11; Mark 4:11; Luke 8:10; Matthew 19:23–24.

6. See, for other examples, Mark 14:61–62; Luke 15:21 and 1 Maccabees 3:50 (NRSV).

7. For a brief but effective summary of 'kingdom' threads and thought in the Hebrew Bible see Beasley-Murray, chapters 1–4.

8. Mark 3:27; Matthew 11:29; Luke 11:22.

9. Matthew 13:44–46.

10. Luke 15:4–32.

11. Matthew 18:23–25.

12. Matthew 20:1–16.

13. Matthew 22:1–14; Luke 14:16–24.

14. Mark 4:30–32; Matthew 13:31–32; Luke 13:18–19.

15. Mark 4:26–39.

16. Mark 4:1–9; Matthew 13:1–9; Luke 8:4–8.

17. Matthew 13:24–30.

18. Matthew 13:47–50.

19. Luke 16:1–8.

20. Luke 18:1–8

21. Matthew 24:43–44; Luke 12:39–40

22. Matthew 25:1–13

23. Matthew 25:14–20; Luke 19:11–27

24. See the disciples' prayer in Matthew 6:9-13 and Luke 11:2-4; the teaching in the beatitudes in Matthew 5:3–12 and Luke 6:20–23; the teaching around the feast in the kingdom of God in Matthew 8:11–12 and Luke 13:28–29.

   In addition see Mark 9:43–48 and Matthew 8:8–9; Matthew 7:21; Mark 10:23, Matthew 19:23 and Luke 18:24; Mark 10:15, Matthew 18:3 and Luke 18:17; Matthew 5:20; Matthew 21:31, 23:13 and Luke 11:52; the teaching concerning the keys of the kingdom in Matthew 16:19; the teaching concerning the 'little flock' in Luke 12:32 and the kingdom coming in power in Mark 9:1 and Matthew 16:28 and Luke 9:27.

25. See G.R. Beasley-Murray, *Jesus and the Kingdom of God*, Grand Rapids: William B. Eerdmans, 1996, chapter 13.

26. See G.R. Beasley-Murray, *Jesus and the Kingdom of God*, Grand Rapids: William B. Eerdmans, 1996, chapter 14.

27. See G.R. Beasley-Murray, *Jesus and the Kingdom of God*, Grand Rapids: William B. Eerdmans, 1996, chapters 1–4.

28. For the fuller context see Isaiah 40:1–9, see also Mark 1:1–15.

29. See P.A. Mickey, 'Kingdom of God' in David Atkinson and David Field, *New Dictionary of Christian Ethics and Pastoral Theology*, Nottingham: Inter-Varsity Press, 1995, p. 530.

30. By this I mean His miracles of the natural and created order.

31. For example Mark 4:26–32.

32. Geoff Bullock, Copyright © 1995 Word Music Inc./Maranatha! Music/Adm by Copycare. Used with permission.

33. The phrase was originally coined by a groups of academics, theologians and practitioners who met in Oxford in 2001 to write the Micah Declaration. For more information see http://en.micahnetwork.org/home/integral_mission/micah_declaration. I have been involved in the Micah Challenge movement for the last three years and count it a privilege to support their campaign to see the millennium development goals of the United Nations met by 2015.

34. I am grateful to a member of my church, Clare Pritchard, for pointing out that the original word for 'great' in the Greek New Testament (*megale*) is the root word for our word 'mega'. This is a helpful aid for remembering just how central the mega-commandment is.

35. For more information on the scheme contact info@faithworks.info

36. For more information on Torch Trust for the Blind see www.torchtrust.org. For more information on Churches for All and related agencies and charities see www.faithworks.info/churchesforall.

37. John 14–16; Acts 1:4,8; Acts 2.

39. For more information contact info@faithworks.info.

40. Contact info@faithworks.info for more details.

41. For information on both The Terminus Initiative and One 25 Limited, please contact info@faithworks.info

42. See Amos 5:21–24; Isaiah 58 and Micah 6:8.

43. For more information, contact info@faithworks.info.

44. For more information see www.chaste.org.uk.

6

What Do We Do?

But be doers of the word, and not merely hearers who deceive themselves. For if any are hearers of the word and not doers, they are like those who look at themselves in a mirror; for they look at themselves and, on going away, immediately forget what they were like. But those who look into the perfect law, the law of liberty, and persevere, being not hearers who forget but doers who act – they will be blessed in their doing.

(James 1:22–25, NRSV)

Very truly, I tell you, servants are not greater than their master, nor are messengers greater than the one who sent them. If you know these things, you are blessed if you do them.

(John 13:16–17, NRSV)

Having established what we believe about the kingdom and integral mission, we must then work out the right way for us to put our convictions into practice. A doctor is not just someone who simply knows about medicine, she must also be a practitioner of some sort, putting what she knows into effect through what she does. It is immaterial how much knowledge we may acquire if we never use it. We have now considered the kingdom and proposed that to be kingdom people is to be involved in the transformation of our communities at every level. What on earth do we do now? It is in working out what we *do* with what we *know* that we ensure that our convictions give shape to our commitments. This is the heart of integral mission:

Integral:

1. of, pertaining to or belonging as a part of the whole; constituent or component ...
2. necessary to the completeness of the whole ...
3. consisting or composed of parts that together constitute a whole.[1]

As I begin to explore what we can do to live out the kingdom in our communities I am very aware that there are thousands of local churches who have already made this commitment. Faithworks has the privilege of working with many of them but there are many more, who are not members of the Faithworks movement, whose lives and actions are living out the reality of God's kingdom all around them. Commitments to local communities span theological divides and doctrinal differences. Roman Catholic churches and agencies, committed to the deep vein of Catholic social justice teaching, engage in their communities through support and outreach and specific social action such as the work of the Society of St Vincent de Paul, which is committed to helping those in need regardless of their social or religious background.[2] I cited the example of the amazing work of The Salvation Army in a previous chapter, but the work of both the United Reformed Church and the Methodist Church in the United Kingdom also demonstrate the breadth of engagement in kingdom living that takes place across the United Kingdom.

Faithworks is delighted to have local churches from across every major denomination as members of the movement, but we also recognise the immense work that is done by those churches and local congregations who do not have formal membership of Faithworks but share our vision of communities and lives transformed by the power of the good news. Faithworks plays one small part in the building of the kingdom, and it is our privilege to work with and alongside millions of Christ's followers around the world who offer themselves to be the voice, hands and feet of Jesus to those around them.

It is simply impossible to pack into one book all the encouragement and support that I would like to share with you on your journey towards focusing outward as a community of faith and living as kingdom people, but I will highlight just a few ideas and suggestions to inform and inspire you on your adventure of integral mission and kingdom living. The two areas in which we will put the theology of integral mission into practice are the inner and outer worlds of Christian service – the congregation and the community.

1. The Congregation

a. We should begin with what we have and focus on that.

It is easy to be overwhelmed when considering all that a local congregation might do to engage with the local community. The task can seem so enormous and the possibilities so numerous that many local churches fear being swamped by potential demand. It is all too easy to be so daunted by the challenge of engagement with our communities and the fear of change that we end up bound up by our concerns and questions and unable to do anything. We take heart as we realise that there are some simple straightforward things that a local congregation or individual Christians can do to live out the principles of integral mission, expressing the reality of the kingdom of God. The important things to remember are that we should start where we are, use what we have, and take things one step at a time. God does not ask us to do something that we are unable to do, and he does not expect us to get everything right. I am encouraged by the simplicity of God's requirements of us. All any of us ever needs to accomplish is the next step.

When Moses was called to lead the people of Israel into the promised land, he did not think he could do it. Frozen with fear and anxiety, Moses told God that he would be unable to do what was expected of him, and the people would neither believe or trust him. God's response to Moses releases him from his own inflated expectations and accentuated fears.

> Moses objected, 'They won't trust me. They won't listen to a word I say. They're going to say, "God? Appear to him? Hardly!"'
> So God said, 'What's that in your hand?'
> 'A staff.'
> 'Throw it on the ground.' He threw it. It became a snake...   (Exodus 4:1–3, The Message)

God did not ask Moses to use what he did not have – He asked him to use what was in his hand, simply surrendering the familiar things of his everyday life to God's purposes. The same is true for us. God asks us to use what we do have, what is to hand and familiar to us: we do not have to acquire skills, resources and equipment that are beyond our capacity to provide. The journey into our communities begins when we take the single step of saying 'yes' to God; when like the good Samaritan we see someone who is obviously in trouble, and cross the road to see if we can help.

Visiting Christian groups on my travels with Faithworks, I have been so encouraged in the last few years by the number of people who have said 'yes' to God and met a need. As a result, they have been changed utterly. They did not set out to change the world, they just saw someone in trouble, noticed a need, uncovered an injustice – and they decided to do what they could. Pete Cunningham is the pastor of a local Assemblies of God congregation in Southport. In 1999 he decided it was time to do something about homelessness in the town of Southport. One Sunday morning a young family that was homeless stood on the steps of his church needing help – but no help could be found. Pete wanted to do what he could. So he cashed in his pension and bought a small flat which he then made available to a vulnerable tenant. Eight years later, the not-for-profit company that sprung out of that single act is flourishing, and Green Pastures has a property portfolio of over £10 million, providing housing in Wigan, North Wales, Salford, Blackburn, Wakefield, Flintshire, Stoke-on-Trent and London – all because they did what they could.

They raise deposits for purchasing additional homes from equity in their current properties or from small investors who either buy shares or provide loans with interest paid at 5 per cent gross. They then obtain mortgages from banks or building societies. In around 70 per cent of cases, the mortgage repayments and modest repairs are covered by tenants' housing benefit. Once Green Pastures have purchased a house, they may divide it into smaller self-contained units or keep it as a whole unit. After furnishing and equipping the homes with everything tenants need, they then let the properties. By working with members of local churches they establish pastoral care and support teams of volunteers who help all their tenants according to their needs. These teams often work with the social service departments of their local authorities and other agencies to increase the effectiveness of their support.[3] Green Pastures has eradicated the problem of homelessness in Southport!

As local churches and as individuals we start with what we have. Whether that is some savings, tools, home-making skills (knitting, cleaning, cooking), interest in people, understanding of debt or bereavement or loneliness, good knowledge of the local area, a flair for design, a spare hour or two once a week – even if we have no money and think we have no talents, even if all we can do is make a cup of tea – we will be amazed at what God can do with it when we offer what we can and work together for the service of the kingdom.

> Whatever your hand finds to do, do it with all your might.   (Ecclesiastes 9:10a)

b. We can celebrate the fact that we are already involved in kingdom building.

A church is made up of people, and people live in a neighbourhood – so every single local church in the world is already involved in the community, we just don't always realise that has to give us one tremendous head start.

In evaluating the contribution our church is making to the neighbourhood community, we sometimes overlook a healthy amount of work already in train by placing over-emphasis on our activities as a gathered church at the expense of considering the involvement of the dispersed church. When I ask local churches what they are doing in the community they usually tell me about the projects they are running on church premises: a parents and toddlers group, a café, a youth club, an employment club and so on. Local church leaders will rarely describe what the church is doing in the community in terms of the activity and community involvement of the church family as individuals. This is because we have emphasised what we do when *gathered*, to the extent that church leaders may have focused so exclusively on the activities of the church as an organisation they may never even pause to wonder how the church family expresses kingdom commitment separately and individually. This is especially true of the ordinary people – the homemakers, the teenagers, the unemployed people. A church leader will know if he has an MP and the top executive of a large charity in his congregation, and be very aware of their work. He is less likely to know that one of his students has a part-time job as a cleaner in a hotel, where she has befriended a colleague who is an illegal immigrant and is helping her access food and clothing for her children. Leadership has often focused on what is hierarchical and organisational to the detriment of acquiring useful pastoral knowledge of the flock. While it is vital to meet together and remain committed to our gatherings (Hebrews 10:25–27), it is also useful to remember that we are as much part of the church apart as gathered. In fact, the challenge of Jesus to be salt, and light and yeast in Matthew 5:13–16 and Matthew 17 is more a challenge to us in the dispersal of our daily lives and our individual pursuits than in our corporate activities. The purpose of the ascension gifts described in Ephesians 4: apostle, prophet, evangelist, pastor and teacher are not just for strengthening meetings and gatherings, but (according to Paul's words) given to equip the saints for the work of the ministry.

The work of the ministry is a holistic thing, a matter of the detail of our lives – everything we think, everything we say, everything we choose, everything we do. Consider the encouragement that the apostle Paul gave to the church in Colossae:

> And whatever work you may have to do, do everything in the name of the Lord Jesus, thanking God the Father through Him.
>
> (Colossians 3:16, J.B. Phillips)

There are followers of Christ who work in the health service, schools, commerce, business, local government, retail, banking and the finance industry, and the armed forces. We are scattered across every level and every expression of society around the world. From diplomats to doctors and from managers to mechanics, God's people are like millions of grains of salt scattered across the globe. We are as much the church when we are dispersed as we are when we are gathered. As local congregations we need never feel ashamed of our lack of involvement in the community – only wake up to the reality that it is already happening wherever we are. This calls for a deep change in the way we understand ministry, which most people in congregations will find liberating and invigorating. We have been hampered by our tendency to categorise as 'ministry' only the work of designated church leaders acting within or on behalf of the gathered church. 'Ministry' sounds important, and our everyday lives don't feel important – so we conclude that what we do can't be ministry. This shapes our understanding of 'ministry' and 'the church', which in turn shapes our concept and expectation of teaching, preaching, worship and discipleship. One practical way of enabling the ministries and gifts of the whole church family to be acknowledged is to invite each member to tell a little bit of their story in the church magazine or the Sunday morning service, encouraging the rest of the church family to pray for them. Another idea is to run a 'skills exchange' in the church, where people are able to support others and receive support through the sharing of skills and experience.

In recognising that everyone who is a follower of Christ is a minister of Christ, we break the ceiling on celebrating the impact of the kingdom! Suddenly what we do as parents, teachers or retailers has an impact for

the kingdom. Such a step creates empowering awareness that we are *always* ministers of Christ, and that
our whole lives are connected to the kingdom. By
acknowledging the integration of all of our lives into
the plans and purposes of God, we are able to begin our
return to consciously realising the theological connection between service, mission and worship.

> With eyes wide open to the mercies of God, I beg
> you, my brothers and sisters, as an act of intelligent
> worship, to give Him your bodies, as a living sacri-
> fice, consecrated to Him and acceptable by Him.
> Don't let the world squeeze you into its own mould,
> but let God re-mould your minds from within, so
> that you may prove in practice that the plan of God
> for you is good, meets all His demands and moves
> toward the goal of true maturity.   (Romans 12:1,2,
> J.B. Phillips)

*c. We need to recognise that God has prepared good
work for us to do in the world and that it is a privilege
to serve Him.*

Christians are, in the main, conscientious people motivated by moral imperatives, and are easily tipped over
into a mindset racked by guilt. The pressure to succeed,
to get it right, arising from a mistaken belief that it is
all now up to us to save the world and bring in the kingdom, can be immense and become paralysing.

Some Christians on the other hand, have so profound a faith in the provision of the God of miracles

that they sit back and wait for results to simply drop into their laps.

Psalm 84 points us to a stronger reality with these words:

> Blessed are those whose strength is in you, who have set their hearts on pilgrimage.
>
> As they pass through the Valley of Baca, they make it a place of springs; the autumn rains also cover it with pools.
>
> They go from strength to strength, till each appears before God in Zion.   (Psalm 84:5–7)

The Valley of Baca is a place of rocky adversity – it represents arduous journey through arid country where the going is not easy. But those who find their strength in God, as they set their hearts on making it through, discover springs of grace they did not know would be there. God provides – but you have to make the effort to do the journey if you want to discover the springs.

God's Poem!

> For we are what he has made us, created in Christ Jesus for good works, which God prepared beforehand to be our way of life.
>
>   (Ephesians 2:10, NRSV)

It is both deeply humbling and immensely encouraging to live in the reality of this promise, both on our personal journey and as a local church family. I am what God has made me. I have no need to compare myself with others. I cannot be anything more than God has made me and I should not be anything less. Indeed, it is in working out who I am and what I was born to do that I find the greatest freedom and the deepest sense of fulfilment, purpose and joy – for God has not only made me, he has made me for a purpose! The word behind what the New Revised Standard Version translates as 'what he has made us' is the root word *poeme* in Greek, from which we get the word poem. Literally translated, this means that we are God's poem, or masterpiece, or work of art:

> We are God's work of art, created in Christ Jesus to live the good life as from the beginning he had meant us to live it.
>
> (Ephesians 2:10, Jerusalem Bible)

What an amazing thought! What a privilege – God's poem, God's work of art!

God has not made us (or our congregations) and cast us adrift in the sea of our communities, with no sail or map or direction. Instead, He has fashioned us for the very purpose of achieving those things that He has called us to do. There is something that only our local congregation can do. More than that, there is something that only you or I can do. It is our task to discover the specifics of God's calling on our lives, developing from our reflection on our identity and the nature of integral mission. Once we discover that purpose, the next step is to begin!

I want you to get out there and walk – better yet, run! – on the road God called you to travel. I don't want any of you sitting around on your hands. I don't want anyone strolling off, down some path that goes nowhere. And mark that you do this with humility and discipline – not in fits and starts, but steadily, pouring yourselves out for each other in acts of love, alert at noticing differences and quick at mending fences.

You were all called to travel on the same road and in the same direction, so stay together, both outwardly and inwardly. You have one Master, one faith, one baptism, one God and Father of all, who rules over all, works through all, and is present in all. Everything you are and think and do is permeated with Oneness.

(Ephesians 4:2–6, The Message)

We are energised in rediscovering our sense of privilege in serving God and living out the principles of so majestic a thing as His kingdom. There is an almost inexpressible joy in realising that the short time we have on earth can make a difference for ever. It never ceases to amaze me. I am grateful to God for my family and my siblings and the guidance and care of a loving mother and father who always provided for me. Yet, I am also deeply in awe that God would pluck a young, arrogant boy from a council estate in north Belfast, love him, woo him, disciple him and invite him into a journey of discovery that gets more intriguing, exciting and captivating at every turn. I don't deserve to be leading a local church – no one does. I don't deserve to be leading Faithworks. I don't deserve your time in reading these words. You would have thought there are a thousand ways God could have provided leadership to Faithworks, inspiration to someone to write a book like this, or a pastor for a little flock in Hampshire. Yet he asked me to do it! More than that, He *fashioned* me for these things! Every local congregation is a result of His grace. Every experience, achievement and breakthrough that we encounter in our lives reflects *His* beauty and wonder and power – and He has chosen us to be exactly where we find ourselves right now.

How can we be anything but astounded by the new vision, the transformed understanding of our daily lives that 'being God's poem' gives us? His re-creation of what we are and how we live is evidence of God's incomprehensible, mysterious, overwhelming and transforming grace. It is nothing short of life-changing and world-changing to discover that since God has dealt with our ugliness and deadness, as a pure result of His love for us, we are, therefore, alive and beautiful – a work of art! It is such an unfathomable change: we are lifted out of mundane and monochrome existence into a rainbow of wonder, the sheer beauty of fresh creation. We are set free to do great deeds – which He has got all ready, prepared for us to do! It is as if God has showed us the steps of the most beautiful dance in the world, then set us free to dance! Not only has He enabled us to dance, He has given us a spring in our step and dropped us off with a company of virtuoso dancers all around us, ready to go!

d. We should carry out a church audit

There are a number of routes we can follow in determining what we in our local church have to offer our neighbourhood community. We might carry out an audit of our congregation,[4] working out what we have, and what we do not have. In my experience a church audit can take a couple of months, but it should normally not take any longer than that. Through this process, the capacity and resources of the community of faith will be identified – so it is important to ensure that everyone in the congregation is included and gets involved. It is obviously true that the greatest resource any congregation has is God Himself in the power of the Holy Spirit, but His Spirit lives in people, and will be expressed through their individuality and idiosyncrasy. A church audit should be carried out in such a way that people come alive as they realise they are treasured by God – that they are uniquely gifted and really do have something to contribute.

There is no need to nurse people along asking them to do as little as possible; as they catch the vision of the kingdom they will be eager to contribute, relieved and excited to discover they have the gift that matches the need.

In a local church audit, the first stage is to explore what skills, experience, passions, gifts and talents people have. Then we can identify the practical resources of buildings, finances, contacts, partnerships and current activities the local church has. If we are part of a denomination or movement, we can go on to explore the backing, experience, support and advice we could get from our regional or central resources. As we begin to gather all of this information, it will become apparent what the strengths and the weaknesses of our congregation are.

In ascertaining the resources and strengths of a local church, it is very helpful to discover how the members and attendees already perceive their engagement and relationship with the community beyond the church; and then compare this with the perceptions of the community. I once offered a church congregation my support and advice for the period of a year as they worked out the right way forward for engaging with their neighbourhood community. During the first month, I asked the church family how well they thought the people in the community knew the church. Most of the congregation felt that the community would know about the church and its existence, as the church had prayed faithfully for the community, leafleted the area regularly, and held occasional special services over the church's hundred-year history. However, when we researched the community within just a few streets of the church building, the vast majority of people living in the area did not even know that the church was there. Even asking the question had taken us one step on our journey.

e. We must help people discover their gifts

As we undertake the auditing of the church's life, we may find there are people in the congregation who have no clear awareness of the call of God on their lives, no vision for the 'good works' that God has prepared for them to do. When this happens, it is helpful to support people in their exploration of this issue by setting aside time for an opportunity to discover the areas in which their gifts and skills lie. I have led hundreds of people through a resource produced by Willow Creek Community Church called *The Network Participant's Guide*,[5] adapting the material for use in whole church, small group and weekend settings. By using this tool, or something like it, participants are supported in discovering their personality, their personal profile and their skills and gifts. This is invaluable in helping people to find their role within the local church or the wider work of the kingdom of God. Of course, there are many other resources[6] that can help individuals to work out their strengths and their weaknesses, but what I like about this material is the assistance it offers individuals in identifying their spiritual gifts and role within the local congregation and the wider body of Christ.

f. We must release people, not drain them

The kingdom of God is diverse, mysterious and ubiquitous, found wherever people are engaged in integral mission, sharing the good news of Christ's healing love in practical expressions of kindness, generosity and support.

However, the local church, in order to exist at all, as well as act as a beacon of hope in the community, must maintain the administrative structures, the teaching and preaching programmes, and the numerous projects and ongoing commitments that ensure its financial, legal, institutional, pastoral, liturgical and social obligations continue to be met. These obligations require meetings, personnel and committees – which are time-consuming whatever else they may be.

So an audit of church life, with a view to extending its work in the neighbourhood and enlarging its vision for integral mission, can generate a sense of deep reluctance, or even alarm. Oh no. Does this mean more meetings, more obligations, more pressure to take on more commitments? Will there be occasional spaces for members of the new committees to go home and remind themselves of what their families look like? Will the essential commitments of the church already in place continue to be fulfilled?

I am deeply committed to the local worshipping community. It is my view that every follower of Christ should belong to a church congregation, which in turn should belong to a network or denomination. Such belonging facilitates mutual support and is an

expression of the unity of the whole church, but the loy-
alties resulting from this local commitment must be
held in balance with wider awareness. When Jesus
described Himself as the Good Shepherd, he said that
His care of the sheep involved leading them out of the
sheepfold to find pasture, and back in to find security
and rest. This balance of going forth and returning, of
outreach and gathering, is right for the health of our
souls.

Part of the preparation for integral mission, once a
church audit has identified present structures and commitments, may be a process of streamlining, so that
members of the church family are free to make new
vision come true.

There are simple strategies that make this possible:
choosing either/or rather than both/and in deciding
which projects to pursue; planning fellowship groups
on a system of study courses that end, rather than continue every Tuesday night from now until Jesus returns;
focusing this year on an ecumenical emphasis, next
year on deepening denominational links, rather than
trying to hold down all the balloons in the bathwater at
once; collating the financial or legal administration of
a group of local churches and sharing the cost of an
accountant or administrator. There are many ways to
so organise church life that it resembles something
more orderly than a slime mould; efficiency sounds ter-
rifying, but how liberating when we see how much time
it gives us back.

In evaluating what we can contribute towards the

work of the local congregation, each individual should first ensure that there is some time set aside to fulfil the responsibilities of personal relationships – families, marriages, friends. Some ministers' children have grown up hating the church because it stole every minute of their father's time. As Howard Hendricks[7] said: 'If your Christianity doesn't work at home, it doesn't work. Don't export it.'

No local church can tackle everything. Congregations and their members have many commitments already to fulfil. By clarifying our core beliefs and values, identifying areas of need in the community, carrying out a church audit, and identifying our (personal, individual) resources, we come to the position where a project will emerge representing our appropriate engagement in integral mission.

As we absorb the concept of integral mission, we begin to understand that followers of Christ are missionaries in all they say and do. The local church fulfils its purpose and calling in so far as it reaches out with God's love, serves those around it and enables those who are part of it to do the same. Our lives must reflect the dual nature of our calling, to be a people who worship God and a people who serve others.

We can trace the threads of our calling back to the ancient covenant relationship between God and His people in the story of Hebrew Scripture, and read it passionately expounded in the writings of the prophets. In the Gospels we trace a development of the call of God's chosen people: from faithfulness to God expressed in social justice, to faithfulness to God expressed in service and compassion. Christ was the promised Messiah, but reinterpreted that role in terms of service: 'the Son of Man did not come to be served, but to serve, and to give his life as a ransom for many' (Mark 10:45).

As followers of Christ our lives are still overshone by the twin imperatives of faithfulness to the God who is One, and a life of service, which is our sacrifice of praise.

What Christians individually are called by God to do, the church institutionally must ensure they are free to do. In every expression of its corporate life, the church must prioritise integral mission, because that is what the gospel is about.

To make this possible, local churches may need to do less in terms of programmes or projects and more in terms of supporting the members of the church family in their lives and callings, putting the focus of ministry back onto the community rather than on maintaining the framework of the institution.

g. We need to intentionally place God at the centre of our lives individually and as a local church in all we say and do

Any engagement that we have with our local communities, our friends and colleagues, expresses the reality of intimate relationship with God, the core of our lives and wellspring of our passion. In its work of integral mission, the church is not, and must not allow itself to become, merely a cheap provider of social services to the government or other statutory agencies. It is important to protect our independence from state structures in order to ensure that we preserve our distinct identity. Local churches have a pivotal role to play in the development of healthy communities and one of the reasons that we have such a central contribution to make is precisely the fact that we are independent of statutory agencies and government. Our engagement is motivated and characterised by our faith.

Christian spirituality must baptise all that we do. Our approach to people arises from our commitment to their human dignity, not from the funding pot that we can get because we serve them. We recognise the needs of the whole person, not just the particular area of need we are addressing. Most importantly of all, we recognise that people are spiritual beings and that their physical, emotional and spiritual needs are bound in together. Ultimately, local churches recognise that for lasting change to be effected in the life of an individual – and ultimately therefore in the life of the community – it must have its origin deep within.

By keeping our priorities in mind, and by placing prayer and dependence on God at the centre of what we do both personally and corporately, we ensure that we do not fall into the trap of simply being another service provider. We can take a number of practical steps to ensure that this commitment to Christian spirituality remains steady in our work and lives. We can commit to giving prayer, reflection and conversation enough space in our schedule. We can ensure that we use vocabulary that avoids demeaning those we serve, or reducing our relationship with them to the purely professional – they are not only clients or service users, they are people. We can also commit to the highest standards in our practice and in the way we engage with and treat others. Above all, we ensure that the service we provide, and the way we provide it, stays within the context of a Christian ethos and Christian values. In what we do, and how we do it, we commit to remaining true to Christ. If at any point we need to choose between faithfulness to Christ and the support or approval of others, we ensure that we remain faithful to Christ. If he would not do it, then neither should we.

h. We must teach and live the kingdom as a community

It is vital that a local church places kingdom living right at the heart of its preaching, teaching, discipleship and worship. Ensuring that the local church sees kingdom living in the leaders of the congregation, and hears about kingdom living, is a vital part of doing something about being kingdom people. If we do not practise what we preach, then we have fallen into the very trap that the apostle James warns us to avoid – we become hearers of the word and not doers.

You might like to invite your home group, family, or group of friends to consider the following questions designed to help you explore some of the implications for daily living of integral mission and the kingdom of God:

1. Think of twenty-one people who come to your church. Write down their names. Where do they live? What is their occupation? What are their prayer concerns at the present time? What are their hobbies and interests? If they have children, what are their children's names? In the next week, pray each day for three of these people.

2. Think about the home group you belong to. How well do the people there know you? Is it a safe place to be honest, and to really be yourself?

3. Think about some of the big concerns of the world: drought, climate change, displaced people, modern forms of slavery, torture, fair trade, antisocial behaviour... How are you making a difference in any of these areas? And your church?

4. Think about your partner (if you have one), your family, your friends, your work colleagues, your home group, your congregation... How do/might you plan your time to make sure that there is space to chat, to affirm your relationship, with the individuals in this circle of people?

5. Think about the month that has just gone. Can you identify five choices you have made that were motivated by your Christian faith (not big life decisions necessarily – even small, everyday things)?

6. Think about your church congregation and your town/village. Just at the moment, what would you

say is the biggest challenge facing each of these communities?

7. Think about your Christian beliefs. How many of your friends, family and colleagues have a philosophy of life very different from yours? Is it easy to get on with these people? Do you chat about your different ways of understanding the world?

8. Think back on the conversations you have had with those people. What do you remember as the main issues and concerns that preoccupied their minds? What do you think your life and faith might have to say to people preoccupied with those issues? What are your own attitudes in these areas – do you notice a difference between your approach and theirs?

9. Think about the creative arts. Do you enjoy painting, or writing poetry, or dancing, or playing a musical instrument? If not, would you be prepared to have a go?

10. Think about the kingdom of God. Imagine it as a real place. What might be on the statute books? Now imagine you are an ambassador of the kingdom, and your church (or your home) is an embassy. How could visitors to the embassy tell which kingdom you represent? In what ways would your embassy like to make its mark on the surrounding society?[8]

2. The Community

a. Understand the needs of the community and those around you

The members of a local church do not always worship where they live, especially in rural areas where people often worship in a town around which villages cluster. (Conversely, some town-dwellers worship in small country churches to support the Christian witness in the village.) Church members may also travel to work in a place which is neither near their home nor their place of worship. In such circumstances, which is their community?

The individual Christian who would like to make positive steps towards making a difference in the community must first therefore decide which is the most appropriate community setting: for some this will be obvious, for others less so. Similarly, a church may be part of a benefice or other grouping, and may have to choose from a group of discrete neighbourhoods in settling on a mission project.

Whatever the choices involved, it is essential that Christians understand the issues that create the profile of their neighbourhood.

It is important to listen, to notice, and to research – otherwise time, money and effort can be wasted addressing secondary or obsolete issues, while ignoring urgent or growing concerns.

One local church that I know decided that they wanted to engage with the community by providing a parent and toddler group. They thought this was a good idea and duly spent a lot of time and money setting up the group. However when numbers did not seem to pick up and the group had a low attendance, they began to wonder why. They soon discovered two things. Firstly, the local council was funding a new parent and toddler group that began on the same day as the one the church decided to run, and secondly the council group had better equipment, more support, better facilities and was desperately trying to get volunteers to help run it. So, after discussion with the helpers in the church parent and toddler group, and meetings with the local council and the organisers of the other, the local church closed their project and released all the volunteers to help with the other one. The result was a room full of happy parents – and followers of Christ who knew they were making a difference in their community. To have researched more carefully in the first place would have been a more efficient way to proceed, but the graciousness of the church representatives in the negotiations that took place answered the purpose of forming new links with the community.

b. Listening to the community

Having established what we believe and what we are called to do; having done our church audit and identified what we have to offer and are free to contribute, the next step in integral mission is to listen. The ability to listen to our communities is an essential characteristic of a local church committed to living out kingdom principles. Listening is of itself an act of love. When someone takes the time to listen to our concerns and fears, our hopes and aspirations, we know we matter to them. Listening is not just part of our preparation for mission – it is itself mission. As a pastor, one of the most important things I can do is listen to the teachers, doctors, local police officers and social workers who are already active and committed to my local area. I can take careful note of what they think is happening in the community and what they perceive the needs to be.

If we rely on our church leaders alone to do the listening, we will drastically limit our possibilities. Encouraging and enabling a whole congregation to listen to their neighbours, friends and colleagues will create a huge bank of expertise and wisdom and understanding. What if we simply ask a couple of questions of our neighbours, or of the people in the corner shop, or of people at the school gate – questions like:

- What do you think is our community's greatest asset?
- What do you think is our community's greatest need?
- If you could change one thing about our community, what would it be?
- What do you think is the best thing about living or working here?
- How do you think the local church could best help the community?

It is probably a good idea to ensure consistency in the questions that the congregation are asking of their neighbours, friends, colleagues and other contacts. This can be achieved by simply choosing the questions that seem most appropriate for the situation you find yourself in and asking the whole congregation to put those questions to their neighbours and colleagues. It might even be a good idea to try and plan that the conversations will take place across the same period of time, creating a sense of shared purpose in the congregation and ensuring that the responses are more easily analysed and understood. A congregation might designate 'listening' as a specific stage of developing integral mission, and allocate a delineated period of time for listening in their mission project.

This is not a community survey, but a series of friendly conversations between people who know one another, that will inform the individual asking the question, the person answering and the local congregation. It is important to protect confidentiality in handling responses, but there should be some latitude to incorporate them into the intercession that the church makes for the neighbourhood: in Sunday worship, in home groups, in the youth meeting or the children's groups. In this way, the listening of the church is already an instrument of God's love, for as the responses are offered in prayer, the activity becomes part of the Father's listening to the world.

c. Listening to God

Local churches must also listen to God. So often, when it comes to engaging in our communities, prayer becomes an add-on at the end of our list of activities – what is sometimes referred to as 'quarantine prayer', briefly isolating someone in a spiritual atmosphere before returning them to business as usual!

If we are to make a lasting kingdom difference in our communities, prayer must become as much part of what we are and do as our DNA. There is a wide range of organisations and tools to help us to ensure that prayer is at the heart of how we understand the community. For example, the World Prayer Centre in Birmingham can help local churches to connect with prayer groups and networks right across the United Kingdom and beyond.[9] However, nothing beats the persistent and regular commitment of local churches and individual Christians to pray for their communities. It is as we turn to God, asking him to guide and direct us in what we do, that we will be most effective. It is important to remember that even the very best idea, until it is saturated and undergirded in prayer, is still nothing more than an idea.

Two of the groups that help churches to understand and develop the role and importance of prayer in their engagement with their communities are the Shaftesbury Society[10] and Tearfund.[11] The Shaftesbury Society focus their work with churches in the London and Leeds areas of England, helping local churches to envisage God as a partner in their engagement with the community. By doing that, they ensure that God is consulted at every level of decision making and relating to the community. Tearfund, through their programme called 'Church, Community and Change', also ensure that prayer and listening to God are at the heart of the local church's plans and engagement with the local community.

In listening to God, we can also become aware of issues that can be tackled only through God's intervention. Often, as local churches, we can be a little embarrassed or shy when it comes to recognising the importance of spiritual breakthrough in our communities. But the reality is that there are some issues in local communities for which we rely on the intervention of God and His Spirit. The work that we are engaged is holistic – therefore it has dimensions that transcend the physical. It is only through the movement of the Spirit that the kingdom is established. '"Not by might nor by power, but by my Spirit," says the Lord Almighty' (Zechariah 4:6). We must work as if everything depends on us as we engage with our communities, but we must pray *knowing* that it all depends on God.

> Be strong in the Lord and in his mighty power. Put on all of God's armour so that you will be able to stand firm against all strategies of the devil. For we are not fighting against flesh-and-blood enemies, but against evil rulers and authorities of the unseen world, against mighty powers in this dark world, and against evil spirits in the heavenly places.
>
> (Ephesians 6:10–12, NLT)

When we fail to listen or look for God's wisdom, guidance and intervention in our communities, we automatically expose ourselves both to pride (because we assume that we can change things on our own) and vulnerability (because we are failing to use the greatest and strongest asset we have – God's power and wisdom, given to his people for the purpose of building His kingdom). Prayer changes things, and it is an immense privilege to be able to pray for our community. Even people in the community who do not share our faith are often touched and comforted to know that we have prayed for them.

When a local church decides to bring prayer to the top of the agenda, it can be helpful to have some guidance in proceeding. The 24-7 prayer movement[12] began several years ago on the south coast of England and has now spread, like wild-fire, across the globe, offering hundreds of ideas and resources to local churches and individual Christians who want to take prayer for their communities seriously. Not only that, they have also captured the imagination of young people around the world who are committed to connecting the words they use with people to the words they use with God. I recently had a conversation with a young man in Reading in Berkshire. He was part of a prayer group in Reading called The Boiler Room. As we talked he began to share how God had answered prayer for his neighbourhood community. He had been praying about racial tensions in the area, asking God to intervene in the way some newly arrived Polish people were

being treated by their neighbours. One of the neighbours faced a difficulty with their plumbing just after
the young man began to pray, and it turned out that the
father of the Polish family who had moved in next door
was a plumber! Through this seemingly ordinary coin-
cidence, the prejudices and preconceptions creating
tension between the two families dissolved.

The reality is that without prayer and the real intervention of God in our communities, we will never see
lasting and significant change – but our engagement
need never be without prayer! As we listen with all our
hearts to the concerns of our community, we are open
also to the inner voice of God.

God's love and grace soak into the whole situation as
we listen, beginning the gentle miracle of transformation not only in our community but in our own hearts
and lives as well.

> If my people who are called by my name will hum-
> ble themselves and pray and seek my face and turn
> from their wicked ways, I will hear from heaven
> and will forgive their sins and restore their land
>   (2 Chronicles 7:14, NLT)

A commitment to pray and listen to God for the community brings real and lasting change. Diane Briggs
works as a manager in a church-based playgroup. She
is committed to her local church and the church is
committed to serving the community. Diane's
congregation works on the principle of firm belief that

wherever they go, they bring Jesus with them. As part of the playgroup structure, a group of people from the congregation regularly pray for the staff, volunteers, parents and children in the group. As well as that, Diane ensures that the staff and volunteers pray together regularly. Even those on the staff who are not yet Christians are invited to pray and they often request prayer for themselves, their friends or people in the playgroup. The playgroup itself has a box where people can place prayer requests.

One of the mums in the playgroup was having diffi-cultly in feeding her second child, Shawn. For three months Diane prayed for Shawn – and his feeding problems disappeared. Another mum attending the playgroup asked Diane to pray for Lisa's family because they were facing real financial pressure and there was a real possibility they would lose their home. Once again, the situation was turned around, and Lisa's hus-band found work shortly after Diane prayed.[13]

Of course it is not possible to know what the out-come would have been if no one had prayed. The fact is someone did pray, and not only did the situations change, but the people concerned were drawn closer. People are warmed and encouraged to know that some-one cares for them and is holding them up in prayer day by day. People for whom we are praying become dearer to us; we come to care about them very much as we pray. Whatever would have happened if no one had prayed, prayer changes things on many levels. If we do not listen to God at the same time as listening to our communities, then we are only using one half of the listening ability that God has given to us.

d. Learn about the community

The call to love and serve our neighbours as ourselves (Matthew 22) is directly connected to the call to love God with all of our heart, soul, mind and strength. That means that our engagement with our communities should be intelligent, directed, considered and informed. God does sometimes surprise us with a persistent prompting unconnected with anything we have been thinking or praying about before ('Noah, you should be building an ark', for example!), but more often than not it is as we find out about the community and spend time in prayer listening quietly to God, that the vision and ideas start to come.

As well as listening to our neighbours, in order to learn about our communities, we need to research them.

e. Hard data

Learning about the challenges that face your community and the services that are already being provided involves collecting hard data. This includes such information as the size and age profile of the local population, mortality rates, unemployment levels, geographical features that may have an unexpected influence, types of housing in the area, local businesses (What type? How many? How big? Small family firms or owned by large conglomerates?), schools, doctors' surgeries, arts facilities, community organisations in the area and any recreational facilities or services that might already be in the local community. This hard data can relate to either the general statistics of the community or to the specific area in which you have something to offer, such as education or care of the elderly.

A good place to start collecting hard data is the census. This is available in your local library and it will help you to understand the general trends and social demographics of your community. The office of national statistics can be very helpful in explaining the data contained in census information.[14] Another source of helpful information is the Department for Communities and Local Government. This government department has a whole range of statistics and research that can help you understand the people who live in your community and the challenges that they face.[15] It is particularly helpful in exploring any issues of poverty and deprivation in your community, discovering whether or not your community is part of a 'Super Output Area' (a government term defining a neighbourhood as deserving special help and support in regeneration), and in researching information about employment, issues facing pensioners,[16] families, schools and children,[17] education,[18] or crime.[19] Your MP will also have a very good grasp of all the hard data that relates to his or her constituency.

On top of this basic information, if you contact your local council and ask for a copy of your local strategic plan you will be able to discover what the perceived needs of the community are, what the specific challenges are in your community and what the council is suggesting should be done about these challenges. The strategic plan will also be available from your council's website or in a library. Alongside this, you can access information on health needs by contacting the primary care trust and other localised needs or initiatives by contacting your council and asking to speak to the relevant department. At the same time you can request any information they might have on community development plans or local area agreements. These are plans that are put together across the various government departments at local level to ensure that community development is managed in an efficient and integrated manner.[20]

The National Council for Voluntary Organisations[21] or your local council for voluntary service may also be able to supply you with a profile of voluntary and community group activity in your area.

If you are not used to gathering data, this task may feel overwhelming and bewildering, but the enterprise will be far less intimidating if it is undertaken in small groups, subdividing into pairs for visits to institutional bodies, meeting up to compare notes, discuss and pray through findings over a cup of coffee. It is important to bear in mind that you are not just gathering information for its own sake. You are doing all you can to listen with God to discover the challenges and needs – the silent prayers – of your neighbourhood community. You are using your intelligence and your creativity to understand the needs of your community. The internet can prove a valuable aid in sorting out all of this information and putting it into some semblance of order, so sites such as www.upmystreet.com can really help you to understand the community in which you live.

f. Soft data

'Soft' data complements 'hard' data in creating a balanced picture of your community. Facts and figures go some way towards describing neighbourhood life, but to put together a more detailed and accurate picture you will need to talk to the community and include their stories, memories, opinions, viewpoints and outlooks. It is vital to give breadth (quantity) and depth (quality) to your 'soft' research, for which there is a wide range of techniques and tools to assist you. While questionnaires will give you breadth of information, depth will come from interviewing a smaller, carefully selected sample, or running focus groups. Combining these two approaches to gathering information will always give you a clearer indication of the real needs of your community than adopting one approach alone – and so will facilitate a more effective response to them.[22]

g. Using questionnaires and interviews

Questionnaires are the quickest way of gathering basic, broad-brush, 'quantity' information about your community, and are very useful for that reason. But bear in mind that careful planning and phrasing of your questions is necessary to ensure that the information collected is clear, meaningful and suitable for analysis. This is where working together in a group can be help-ful – what seems abundantly clear to a question-setter can seem bafflingly ambiguous to a checking partner. It is also worth noting that multiple choice questions where interviewees answer by selecting A, B, C or D, for example, are by far the easiest to collate (though the information they gather may miss the people whose lives do not fit standard categories – and these may be most urgently in need of help). When formulating a questionnaire, it is important to keep it simple and short, check that it flows naturally and that it includes monitoring information (e.g. age, gender, etc.). Any controversial or difficult questions should be left until the end.

It's always a good idea to run a 'test' on a small but representative group of people first to ensure that your questions are clear and that the answers can be accu-rately analysed and provide useful feedback. Make sure that the people you survey know who you are, why you are asking them for information, what you will be doing with it and how and when they can access the results. It is also important to hold a training session for all those who will administer the questionnaire. Give them a chance to practise using it on one another and carefully explain how to deal with the different reactions they are likely to encounter, ranging from eager helpfulness through indifference to open hostility. Questionnaires are far more successful when someone proactively carries out the interviews, rather than leaving forms and then expecting people to complete and return them; so, in organising the collection of information, a local congregation should try to arrange an interview system rather than posting questionnaires through the door of the local community to be collected later. As well as door-to-door questionnaires, it is worth thinking about other places you might conduct interviews, such as the local shopping centre, train station, youth club, toddler group, etc. One town in the east of England arranged for members of churches to conduct their interviews at either end of the school day, providing a tea and coffee stand for parents and carers, as an encouragement to stay and answer questions.

Questionnaires are helpful in gathering information anonymously, getting answers to defined questions, and contacting large numbers of people. As the responses are gathered, the interesting variation in responses to the same question offers a helpful insight into the variety that is present in the local population. However, questionnaires do also have shortcomings. Most people are naturally suspicious of strangers asking them questions, so the answers can be inspired by all sorts of motives. The interviewee may be wondering 'How do I get rid of this person as soon as possible?', 'I'm not telling him what I really think – it will be used against me', 'I don't like these people prying into my life', or 'What is all this information going to be used for?'. Not only that, but people are often busy when you call on them unannounced, or stop them in the street, and may be preoccupied with other issues.

Because they are less rigidly tied to a specific question with a small space for a specific answer, interviews enable much broader exploration of ideas and opinions, providing a better quality and greater depth of insight and information. Interviews are more personal, having the added advantage of the opportunity to probe deeper by asking supplementary questions where appropriate. Although time-consuming, interviews are an excellent way to discover more about the life of the community. They are useful for learning from teachers, social workers, playgroup leaders, youth workers, doctors, other service providers, residents – anyone who is likely to have depth of insight into the specific issue being researched. There is no requirement for the interviewee to be literate, and for this reason interviews are helpful for understanding the perspective of people whose first language is not English, or who are dyslexic, or for whom the written word presents other difficulties. Interviews have also the advantage of creating a sense of involvement for the interviewee – to be face-to-face with another person, to be listened to and have one's opinions recorded, feels affirming and inclusive.

Drawbacks to interviewing as a system for gathering information include the lack of anonymity, the time-consuming nature of interviewing, the need for a place to sit and talk and take notes, the need for reasonably personable individuals to conduct the interviews, and the reality that the answers recorded can be affected by the perspective and interpretation of the interviewer as much as by the person being interviewed.[23]

However we go about it, if we are to engage with our communities meaningfully, then we must be able to learn from them and about them.

An Example of Learning

The Saltbox Christian Centre[24] in Stoke-on-Trent, led by Lloyd Cooke, exists to support Christians engaged in work in their neighbourhood communities and to promote the role of faith groups in community enterprises in North Staffordshire. In 2004 and 2005, using the techniques we have just discussed, Saltbox began to research the challenges faced by the city of Stoke-on-Trent, and the contributions being made to the wellbeing of the area by local churches and other faith groups. As a result they published a report entitled 'Faith Action Audit'[25] which has led to a strong and growing relationship across the churches as they continue to work in their local communities.

The success of the initiative resulted from the desire to understand the needs and concerns of that region, to consider the role and contribution of local churches, to help the people of the city and to serve the purposes of God. The process of gathering information may seem daunting when it is unfamiliar, and requires a meticulous, even painstaking approach which can seem tedious at times – apparently more administrative than visionary: but it is vital if we are to connect with our local communities authentically.

As Paul Sanderson, coordinator of the WIRE project in Southampton, recalls:

> I began by researching the local area to find out what was going on. I arrived ready to change the world, but for three months I simply visited local schools, families and the local library to chat to people there, in order to build my information about the area. At the time it was frustrating, but as I look back now I am incredibly grateful for it.[26]

An A–Z of Getting Involved in the Community

Having engaged the members of the congregation and made the commitment to listening to and learning about the needs of the community, local churches are then in a place to ascertain what they can usefully contribute and how they can best bring their vision into practical effect. The ways in which we can engage with our communities are limited only by our imagination. Below is a starter A–Z list to encourage and assist churches in exploring some of the many options open to them, practical suggestions for effective planning and action along with pointers and tips to help remember important principles.

Acclaim the past

So often local churches feel that in order to move into the community or introduce something new, we have to prove that everything that has gone before is wrong. This is an approach that will destroy your engagement with the community before you have even begun. It is much better to start by acclaiming the past and thanking God for the faithful service of the people who have gone before the current generation. A service of thanksgiving to celebrate the history of the church/neighbourhood/project may also look forward optimistically to the new vision, and is an opportunity to invite the participation of people who have drifted away.

Build one vision

A local congregation needs a clear vision. Without it, the local church will amble along directionless. Too often, when the pastor or vicar changes, so does the focus of the church – but the vision of every local church is to be at the heart of its community, serving unconditionally and seeing God's kingdom come. This is what will unite the people of the congregation in the long term, nothing else. Whatever your vision, ensure it is on the front of your bulletin or in announcements, or on your screen at the beginning the service (ring the changes in your presentation – people blank out what they see every week). Build the vision by keeping it before the attention of the people; take opportunities to write a progress journal in the church/community newsletter, or to feature in a local newspaper article.

Keep a 'vision board' with an attractively presented collage of photographs, headlines, inspirational quotations and brief updates in the foyer of your church's place of worship.

Cultivate an understanding of integral mission
Integral mission can never be taught in one meeting or through the occasional reference to the concerns of the community. It must lie at the heart of all that the local congregation does, informing preaching, teaching, fellowship and social activities; shaping everything the local church is and does. Create opportunities for sharing experiences that highlight the connection between the church's worship and teaching programme and everyday life out and about in the community. Make yourself some inspirational notices for your fridge door or your desk: 'Your Kingdom come, O Lord – and let it begin with me!' 'Think global, act local' 'What on earth are you doing?' 'Have you loved your neighbour today?' – anything that will make you smile, make you think, and remind you of your chosen focus.

Do your homework – research
In order to serve the purposes of God, the local church must understand who we are, who the community is, and how to connect the two – this is the hard work we have explored in this chapter. Put together a working team to carry out the research of the area that you need. Doggedly identify dreams, disasters and daily reality in your district – do your research!

Encourage people to see the bigger picture

The bigger picture is not just a full church building, or really exciting meetings! It is lives transformed by God's grace and a whole community discovering its purpose and its significance because of God's power and love at work. Local churches are kingdom communities! Have a slot in every meeting for someone to tell their own story that will help people understand that they are loved and valued for who they are, not just for what they do. Encourage people in their participation, in their motivation, and in their vision.

Focus on what you have

It is all too easy for a local church to draw back from attempting community engagement because of a perceived lack of experience, resources or skill. But once we begin to focus on what we have, rather than on what we do not have, we begin to see that we have all that we need to bring hope to our communities – because we have God's Spirit, God's command and God's heart. Make a list of all the skills and talents and resources you have as a local church. Focus on, and celebrate, what you have.

Guard your distinctiveness and *give* yourself away

The local church must not sacrifice its allegiance to Christ on the altars of political correctness, power or popularity. We are called to be the voice, hands and feet of Christ in our communities. Therefore, we must never apologise for Him. At the same time, we must take seriously the call to serve those around us and to love people into God's arms. We are called to be faithful, but not to be inquisitors. Before you make any decision as a church or as an individual, ask yourself – what would Jesus do?

Hold to clear and measurable aims and objectives

If we do not know what we are aiming for, we will miss it every time! We need to know what our principles, objectives, plans and methods are, and hold ourselves and one another accountable. Take time to write out your goals and stages of implementation, and discuss these regularly.

Identify champions in the community/mission

There are people in every church family whose enthusiasm is inspiring and catching. The job of a good church leader and the task of a good team is to identify what fires the imagination of individuals and then help them to live out of their passion. In your local church, who feels passionately about community concerns? How might you release their passion? An enjoyable exercise in small groups is to work in pairs identifying *each other's* area of passionate concern. From these observations, the passion of particular individuals for key areas of work will emerge.

Justify our thinking biblically/theologically

We must never treat the biblical underpinning of integral mission and kingdom thinking lightly. Instead, we must make sure that we understand biblically what we are called to do and be. Our choices and inspiration grow from our rootedness in Scripture – it is not a matter of thinking up a verse to go with plans we have already made. Develop a teaching and preaching programme and prayer diary that puts biblical kingdom thinking at the heart of your church's life.

Keep reminding people of the vision

Nehemiah reminded the people of the vision of rebuilding Jerusalem at least every twenty-eight days! We should at least match that by reminding people of the mission and vision of the local church regularly and clearly. Articulate the vision of the church every month and ask the congregation to pray into it regularly as a whole body.

Let people experiment

It is not an unpardonable sin to fail. Local churches need to allow members and regular attendees the room to try new things – even if they do not always work. Better to have a go at doing something for the kingdom than to criticise everyone else for not doing anything! Have a 'blue sky' ideas time regularly in a church family meeting or with a small group or planning team, with no idea off limits and no comment too silly!

Make involvement easy

Sometimes the process of commitment to a local congregation can feel a bit like sitting an entrance exam!

Instead we should make it easy for people to get involved, though without compromising our faith identity. For people who are attending worship and would like to participate in community projects, but are not yet church members, why not develop a volunteer contract that is renewable every six months? Then people know what they are being asked to do and they do not feel as if they are signing their lives away in the process.

Never *take criticism personally*

This is hard! When people do not like what is happening in a church they more often than not turn on the leader or the people with the vision. However, it is vital to understand that even within the sharpest criticism there is a kernel of truth. Try to learn to ask these three questions when you are criticised – What do you think went well? What do you think we could do better? How can you help? Perhaps all the congregation could be encouraged to ask these questions when formulating any criticisms, too.

Offer *people different ways of engaging*

Not everyone will want to be on the streets on a Friday night working with the homeless men and women of the town. Make sure that you allow different ways for people to get involved. Why not put together a list of ways in which people can get involved from prayer and giving, to writing letters, physical work or encouragement and advice? Then give people the opportunity to choose how they can help in a way that will play to their strengths.

Praise current activities

Often local churches are keen to start new projects, when current ones are under-resourced and undervalued. Make sure that you encourage and support those current activities that are vital to the church's life and mission. To create links between areas of work in the life of the church, and to affirm and acknowledge the current work while encouraging and making links with the new, buddy new teams with current teams for sharing of wisdom, ideas, support, encouragement and prayer. Invite workers from current projects to share their stories on a Sunday or in a gathering as well as promoting new visions.

Question the status quo

Do not let your church become an 'add-on' congregation, perpetuating traditional practices that may have long passed their use-by date at the same time as taking on new projects and visions. Encourage the congregation to have a healthy attitude to change by regularly reviewing the congregation's time, budget and 'best practice' standards. Allow some space around each event, so that it receives the focus of planning, publicity and celebration it deserves. Be willing to prune programmes and projects that have become irrelevant or tired. When setting up a new programme or project, include an end date in the planning. To help you review what is still vibrant and useful in the church's life (and what may be missing), ask people who have only recently or occasionally attended to write a short piece for the church newsletter about what they found helpful in the church's life and what they struggled with.

Recognise your greatest resources

People, people, people! Never treat them with less dignity than God has treated you; and always encourage them. Do this by ensuring that you are always both honest and loving, and that you value their potential as well as their achievements. Always thank people for their commitment and work, holding a 'thank you' party on a regular basis (once a year is probably about right) where the whole church celebrates all the work and commitment shown in the last twelve months.

Show the benefits of engagement

If people hardly ever hear about the work in the community and the things that the church is involved in, they will not perceive its importance or be inspired to participate. Make sure that you regularly update the wider church family on the work in the community, with a regular spot for prayer, thanksgiving and honest sharing of struggles and stories.

Take risks

Nobody can guarantee the outcome of a project before it begins. Celebrate an entrepreneurial, optimistic spirit and a 'can do' attitude in the congregation by encouraging people to experiment, to try, to take risks. If you love them and set boundaries that are clear, people can be free to fail. To help this, make sure that you share from your own weaknesses and failings, not just from your own strengths.

Use the building, don't worship it

For many people in local churches, the building is a sacred space because of its significance in their personal faith history. Treat with reverence, and never belittle, those memories of sacred moments and treasured relationships, but firmly encourage the understanding of church buildings as instruments of, not monuments to, God's grace in human lives.

Value one another

No one is encouraged to give their best by aggression or complaints. A central principle of kingdom living is that our relationships are as important as the work that we do. Learn to bless and encourage one another. For example, regularly encourage the congregation to pray for one another and to thank one another – over communion can be a great time to do this. Remember that any criticism or necessary rebuke will be better received by people who have been often thanked and appreciated for their contribution, and know themselves to be valued and loved. Avoid negative humour – greeting someone who enters the room with the words 'Oh no, not you again' or 'Look out, here comes trouble!' can be intended as affectionate and funny, but has an insidious, cumulative effect, establishing a negative culture and encouraging low self-esteem. As people with low self-esteem sometimes find a haven in the church, gentle encouragement toward positive speech may be helpful, so that people learn to say positive things: 'Oh look! It's my favourite church caretaker!'; 'That's the best cup of tea I've had all day!', etc. Remember the power of your smile.

Work with others

Individuals and local churches are part of the meta-narrative of the kingdom of God, but we are not the whole story. We must work together with other groups, churches and individuals if we are to make a lasting difference in our communities. To help this, arrange a couple of opportunities to celebrate the work of other churches. Your local expression of Churches Together may offer a valuable opportunity for united worship and planning shared events with other churches in the community

eXamine your progress regularly!

Review and accountability are vital in monitoring both your practice and your vision, helping you to stay on target in working towards your intention. Seek the advice and guidance of the church family on a regular basis, by building in evaluation meetings to your project schedule, distributing evaluation forms, or having a bright, prominent, suggestions and comments box in the church building or project location.

You *need to model what you say*

People will not follow us if they cannot see us to be authentic. We must model what we ask others to do and be. Help yourself to model your words by becoming part of an accountability group or a prayer triplet.

Zeal *makes all the difference*

Too often we run out of ideas and passion because we forget why we are doing what we do – but if we can remember that we are kingdom people, motivated and sustained by the unconditional love of God, offering our work as a 'thank you' for His goodness to us, we will be more likely to keep going. Help people remember this by encouraging regular prayer, praise and ministry together and towards one another. Remember Jesus' teaching about keeping focused in Matthew's Gospel (6:22). The traditional words of the King James Version capture the meaning well: 'if … thine eye be single, thy whole body shall be full of light'. As we focus on what we are called to do, light builds and fills our whole being.

Conclusion

We have discussed ideas and practical suggestions around making a difference in our communities. We have affirmed the necessity for joined up thinking and action. We have seen that we need to be moving forward carefully, clearly and confidently, whether in the congregation or in the community. At the heart of all that we have considered abides the conviction that we are kingdom people whose lives are designed to reflect the wonder and love of God into our homes, our streets and our communities. Everything that we do is connected. God's presence in our lives is an invisible thread running through our private lives, family lives, working lives, friendships and faith community. Our calling is to live confidently in our awareness of this integration of all that we say, do, think and are, for the glory of God. In so doing, we become conduits into the world of the already-present kingdom of God.

Our mission, should we choose to accept it, is the transformation of the world!

Let us pray.

Father,

Let us not become weary in doing good. Help us to continually remember that You are with us in every act of kindness and every word of truth. Keep our focus on You and help us to remember that everything we say and everything we do is for You. We pray that You will use us as channels through which Your love pours into our communities. Help us to be Your agents of change in a broken and needy world. Help us to listen to You, to be willing to do what You ask, and open to doing something new for You.

Help our love of You and of other people to be practical and tangible. Guide us in our use of resources and help us to see those around us as You have made them. Banish despair and heal the pain in the lives and experiences of our communities. May faith bring wholeness as it always has to those whose lives touch Christ's.

We pray that You will connect us with others who love You and long to see your kingdom come. Let local churches rise as forces of good and grace in our communities and keep us true to You, and to what You have called us to be.

Amen.

NOTES

1. Definition from *Dictionary.com Unabridged (v 1.1)*, New York: Random House, http://dictionary.reference.com/browse/integral (accessed 4 July 2007).

2. For example, in Northern Ireland, the SVP visits 2,600 people in need per week, has 185 'branches' or 'conferences', spends £2.2 million a year and has almost 2,000 volunteers. For more information see www.svp-ni.org. The charity has also been active in England and Wales since 1844, see www.svp.org.uk.

3. For more information on Green Pastures and the work they do see www.greenpastureshousing.co.uk.

4. For help with church auditing, contact Faithworks.

5. Bruce L. Bugbee and Don Cousins, *Network Participant's Guide*, Grand Rapids: Zondervan, 1994.

6. Myers Briggs, for example, is a helpful tool for profiling – see www.myersbriggs.org. Likewise Belbin psychometric testing – see www.belbin.com. Other, more traditional approaches to helping people work out their 'life' purpose include mentoring, the appointment of a spiritual director, or regular, planned spiritual retreats.

7. Dr Howard G. Hendricks is Distinguished Professor and Chairman of the Center for Christian Leadership at Dallas Theological Seminary.

8. The London Institute of Contemporary Christianity has suggestions for more ways of creating a 'kingdom dialogue' in your local church: see www.licc.org.uk.

9. See www.worldprayer.org.

10. The Shaftesbury Society has merged with John Grooms. For more information see www.shaftesburysoc.org.uk.

11. See www.tearfund.org.

12. See www.24-7.com.

13. See *Prayerworks: The Manual*, Milton Keynes: Authentic, 2005, from p. 58.

14. See www.statistics.gov.uk.

15. For more information see www.communities.gov.uk.

16. For more information see the Department for Works and Pensions – www.dwp.gov.uk.

17. For more information see the Department for Families, Schools and Children – www.dfes.gov.uk.

18. At the time of writing, the government in the UK has just undergone a major reshaping. A new department entitled the Department for Higher Education and Vocation training is being established. For more details see http://www.dfes.gov.uk/hegateway

19. For more information see www.crimestatistics.org.uk

20. For more information on local area agreements see the Department for Communities and Local Government website, www.communities.gov.uk.

21. See www.ncvo-vol.org.uk for more information.

22. For more information on conducting a community audit and understanding the needs of your community, please see www.faithworks. info and explore our community audit tools.

23. The Neighbourhood Initiatives Foundation provide some very helpful tips around auditing of communities. See www.nif.co.uk for more details.

24. See www.saltbox.org.uk.

25. More information can be obtained either from Saltbox or from Faithworks.

26. Paul Sanderson, a manager for Spurgeon's Childcare and the coordinator of the WIRE project, Southampton. For more details, contact www.thewireproject.com.

7

How Do We Behave?

But in your hearts sanctify Christ as Lord. Always be ready to make your defence to anyone who demands from you an account of the hope that is in you; yet do it with gentleness and reverence. Keep your conscience clear, so that, when you are maligned, those who abuse you for your good conduct in Christ may be put to shame. For it is better to suffer for doing good, if suffering should be God's will, than to suffer for doing evil.   (1 Peter 3:15–17, NRSV)

Let the same mind be in you, that was in Christ Jesus.   (Philippians 2:5, NRSV)

I love being part of the church. There is no greater privilege for me than to be part of the bride of Christ. I want to celebrate what it means to be part of a group of people who are committed to God, to their community, to one another and to a right understanding of themselves. It constantly amazes me that God has decided to entrust the purpose of kingdom building to a ragtag group of people like us. We fall and stumble so many times, and manage to get it wrong so often – yet God remains committed to working out His purposes and his plans through us. It's breathtaking. It's intoxicating. It's exhilarating. It's also at times frustrating!

Whilst I am not a deconstructionist, and I believe firmly in the purpose and place of the local church, I also want to be a realist – and the reality is that the church does not always behave well. Perhaps because matters of protest make more headlines than people living in harmony together, we have become better known for what we stand against than what we stand for. To make matters worse, our voices often sound aggressive and moralistic, until we appear more like an angry mob than of the people of God. Instead of living in the responsibilities of our calling to be the servant church – the anointed people of God in His unconditional love, the followers of Jesus who came not to condemn but to save the world – we are perceived as being elitist, aloof and separatist. Like Israel in the Old Testament, it appears that we sometimes want to live in the blessing of being the people of God, without actually accepting the responsibility. The stridency that has been on public display has managed to alienate the public, disconnect us from the nourishing roots of our calling and separate us from our meaningful role in society. If we really are to be a kingdom people, then our behaviour is going to have to change.

I am not suggesting that we may never be angry. Constructively channelled and expressed, anger is a most effective force for positive social change. But we need to be angry at the right things and express that anger in a godly way. We should be angry at the injustice in the world. We should speak out on issues of exclusion and pain and sin – but in our speaking out we have to learn to use the right words to the right audience. We must not permit ourselves to be boxed into a corner – allowing those who like to caricature the church to show us waving placards on issues of personal morality, condemning others in a shrill and aggressive voice, whilst remaining silent on injustice that should have the whole world shouting. We have condensed down 'morality' to sexual (especially homosexual) behaviour, abortion and marriage. These are very important issues, and we should not be afraid to speak out on them – but gently, and with understanding, for we touch on people's loneliness and love, their vulnerability and choices that have broken their hearts: they don't need our condemnation as well. And how did we manage to reduce biblical morality – *kingdom living* – to just these issues? Why does the church not say more about housing, healthcare, education, employment, debt, asylum, poverty alleviation and the environment, to name just a few areas where our silence is not to our credit? Marriage (or singleness), personal relationships and family life are areas where wise pastoral guidance will always be helpful – for they present challenges to every human being; but it is time the church gave up the ferocious obsession with sexuality, and took a more balanced approach.

Throughout this book I have argued that we need to have an integrated and holistic approach to our mission and purpose in the world. Local churches have a vital and transforming part to play in building healthy, inclusive and safe communities, but local churches will be at the heart of healthy communities only if the people of the community know they can trust us to be gentle and understanding, perceptive and courteous, honest, wise and just. Our public demonstrations and statements, our press releases, and the way we conduct ourselves towards those who are at variance with our outlook, should be positive in expression, so that even those who think we are not right will at least think we are kind.

Mother Teresa said, 'I was once asked why I don't participate in anti-war demonstrations. I said that I will never do that, but as soon as you have a pro-peace rally, I'll be there.'

Not the Whole Story

There are over 48,000 Christian churches in the United Kingdom. The vast majority of them are made up of ordinary people like you and me who want to live out their faith by loving God and loving their neighbours. We are not aggressive, militant, angry, reactive people. We want to obey the Scriptures, we want to act justly, love mercy and walk humbly with our God. Followers of Christ are scattered across every stratum of British society. From local congregations to local projects, we carry on with the work of mission and kingdom-building, day in and day out. We are Christians when we are gathered to worship, and we are Christians when dispersed to work. Followers of Christ live out their faith in every niche of society – from hospitals to hostels, from prisons to pizzerias and from families to factories, individual followers of Christ are at the heart of our communities.

The 8 million or so Christians in the United Kingdom do not all have the same views as those who appear so aggressive and angry in the media. We do not all have the same views on the environment, sexuality, birth control, military force, money, family, healthcare, the point at which life begins (or ends), the role of women, or even the way in which the church should be governed or led. The Christian church is united in its commitment to Christ and its commitment to the world, but we are a diverse and colourful bunch of people. We may have strong and clear views on many things – but we also have varied views on innumerable matters. Therefore, while it is important that we stand together, it is also equally important that we do not allow ourselves to be caricatured into one 'personality'. There are millions of Christians who want their leaders to speak out – compassionately, graciously, but clearly – on issues such as community cohesion, the responsibility of the state to protect the vulnerable, the need for a better policy towards those seeking asylum, and the desperate need for a better approach to environmental responsibility. We are uncomfortable with being perceived as angry, aggressive and narrow moralists. That doesn't mean we have no wisdom to offer in the area of personal morality, but that our horizons are broader than the bedroom. For us, a budget is a moral issue. The decision to go to war is a moral issue. The right of the poor to justice is a moral issue. The ownership of land, energy sources, genetic manipulation, racial harmony, transport policies, clean water provision, farming techniques and literacy and deforestation are moral issues. Morality is holistic, because morality is about the art of living. We want to speak out and live out our faith – but we also want those who claim to speak on our behalf to be mindful of how they represent us. Angry voices are not even half the story.

A Case in Point

I personally hold a conservative view of human sexuality. It is my conviction that God designed human beings to exist in partnership with one another and that the best environment for sexual activity is within the context of marriage – which is a lifelong commitment of monogamy and faithfulness publicly declared between a man and a woman. I also believe this is the best environment in which to bring up children. I believe this to be God's design. Yet, even though I believe all of that, I also recognise that there are other Christians who hold different views. I might disagree with them, but I also respect them. So when the press and media reported 'the church's' views on the proposed Sexual Orientation Regulations in England and Wales in January 2007, I felt compelled to speak out.

The impression given by the coverage was that every single Christian in the United Kingdom, and therefore every local church, disagreed with the SORs. Furthermore, that gave the impression that the whole church was against gay couples. I became involved in the debate very publicly because I took the view that the proposed regulations themselves did not pose a threat to Christian freedom. I was also concerned that the church was being misrepresented by some of those who had stepped into the limelight on the issue. I spoke out because I believe passionately that acceptance of people is a Christian duty and that acceptance of a person and service of others does not equate to endorsement of their lifestyle. I wanted to challenge the idea that if you were a Christian, you were bound to be opposed to the Sexual Orientation Regulations. Most importantly of all, I spoke out because I wanted to challenge the way in which some Christian agencies were articulating their arguments. Rather than speaking compassionately and graciously, and speaking the truth in love, the church was portrayed as a snarling mob who thought that their views and their rights and their ideas should be imposed upon everybody else. That misrepresentation of my faith and convictions was something I was unwilling to allow to go unchecked, so I spoke out. My challenge was simple then, and remains so now. To be a believer is to live by the light of the whole gospel – and there is far more in the New Testament about our demeanour, and our conduct and attitude to our fellow human beings, than there is about being heterosexual, married or right.

The Example of Jesus

We must make sure that our behaviour is in line with the example and life of Jesus. As we become familiar with him, we should seek to mirror him. To be a follower of Christ – to be a kingdom builder – is not just about what we believe or the projects or work that we do, it is also about how we behave, and our behaviour is shaped by our attitudes. Jesus as we encounter Him in the gospel narratives told the truth in an uncompromising manner; but He was neither negative nor aggressive – and He won the right to speak so directly by healing the sick and embracing the leper and binding up the raw wounds of the broken-hearted. Jesus knew who He was, but had no hesitation in taking the role of the lowliest household servant. When He was angry, it was on behalf of others, because they had been rejected and shut out. His purity remained whole and beautiful, but it was warm and loving – not the purity of snow. Jesus was not choosy about the company He kept. Several of His friends seem to have been prostitutes; but that friendship occasioned no nudging and winking. He was honest through and through, and respectful of other human beings; direct in his dealings and whole and true right through to the middle. It would have been a waste of time trying to slur Jesus with smut – His trustworthiness was simply apparent. Jesus didn't hurt people, He healed them. We are called to be the same. That's what being a follower means.

Our self-awareness, self-understanding and attitudes toward others are at the heart of a strong commitment to being the people of God and seeing God's kingdom come. *How* we do things is as important as *why* we do them.

In chapter 4 we considered the way the church is perceived in modern society, and how we might respond to those perceptions, developing them into constructive dialogue. The perceptions of others arise (in part) from our behaviour towards them; therefore this dialogue matters to us, because we aspire to authentic and honest communication. But what others think of us is not the force that drives us. Our concern is not the image of the people of God, but the image of God in the people.

Taking our approach, attitude and conduct seriously is not a public relations campaign, it is foundational to establishing the reign of Christ's kingdom on earth. Let's look specifically now at five key focal issues of attitude and conduct:

- identity
- equality
- influence
- conscience
- diversity

The vast majority of Christians around the world do not grab the headlines in the way that they speak and behave. 'Make it your ambition to lead a quiet life, to mind your own business and to work with your hands,' says the letter to the Thessalonians (1 Thessalonians 4:11), and most Christians live exactly in that way – occupied in healthcare, education, housing, crime reduction, parenting classes and community groups every day. Perhaps those who criticise and condemn, who shout and attack, attract the attention of the media; but they are not representative of the main body of Christian people. Most Christians understand that what we see in Jesus is supposed to be the role model for our own lives.

Attitudes that Spring from Inclusion and Justice

Because Jesus could accurately describe Himself as having come here not to be served but to serve, and to lay down His life for the benefit of other people, the church must be committed to loving service in the community in order for it to be the church of Christ at all. Our attitudes should be positive and encouraging, believing the best of our communities, looking for what is good:

> Finally, brothers, whatever is true, whatever is noble, whatever is right, whatever is pure, whatever is lovely, whatever is admirable – if anything is excellent or praiseworthy – think about such things.

Whatever you have learned or received or heard
from me, or seen in me – put it into practice. And the
God of peace will be with you.

(Philippians 4:8–9)

Something precious and central is lost if the local
church offers to the community only conditional love.
At the heart of a commitment to being *kingdom people*,
as we have already discovered, there is a commitment
to inclusion and justice. We hold a clear and strong
commitment to human dignity in all people, irrespec-
tive of their creed, colour, orientation or preferences
because we are committed to the belief that all people
are made in the image of God (see, for example,
Genesis 1:29, Psalm 139). As individual Christians and
as local churches, we must ensure that we both recognise and articulate these convictions, and ensure that
our behaviour and approach to others is consistent
with our teaching about inclusion and justice.

For local churches to gain the trust of people in the
community, it is important to create living relationships, overcoming the mistaken perception of the
church as a monolithic, detached institution shrouded
in the traditions of the past. The body of Christ is made
up of people who are called to love God and love their
neighbour (Matthew 22). It is made up of real people
(1 Corinthians 12), exists to serve real people
(Colossians 3) and is a group of real people drawn
together because of their relationships with God and
with one another (Ephesians 1). It is not a vague,

disembodied, authoritarian, remote institution. The tendency of both government and elements of the church itself to view it in that light have become obstacles to the true mission of Christians, which is to be engaging with the world around us for the glory of God and the extension of God's kingdom.

In the interests of all that is good in the church, and of the future of our work in the community, we must avoid being represented by an aggressive and angry right-wing lobby. It is vital to bear in mind that there is more at stake in this dialogue than whether the church is popular or not. Securing good opinion and wooing the approbation of our critics is not the issue. What is at stake is that the way we behave and talk in public, and the implications of our decisions affect the lives of real human beings – often the most marginalised and excluded people in our communities. What a travesty, indeed what a pyrrhic victory it would be, if the church enjoyed a good reputation for itself institutionally at the expense of its commitment at the grass roots to vulnerable people and the local community.

Called to love without fear, we must understand that our commitment to service and to befriending and caring for people does not imply an endorsement of their lifestyle (John 4: 13). As we make links and connections among the diverse folk of our community, we need not fear that we will be compromised or tainted by that connection. Maintaining our own boundaries and staying strong in our own identity is part of the requirements of our discipleship, but we are not here to judge others and condemn them.

We must also ensure that we do not categorise people purely in terms of our view of their conduct and behaviour. In the Gospels, there are various references to an occasion when Jesus was a guest at the house of a man called Simon (Luke 7:36–50, Matthew 26:6, Mark 14:3, also John 12:3). Simon is described as 'Simon the leper' (perhaps Jesus healed him?) and as 'Simon the pharisee', so he belonged simultaneously in the category of the excluded and the category of the righteous inner ring. At dinner, a woman with a tarnished reputation came into the place, and began to wash Christ's feet with her tears, drying his feet with her unbound hair. Simon (fully in persona as 'pharisee'!) was scandalised, making the judgement that if Jesus were really a prophet He would know what kind of person this woman was and not permit her to get close to Him or touch Him. Christ's response to this judgement should determine our attitude and approach to all the lost and the outcast in society. He said, 'Simon, do you *see* this woman?' (my emphasis).

He calls the man by his name – responding to him neither as a leper nor as a pharisee, but as a person, and requires that Simon extend the same courtesy and compassion to the woman. It follows that Christ asks no less of us; the compassion to really see.

Kingdom theology believes that each of us is a whole person and that salvation is good news at every level for every person. We must show that our faith works. Those of us who have a personal faith must ensure that we both articulate *and* demonstrate that Christian faith is good for our community and for wider society. It is our responsibility to demonstrate that the idea that our faith can be separated from our life is as preposterous as arguing that our political principles should be divorced from our political actions. It is logically impossible for a Christian not to allow their faith to shape both their ideology and their lifestyle. It must also be equally impossible for a Christian's commitment to serve other people to be divorced from their commitment to love and serve God.

Having said all of that, there are some things that we as Christians will object to on issues of conscience. We should remember that it is a philosophical impossibility to legislate against our conscience and belief in any genuinely effective way. No one can stop us from believing. Not only is it intellectually suspect, it is pragmatically impossible – and against the law. Issues of true conscience must remain intact according to Article Nine of the European Convention of Human Rights, and it is a deeply held principle of democratic society that its citizens should be free to live according to their conscience – without obviating the freedom of others to do the same.

This exercise of our freedom of conscience must be set alongside the inherently good principles of non-discrimination, fairness and service provision for all if we are to thrive as a diverse society, rather than simply endure difference. In words attributed to Voltaire,

> I disagree profoundly with what you say, but I would
> defend to the death your right to say it.

We are free to differ from one another's viewpoints, but
we do well to create a cohesive society by caring for
each other.

One of the principles of integral mission that we
have already established and affirmed is that distinctive
identity, when properly understood, leads to strong and
positive diversity. There are issues of conscience for
those of Christian faith that result in us being unable to
provide certain services or receive funding for certain
areas of our work. Members of the Faithworks movement live with these choices every day. We are over-
looked for funding, or may feel unable to apply for
funding because of the distinctive commitments that
spring from our faith. We are often misconstrued and
misunderstood. We can be attacked and criticised. Yet
we carry on our work, paying for it from our own
resources and the support of our own local faith communities because we are committed to serving and
engaging in our communities at the same time as being
committed to our faith. For us, and for thousands of
other people and projects, this is part of the cost of
being committed to both unconditional engagement
with our communities and the standards of Christian
morality. This is one of the challenges of kingdom living. In short, millions of Christians, and thousands of
projects run by them, get on with the work of serving
people unconditionally every day. We do it because it's

right, and we won't stop doing it. No one can stop us from being distinctive but ourselves. The consequences of our faith commitments are felt every day. Our service is offered freely, but some of our distinctives are non-negotiable.

While we must avoid the language of demands and threats we must also make our position and its consequences clear. Part of the commitment that we make to our society is to recognise and celebrate its diversity while living and behaving in a way that is in keeping with our own religious ethos and values. We do not have the right to demand that our society adopts our ethos, but we can help them to understand it. We must understand that our own rights are no more important than the rights of those who disagree with us. Healthy societies and communities do not just endure difference and diversity, they embrace it.

We as followers of Christ must take the trouble to be self-aware, pausing to reflect upon our own thinking and behaviour as ambassadors of the kingdom of God. We must be diligent to maintain Christ-like attitudes. The world around us is shifting, and the secularisation consequent upon postmodern thought alters radically what the church may assume about its position in society. Even though the establishment of the church is still part of British legislature and tradition, the combination of the rise of postmodern secular philosophy and increasing religious diversity has massively diminished our political influence and power *as an institution*. The age of the church and the state sharing political power is over. We are returning to a pre-Constantinian model of Christian community. In so doing, we may well also be returning to a more authentic place of spirituality and service. We are returning to a dependency on the voice and conscience of every Christian individual. When the voice of the church as institution no longer signifies very greatly in forming social opinion, it becomes crucially important for its members to fulfil their individual responsibility as citizens to shaping what their community will become.

Identity

Our understanding of Christian identity prompts us to a commitment to give our service rather than make demands (John 13). It seems very clear to me that it was the assurance of His identity and purpose that led and enabled Christ to serve those around Him unconditionally. His confidence in what God had called Him to do enabled Him to engage with those around Him compassionately and authentically – even those who would ultimately betray Him.

> Jesus knew that the Father had put all things under his power, and that he had come from God and was returning to God; so he got up from the meal, took off his outer clothing, and wrapped a towel around his waist. After that, he poured water into a basin and began to wash his disciples' feet, drying them with the towel that was wrapped around him.
> (John 13:3–5)

Our call is to follow his example, in both assurance and service. The New Testament offers no model for a demands-based approach to engagement with the community, nor can I see it in the life and example of Christ. The driving out of the tax-collectors from the temple does not represent demand and protest at the state, rather it is a challenge to the church and our own institutions to ensure that we do not exploit our position and our power at the expense of those who need access to God and his love. In our rush to demand what we think is important, we must not allow ourselves to make our service the bargaining tool. Once again, I think of the work of thousands of local churches across the UK. So many of them embody this quiet choice to be like Jesus every day. They serve, love and embrace, declining to push and shove for recognition, continuing to practise a gospel of welcome and hospitality. There are times when the work flows easily, delivered in happy partnership with other agencies; and there are times when we work in isolated and unsupported situations – but we must never lay down a set of demands to be fulfilled before we offer our service. We serve because God asks it of us, so it is part of our identity to serve, the expression of the faith we have embraced. Mission is not another form of trade.

Equality

The Christian faith teaches and recognises the absolute equality of every human being (see Genesis 1:29, Colossians 3:11, Acts 10:34) as well as challenging individuals and communities to live within the best framework possible (Exodus 20). Our affirmation of equality implies a definition of citizenship in terms of duties rather than of rights (Philippians 2). But what should we do when, in recognising the equality of all people, we have invited equal expression of views that are narrow and oppressive? When tolerance of all leads to intolerance of us, what do we do?

> Think of yourselves the way Christ Jesus thought of himself. He had equal status with God but didn't think so much of himself that he had to cling to the advantages of that status no matter what. Not at all. When the time came, he set aside the privileges of deity and took on the status of a slave, became human! Having become human, he stayed human. It was an incredibly humbling process. He didn't claim special privileges. Instead, he lived a selfless, obedient life and then died a selfless, obedient death – and the worst kind of death at that – a crucifixion.
>
> (Philippians 2:5–8, The Message)

I am deeply challenged by these words from the apostle Paul, the more so when I remind myself that the challenge is not just for an individual follower of Christ, but was for the whole Christian community in Philippi. In what way can we protect our rights and remain true to the example and teaching of the New Testament? Our social conditioning, our instinct for self-preservation, and our failure to understand the spiritual power that is ours in Christ, together mean that our knee-jerk reaction is usually to defend ourselves most vigorously.

The challenge for us as Christ's followers is to recognise the equality of all people, and defend that equality; then when faced with those who treat us as less than equal, to be able to maintain our Christ-likeness by refusing to abandon our principles to grab for our own rights. We clearly must present the case for our rights, but we must not walk away from society if we do not get them. This is one of the paradoxes of the kingdom. It seems an impossible position to defend – that we are willing to give away our rights because of our love of God and commitment to others; and yet it is the call that is placed upon our lives, if we are to take seriously the teaching of the New Testament in its fullness and not just in its parts. The key question we must answer here is whether or not we are willing, if faced with the decision, to lay down our own rights in order to remain engaged in the community. The teaching of the New Testament and the example of Christ demonstrate that our identity is not affected at all by doing so – but our political influence and power may well be.

Influence

The Christian understanding of influence encourages us to accept responsibility rather than demanding privilege (Luke 22:25–27). The understanding of authority (as prophets, judges, kings) in the Hebrew scriptures was in terms of accountability – for authority could ultimately be validated only by God. This understanding is perpetuated into the New Testament, for example in the story of Christ's healing of the centurion's servant, where the centurion expresses his understanding of the source of his power as being *subject* to authority:

> Lord, I do not deserve to have you come under my roof. But just say the word, and my servant will be healed. For I myself am a man under authority, with soldiers under me. I tell this one, 'Go,' and he goes; and that one, 'Come,' and he comes. I say to my servant, 'Do this,' and he does it.
>
> (Matthew 8:8–9)

The central call on Israel was to live as the people of God in order to demonstrate to the wider world that God was gracious, just and compassionate. They repeatedly failed to do this. Their central mistake was that they lived in the privilege of their relationship with God without accepting the responsibilities of that relationship. The only power that matters for us is the power of the Holy Spirit that is given to the church by God; but too often, particularly under the persisting influence of the imperialistic mindset of Christendom, followers of Christ have allowed themselves to trade the real and lasting power of God's influence and presence with us for political and temporal power. In short, we try to maintain a place of privilege instead of accepting our responsibilities. When we do this, we diminish rather than increase our real power, for the only influence that lasts is the influence that we are given by God, which is not of this world and so cannot be taken away by any political power.

We must be mindful that as citizens, we have a responsibility to fellow citizens as well as to government and each other. The Christian church is not entitled to special privileges just because it is Christian. We live in a society of competing rights and demands. Our responsibility is to live out our service from our clear sense of identity – knowing who we are, and committing ourselves to live and be like Christ. Just because wider society is vociferous in its demands for privilege does not mean that we should follow suit. I am not, in any way, advocating that in the confusion around equality and diversity Christians should remain awkwardly silent, hoping to be noticed and included. Of course we should engage in the debate, seek to shape opinion, and make our views known. We have the privilege of being members of a democratic society where the opportunity for us to engage also implies a duty. But we must also remember that we are called to be light and salt and yeast (see Matthew 5; 13): hidden, indefinable, dispersed and thoroughly integrated. We have a God-given responsibility to engage in service and to continue doing so, no matter what the political climate might be.

We must also remember both the sovereignty of God in all things and the challenge that evil is at work in the world (see 2 Corinthians 4:4, Ephesians 2:2, Ephesians 6:12, 1 John 5:19). Ultimately we also recognise that

God orders the power of the world – indeed this is what Jesus told Pontius Pilate (see John 18:36) – and we must recognise that our values, our choices and our standards do not reflect those of the society in which we live. We are different. That difference does not, however, exempt us from involvement. It is one of the reasons that we have been given the Holy Spirit – to be effective witnesses in the world and to understand and live out the truth (see John 14–16, Acts 1). Our position is not a privileged position, but carries responsibilities of faithfulness to God and service of others (see Matthew 22). The only privilege we need remember is that of having experienced the grace of God, and the empowering to share that compassionate grace with other people.

Conscience

Christian conscience leads to accepting the consequences of our decisions rather than demanding exemption or protection (see Romans 13). Society proceeds on the basis of consensus; and with the rise of secularisation and religious diversity, we cannot rely on the social consensus to support us. We may encounter situations where our faith means there will be activities we cannot carry out, behaviour we cannot condone, requests we must refuse: and in these situations our conscience is crucial. Article Nine of the European Convention on Human Rights states:

Everyone has the right to freedom of thought, conscience and religion; this right includes freedom to change his religion or belief, and freedom, either alone or in community with others and in public or private, to manifest his religion or belief, in worship, teaching, practice and observance.

Freedom to manifest one's religion or beliefs shall be subject only to such limitations as are prescribed by law and are necessary in a democratic society in the interests of public safety, for the protection of public order, health or morals, or the protection of the rights and freedoms of others.

What, then, should we do when our consciences tell us that we must take actions that contravene the law? What if the *kingdom* thing to do means we will put ourselves in jeopardy of prosecution? The straightforward answer is that we must join with millions of people through the entire history of the church and we must accept the consequences of our allegiance to God.

I am not talking here about parking on double yellow lines because I left home too late to walk to the church where I am preaching, or not declaring taxable income because I would rather give my money to the church offering! I have a sense that many Christians see issues of conscience when actually they are talking about preferences.

That being said, there are undoubtedly situations where our conscience tells us we cannot take a road set out before us. In the Second World War, for example, there were those in occupied territories who defied the Nazis in sheltering Jewish families; similarly, the black followers of Martin Luther King challenged laws of segregation in travelling on buses designated only for whites.

In less dramatic contemporary situations, we occasionally face a crossroads of decision, when we must recognise that certain funding will not be available to us, that certain partnerships are not ones of which we can be part, and certain activities are not appropriate for us. When we have articulated our reasons for this, recognising the challenges that our decisions will create both for others and ourselves, then we must accept the consequences of our decisions.

The more deeply we are engaged in society, the more the consequences of our non-complicity may affect others. For a nation so dependent upon local churches for the delivery of services, the consequences of our choosing to withdraw from some activities could be catastrophic, but we must not use our commitment and the need of vulnerable people as a bargaining tool. Our commitment to serve remains intact. The consequences of our decisions must be borne by us, not by the vulnerable people we serve, even if those consequences involve funding withdrawal and prosecution. Whatever our circumstances, we must not be in any doubt that our first allegiance must be to God (see Romans 13:1, Titus 3:1, 1 Peter 2:13–17, Acts 5:29). Equally, we must beware of confusing 'God' with personal bigotry.

Diversity

The Christian understanding of equality means a commitment to diversity which requires an attitude of humility, not superiority (see Romans 12). The New Testament call to honest self-appraisal and awareness is vitally important when it comes to issues of diversity. I have for some time adopted the approach of comparing my worst attributes with the best attributes of those who criticise me. That way I am careful not to caricature those who are different. If we connect up our commitment to honest appraisal and humility with the belief that all goodness in the world is a reflection of God (see James 1), then we are left with the possibility of seeing the good in others before we see the bad, and of being committed to bringing out the best in others rather than the worst in ourselves. Diversity is something to be celebrated and welcomed, whether in the church or in wider society – not another modern problem to endure!

How we behave is shaped by what we believe and our understanding of issues such as identity, equality, influence, conscience and diversity, not by self-conscious anxiety about what others may be thinking of us. Yet as we think through these issues and allow our responses to shape our actions and sharpen our focus, we do so in awareness that the wider world is watching and listening: and we remember that God is listening too. To hold this awareness in mind recalls to us the need to be gentle in articulating the non-negotiable principles of our faith. When we think about identity, we need to consider our freedom to serve others, not demand extra space for self-expression. When we think about equality, we need to be willing to give our rights away, not insist upon others observing them. When we think about influence, we need to avoid the language of privilege and instead focus on accepting our responsibilities. As we work through issues of conscience, we must be willing to accept the consequences rather than evade them. Lastly, as members of a diverse society, we must adopt the attitude of humility rather than defensiveness, hostility or superiority.

The task of the local church in being an agent of God's kingdom is never about competing in a power struggle – it should always be about service, love and self-understanding.

Conclusion

The church has waxed and waned over its two-thousand-year history. In the United Kingdom, we have been in steady decline since the end of the Second World War. Christian movements for social change have come and gone. A few have continued – like the Young Men's Christian Association and The Salvation Army, which still exhibit massive influence for good, touching and changing the lives of thousands of people every day in pragmatic and in spiritual ways. But at the heart of God's plan for building His kingdom and renewing and transforming the world lies the local church and ordinary people like you and me. We are entrusted with the greatest task of all. What do we need to remember as we put down *Kingdom Come* and set about what God has called us to do and be?

Building the Kingdom

The motivation behind working for transformation in the world is both deeply theological and sociological. Theological because the core mission of the church is to be God's agent in bringing hope and change to the world. Sociological because society is made up of individuals and can only change one person at a time. Far from being isolated and irrelevant, local churches are called to bring the greatest change the world has ever known – the kingdom agenda is nothing short of the transformation of the world!

Christian faith nurtures and reassures us, comforts our sorrow and fills us with joy. It also pushes us out of the comfort zone of our familiar, safe church family into a world that is desperately in need. The honest followers of Christ in every age are participants in the greatest paradigm shift the world has ever seen. We are a community of people whose lives are being transformed by God, agents of transformation in the world. The nineteenth-century evangelical revivalist, Charles Finney, believed passionately in the church's mission to transform the world. In his now famous book, *Lectures on Revival*, he wrote:

The Great Business of the church is to reform the world ... the church of Christ was originally formed to be a body of reformers. The very profession of Christianity implies the profession and virtually an oath to do all that can be done for the universal reformation of the world.

Where Christianity locks itself away from the political and social challenges of its contemporary culture, it becomes irrelevant. It may appear settled and surviving, but it will eventually choke to death because true mission is to the church what air is to the human body. Separation from society leads to stagnation and death for the church. If you forget everything else we have discovered together in the course of *Kingdom Come*, then my prayer is that you will remember these three things.

1. Committed to Christ

Jesus Christ must stand at the heart of any effective local church. Without Him, the local church's ethos, values and distinctiveness will be lost. The modern church may be tempted to turn aside from steadfastly following Jesus in a number of ways. 'Celebrity' Christians and the movements that gather round them face the seduction of power, influence and popularity. Small church and chapel congregations in the mainstream tradition are tempted to settle into nostalgia and preoccupation with procedures and convention. Charismatic evangelical congregations centring in larger urban churches can become victims of their own success, their energies following a closed loop of introspection, disconnected from the experience of even their nearest neighbours. When these things become more important than our commitment to Christ, we lose not only our effectiveness, but also our heart. Once the centrality of Christ as He really is has been denied in a church or a Christian project, the very source of greatest influence is also denied: and it is the whole person of Christ who must remain at the heart of what we do, not just one group's interpretation of Him.

The strongest Christian social action and kingdom living are motivated by a holistic reading of and response to the life and example of Christ. There is plenty of room for a breadth of understanding of Jesus and his ministry. Catholics can stand alongside Evangelicals who can stand alongside Orthodox believers. Pentecostals and Pietists can share this mission with Anabaptists and Charismatics. Each has a particular spotlight to shine upon the person and ministry of the Son of God. The political Jesus *is* the suffering Saviour. The compassionate Christ *is* the holistic Healer. We must allow the birth, life, death and resurrection, with their rich tapestry of meanings and implications, to be interwoven to create the strong, unbreakable fabric of spiritual, social and political transformation. To allow the many facets of Christ's glory to be the jewel at the heart of our lives is to allow ourselves to be strong at the centre and free to be open and completely inclusive at the edge.

At the heart of the American civil rights movement of the 1960s there was quite a diversity of opinion around Christ – from liberal to conservative, black to white, liberator to suffering God. The fact remained, however, that the whole person of Jesus stood at the centre of that movement. He was the embodiment of freedom to those oppressed and of hope to those long discouraged. Yet He was not narrowed by one theology or held down by one denominational view. The same must be true of us as we seek to be agents of God's kingdom in our worlds. Christ is the One from whom we gain our inspiration, our identity and our vision. We must never apologise for Him, for He has never been ashamed of us.

2. Focused on People

Secondly, the projects of integral mission must be focused on people. Policies, procedures and legislation are good servants but poor masters; they are not our ultimate aim or focus. The kingdom comes in one life at a time. We are the ones who wade into the water to help those who are drowning while we figure out a way to stop people falling into the river in the first place! We must not become enamoured of activism, busy about our crusade of endless paternalistic intervention. Positive change always works from the grassroots up, because somebody stopped to listen, somebody saw a need. Christianity is a listening faith, a faith that stops to help because someone is in deep trouble; a faith that sees not a social category but a struggling soul. Revival always starts with the heart of an individual.

Christians do not classify people. We do not regard

some people as more important than others: we recognise that every human being is made in the image of
God and therefore on an equal footing with us and all
other people. A human person is entitled to respect,
dignity, acceptance and love. This clear focus enables
us to serve, not from a position of power and privilege,
but instead from a place of equality and grace. When
we engage in the service of others, we do not 'conde-
scend' to serve. Rather than reaching down to someone
else from the moral high ground of superiority, we
reach across to them because we recognise that they
also are of absolute value to God: and because we know
their weakness is only a mirror of our own. When a
local church gives up its focus on people for a focus on
programmes it becomes nothing more than another
organisation. We may use statistics, but we should
never begin to see people as mere statistics.

This is a crucial component of the local church's
calling because it celebrates the dignity of life wherever
it is found and it levels the place of service. We learn
from St Francis of Assisi who saw an act of compassion
to the poor as a sacrament – a place where the veil
between heaven and earth is truly thin and where we
meet God in a special and sacred way. People are never
simply the objects of our charity: they are individuals
with names, hopes, aspirations and struggles, just like
us. They cry like us and they laugh like us because they
are the same as us. They don't just need our charity,
they need God's justice and mercy in the same way as
we do. To lose the centrality of Christ in what we do

means we lose our inspiration. To lose our focus on people means we will lose our purpose. Both are essential, and we cannot afford to lose either.

There will be times, as well, when we are the ones struggling, sinking, caught in our frailty, dismayed at our failure. These times can be the greatest challenge to all of us – when instead of being the hero come to rescue the situation, we find the sick, the poor, the disadvantaged ministering to our distress, helping us out of the pit, comforting our grief because they've been there. At such times as that, we are glad we chose a faith that is not afraid to be human.

3. Delivered Locally
Every denomination, network and new church stream is called to be part of God's work of transforming grace, reconciling the world to himself. This change, to be effective, must percolate through to every level – spiritual, social and political, intellectual awakening, and a change of heart.

Working as agents for social change of this kind, the individual local expressions of the church need each other. None of us can do this on our own, not just because the task is too big, but because its nature is love, and love doesn't happen in isolation. Without one another we have failed in the greatest commission and commandment of the Scriptures – to love God with all our hearts and our neighbours as ourselves. The kingdom of God can enter society through the church where the church is simple and humble and kind and free – for then it finds its place at the heart of the kingdom.

The ancient Chinese philosopher, Lao Tsu, spoke of something he described as the 'valley spirit' – he put it like this:

Why is the sea the king of a hundred streams?
Because it is content to lie below them.

One of the greatest mistakes the church makes is when we begin to exalt our own interests and priorities, functioning for our own sake rather than for the sake of others. There is no sense in which the church is called to self-preservation. Part of Christian freedom is the willingness to let go, to be content with the place that God chooses for us.

Into a world frantic with grabbing and getting, addicted to excess and speed, the freedom of humility and simplicity that we see in Christ runs like a stream of peace; permeating society, through myriad instances of engagement with the community, as agent of change and redemption. This healing of society touches our own lives too, for we also are part of the community. Those congregations, committees and faith communities that engage in integral mission will never be the same again. The miracle of hope and grace blesses us too, birthing strong and effective Christian communities.

The commitment to local church does not imply endorsement of one form of church[1] alone. Integral mission embraces the partnership of many strands of church. From the innovative and new to the traditional and established, the church in its local expression becomes a gloriously diverse vehicle of transformation. Christianity, like Judaism, its parent faith, understands spirituality in terms of community, and affirms the human need to belong.

A Christian who avoids commitment to the local church is like a river without a riverbed or an arrow without a bow. As Christians catch the vision of integral mission, they see the strength that lies in the many small contributions of the whole group.

The art of singing well in a choir is to sing loudly enough for your neighbour to hear your voice, and quietly enough for you to hear your neighbour's voice. This is what makes harmony blend into beauty. Integral mission is not a solo performance; it is a harmony, a symphony, a blend.

Staying Centred in the Purposes of God

Without Faithworks, *Kingdom Come* might not have been written: but *Kingdom Come* is not just about Faithworks. Faithworks is just one expression of the vision for integral mission, a Christian social movement, and an instrument of the Holy Spirit in bringing in the kingdom Christ began. Only as local churches, projects and individual followers of Christ allow their own agenda to be subject to the common cause and higher goal of God's kingdom will we see lasting transformation spread through our local communities and beyond to the wider world. The time for narrow-mindedness, exclusive deals and defensive doctrinal posturing has long since past. Unity without a purpose is both unbiblical and unnecessary. I do not need to agree with all of your theology in order to work with you as a fellow Christian, nor do I need you to agree with all of my thinking for you to work with me. We may disagree about many things, but if we can put Jesus at the centre, people first, and remain committed to the body of Christ, then we have all the grounds that we need for unity and collaboration. There is too much to be done for us to waste time arguing about the finer points of our theology. The world needs us, Christ calls us, and it is time for us to answer – together.

Just before completing this manuscript I had to go to Glasgow for a series of meetings. I was looking forward to the few days I would spend there because of the opportunities it would present to work in partnership with Christian agencies serving the excluded and the poor. On my arrival in Glasgow, my first meeting was scheduled for 11:00am at the end of Argyll Street. I set off on foot and before long realised I was lost. I phoned Martin, the colleague I was due to meet, and he told me that I had made only a small mistake. As I headed along the side of the Glasgow expressway, I could see the copper dome of the church building where I was due to meet him – on the other side of the dual carriageway! Undeterred, and with his directions fresh in my mind, I set off.

About twenty yards after the place where I had spoken to Martin on my mobile phone, a man approached me from a side street to my left. He was clearly worse for wear and I wondered if he might be homeless. He spoke to me, but my attention was focused on getting to my meeting, so I quickly and far too sharply responded to him, telling him I would buy him a sandwich, but I wouldn't give him money. To my utter shame and embarrassment, he replied, 'I don't want you to buy me a sandwich, I want you to talk to me about God.'

I was dumbfounded. In my professionalism and haste to talk to church leaders about the poor, I was ignoring the poor. In my passion for the purposes of the kingdom, I was walking past a human being who was yearning for the kingdom. Utterly convicted by God, I stopped, apologised and spent a few minutes talking with him. The conversation ended and I continued on my journey – but God now had my attention properly, and intended to make the most of the opportunity! Crossing the road at a roundabout and walking back up the other side of the expressway toward the church, someone had written in huge black letters across the pavement, 'I miss being close to God.' It was a message; but was it about the other man, or was it about me?

As I reflect on my work as a local pastor, the leader of Faithworks, a Christian speaker, broadcaster, commentator and writer, it strikes me that this one phrase perfectly encapsulates what all that we do is about. As long as there is one person who 'misses being close to

God' there is work for us to do. The kingdom of God is not about power, politics or pride. It is not about us – it is about the relationship of ordinary people with God whose very being is love. God has called us to the task of changing the world – and we do it in the most ordinary and yet extraordinary way – one life at a time.

God's kingdom is here, is coming and will come fully when the Lord Jesus bursts the skies and returns. But until that moment, he asks us to join him in the greatest adventure possible. May he give you the grace to love others unconditionally, serve them passionately and work wholeheartedly for that kingdom. May we love God with all our heart, mind, soul and strength, and love the neighbours God has sent us as ourselves. It is only as we do this that we will see the answer to prayer as Jesus himself taught us to pray.

Let us pray:

Father,

Your name is holy and we count it an honour and a privilege to be part of your family. We thank You that You have promised that You will put right all that is wrong with us, with human society and with creation.

We give You our churches and projects and lives afresh today. We give You our hands, our feet, our hearts. We give You our intellect and our creativity, asking that You will take every word that we speak, everything that we do, every smallest thought that we think – the whole of what we are – and use us for Your kingdom and Your glory.

Change our communities by the power of Your love and grace until every injustice is destroyed, every evil is vanquished and our world is transformed. Renew the lives of all we meet with Your love and let them find grace and peace and new life in Christ.

May our churches be beacons of hope and joy and welcome. May our words speak of wisdom and love. May our simplest actions be movements of kindness and our stillness be a stronghold of truth.

Change us, renew us, revive us.

Let Your kingdom come on earth as it is in heaven.

Amen.

NOTES

1. For an excellent exploration of some of the challenges and opportunities of new forms of church, see Tim Conder, *The Church in Transition: The Journey of Existing Churches into the Emerging Culture*, Grand Rapids: Zondervan, 2006.

Further Information

To find out more about Faithworks,

visit	www.faithworks.info
write to	Faithworks
	1 Kennington Road
	London
	SE1 7QP
call	0845 070 3571
email	info@faithworks.info

About Faithworks

Faithworks exists to celebrate, resource, inspire and speak up for the many thousands of vital initiatives that are transforming lives and communities, because of their Christian faith.

Faithworks has a growing membership of over 20,000 people, churches and organisations within the UK. Members share a motivation, which comes from their faith in Christ, to serve their local communities and positively influence society as a whole. As we work together to serve unconditionally, in a way that is both credible and accessible, we believe that lives, communities and ultimately our nation will be transformed through Christ.

Faithworks has three main objectives:

- To inspire, resource and equip individual Christians and every local church to develop their role at the hub of their community, serving unconditionally.
- To challenge and change the public perception of the church by engaging with both media and government.
- To encourage partnership across churches and other groups to avoid unnecessary competition and build collaboration.

The Faithworks movement was founded in 2001 by Steve Chalke MBE and eleven partner organizations including Oasis UK, the YMCA, Care for the Family, Stewardship, and *Christianity* magazine. These partners have been joined by many other Christian organisations and networks who are part of the Faithworks movement, delivering with and through the local church, and enabling churches to deliver, professional, inclusive and authentic service provision within their communities. Malcolm Duncan has led Faithworks since January 2005.

Oasis UK continues to be the lead partner of Faithworks, providing financial support, staff and office space as well as models of inclusive activity and good practice.

Resources and Services

Faithworks has developed a number of resources and provides a range of services that aim to help individuals, churches and organisations engage effectively with the challenges facing their local community. These include:

- Published materials such as books, manuals, DVDs and guides that help projects with the principles and pragmatics of engaging with the community, working with other voluntary/faith groups and with the government and local media.
- Web-based resources including articles, prayer notes, monthly emails, a directory of Christian community projects, and updates on issues such as funding, key opportunities, policy developments and events.
- *Faithworks* magazine, a quarterly publication featuring comment and advice from practitioners in community engagement, as well as reviews of useful resources and relevant news.
- An annual awards programme providing much-deserved funding and recognition for the excellent community work, motivated by Christian faith, carried out by projects in the UK.
- Campaigns to promote the transformational work that is being done by members of the movement. The 'My Faith Works' campaign celebrates real examples of Christian faith working in difficult situations to bring hope and positive change.

- Training and conferences to enable local projects and churches to run professional projects, be equipped and trained for engagement with the community and wider society, and work effectively in partnership.
- National leadership, engaging on behalf of all those involved in the Faithworks movement, with denominational bodies, the Government, the media and wider society on issues of social action, social justice and inclusion.
- Speakers for local, regional, national and international events, who aim to inspire, challenge and encourage the church to engage with the community unconditionally.
- Working groups that focus on particular areas of engagement within society, so that projects and churches can be best equipped in addressing key issues such as diversity, education, healthcare, housing and crime prevention.

Getting Involved in the Faithworks Movement

There are lots of ways to get involved in the Faithworks movement. All of them involve Christians becoming activists, not just observers. Here are just a few:

Individual Membership

Faithworks membership is free. Sign up today at www.faithworks.info/join. Membership gives you access to the resources and information that

Faithworks provides. Membership of Faithworks is more than putting your name on a mailing list. As a member you become part of a growing movement across the world that is working for radical and lasting change in communities through Christ.

By joining the Faithworks movement, you can inform and authenticate our voice. It is the Faithworks membership on the ground, serving their local communities unconditionally with commitment and professionalism, that provides Faithworks with a credible platform to engage with both government and the media.

Support Faithworks in Prayer and Financially

Faithworks is almost entirely financed by voluntary donations. For the movement to develop and grow it needs supporters in the form of individuals, churches and organisations willing to commit to regular financial and prayer support. Daily prayer points with biblical reflections can be downloaded from the Faithworks website each week. You can give financially online at www.faithworks.info/give, or call 0845 070 3571.

Declare that Your Faith Works

Faithworks is calling on all those who do what they do because of their love for Christ to testify that 'my faith works'. Be part of this national campaign – sign up and celebrate what you do and why you do it at www.myfaithworks.info.

Partnership

Faithworks actively encourages partnership built around four fundamental pillars – purpose, principles, priorities and processes. Formal partnership in the Faithworks movement is open to all Christian churches, organisations, networks and individuals through signing the Faithworks Charter and Partnership Agreement. The charter sets out commitments and principles for service delivery and the partnership agreement sets out how partnership in the movement works.

Faithworks Affiliates

You can partner with Faithworks by officially affiliating your church, Christian community project or organisation to Faithworks. Affiliation is a way of ensuring that your local efforts and initiatives make a difference at a national level as together we speak with a louder, more influential voice.

As a Faithworks affiliate you will receive a certificate recognising your affiliation, an annual subscription to the quarterly *Faithworks* magazine, the right to use the Faithworks registered logo and a link to the Faithworks website. In addition to all the benefits of personal membership, affiliates also have access to free downloads of the growing number of practical tools produced by Faithworks to assist their church, organisation or project in developing effective work in the local community. We also offer affiliate discounts on events and training and we are constantly reviewing how best we can serve you.

We ask that affiliates sign the Faithworks Charter to demonstrate their commitment to excellence and trustworthiness in community engagement, and make a financial contribution of £40 per annum. To become a Faithworks affiliate, visit www.faithworks.info/affiliation.

Networks

Locally – you can partner with Faithworks as a local network of churches, projects and organisations across a town, county or region. If you are starting a network, we ask you to ensure that the churches and projects that join your network individually affiliate with Faithworks nationally, entitling them to all the benefits of affiliation. However, beyond these simple principles we recognise that each local network will be unique and established in a way that is right for their own locality and that flexibility should be encouraged in formation or running of networks.

It may be that you are already involved in an effective network. This whole network can join the Faithworks movement. Where there is a strong local network, there is no need to start another one, but there may well be added value in the network and Faithworks learning from each other and working together. The name of a local network is not the most important thing – what matters is that it is working to unconditionally serve the local community and is committed to good working principles, practices and partnership.

As a Faithworks local network, you will be given the opportunity to host Faithworks regional events to inspire and resource your members and beyond. If you want it, your local network will receive a specially designed Faithworks logo, which will include the name of the town, region or area in which you operate, for use on all literature and publicity that you produce in relation to your Faithworks-affiliated activity.

Regionally – Faithworks is committed to effective regional working. Working with a regional leader and a small number of people who make up a voluntary advisory group in each of the twelve regions in the UK, Faithworks serves the church in partnership with networks such as the Churches' Regional Network, the YMCA and others. The aims of regional working are:

- to ensure the best informed development of local networks;
- to highlight particular regional issues and appropriate responses;
- to develop the most effective models for a particular region;
- to allow for regional diversity whilst ensuring a sense of unity and purpose across the whole movement;
- to enable effective access to regional resources, funding and specialisms;

- to be a first point of contact for existing Faithworks members and partners in the region.

National and International Networks

Faithworks is committed to working in partnership with other organisations that have a national presence. This includes major organisations such as the Shaftesbury Society, the Evangelical Alliance, Churches Together in Britain and Ireland and all of the denominations. All of these organisations, including Faithworks, must recognise that if we expect local churches and projects to work together, then we must also model partnership, joined-up thinking and networking. For that reason, Faithworks is committed to ongoing dialogue, shared resources and joint working at a national and international level. This can be improved in a number of areas – from work with government through to the delivery of training and resources. Faithworks is keen to explore national and international networking with as many groups and organisations as possible to avoid duplication and strengthen delivery to local projects, churches and communities.

The Future for Faithworks

The transformation of individuals, communities and society as a whole is possible. Faithworks is committed to providing the best network possible across the UK and beyond to enable that transformation to take place.

While there is one community that suffers from exclusion or one church that does not open its arms to embrace those whom God has made, the mission God gave to His people is not complete. The task may be daunting, and the challenges great, but as we work together, we can and will see our world changed: we can build a better world and see God's kingdom come – but we can only do it together.

Bibliography

Alan Aldridge, *Religion in the Contemporary World*, Cambridge: Polity, 1999.

Richard Appignanesi and Chris Garratt, *Introducing Postmodernism*, Cambridge: Icon, 1999.

Craig Bartholomew and Thorsten Moritz, *Christ and Consumerism: A Critical Analysis of the Spirit of the Age*, Exeter: Paternoster, 2000.

John Benton, *Christians in a Consumer Culture*, Fearn: Christian Focus, 1999.

G.R. Beasley-Murray, *Jesus and the Kingdom of God*, Grand Rapids: William B. Eerdmans, 1996.

Mike Booker and Mark Ireland, *Evangelism – Which Way Now? An Evaluation of Alpha, Emmaus, Cell Church and other Contemporary Strategies for Evangelism*, London: Church House, 2003.

M.J. Borg, *A New Vision: Spirit, Culture and the Life of Discipleship*, New York: HarperCollins, 1987.

Callum G. Brown, *The Death of Christian Britain*, London: Routledge, 2000

Walter Brueggermann and Patrick D. Miller, *The Word That Redescribes the World: The Bible and Discipleship*, Minneapolis: Fortress, 2006.

Walter Brueggermann, *Texts that Linger, Words that*

Explode: Listening to Prophetic Voices, Minneapolis: Fortress, 2000.

Walter Brueggermann, *Hopeful Imagination: Prophetic Voices in Exile*, London: SCM, 1996.

Walter Brueggermann, *Biblical Perspectives on Evangelism: Living in a Three-Storied Universe*, Nashville: Abingdon Press, 1993.

Walter Brueggermann, *Texts Under Negotiation: The Bible and the Postmodern Imagination*, Minneapolis: Fortress, 1993.

Walter Brueggermann, *Finally Comes the Poet: Daring Speech for Proclamation*, Minneapolis: Fortress, 1989.

Walter Brueggermann, *The Prophetic Imagination*, Augsburg: Fortress Press, 2001.

Bruce L. Bugbee, *Network Participant's Guide*, Grand Rapids: Zondervan, 1994.

David G. Burnett, *The Healing of the Nations: The Biblical Basis of the Mission of God*, Carlisle: Paternoster Press, 1996.

D.A. Carson, *The Gagging of God*, Leicester: Apollos, 1996.

Tim Chester, *Good News to the Poor: The Gospel and Social Action*, Leicester: Inter-Varsity Press, 2003.

The Churches Regional Commission in Yorkshire and Humber, *Angels and Advocates*, www.crc-online.org.uk.

Tim Conder, *The Church in Transition: The Journey of Existing Churches into the Emerging Culture*, Grand Rapids: Zondervan, 2006.

George Grant, *The Micah Mandate*, Chicago: Moody Press, 1995.

Steven Connor, *Postmodernist Culture: An Introduction to Theories of the Contemporary*, Oxford: Blackwell, 1989.

Caroline Cox and John Marks, *This Immoral Trade: Slavery in the 21st Century*, Oxford: Monarch, 2006.

Richard Dawkins, *The God Delusion*, London: Bantam Press, 2006.

Vincent J. Donovan, *Christianity Rediscovered*, Orbis Books, Maryknoll, New York, 2003.

John W. Drane, *Cultural Change and Biblical Faith: The Future of the Church – Biblical and Missiological Essays for the New Century*, Carlisle: Paternoster, 2000.

John W. Drane, *Faith in a Changing Culture: Creating Churches for the Next Century*, London: Marshall Pickering, 1994.

Malcolm Duncan, *Building a Better World: Faith at Work for Change in Society*, London: Continuum, 2006.

Terry Eagleton, *The Idea of Culture*, Oxford: Blackwell, 2000.

John Finney, *Finding Faith Today*, Swindon: Bible Society, 1992.

David Greenlee (editor), *Global Passion: Marking George Verwer's Contribution to World Mission*, Carlisle: Authentic, 2003.

David Held, Anthony McGrew, David Goldblatt and Jonathan Perraton, *Global Transformations: Politics, Economics, and Culture*, Cambridge: Polity, 1999.

William D. Hendricks, *Exit Interviews*, Chicago: Moody Press, 1993.

Christopher Hitchens, *God is Not Great: How Religion Poisons Everything*, New York: Hachette, 2007.

Holy Trinity Brompton, *Alpha News: May–October 2007*, London: Holy Trinity Brompton, 2007.

Alan Jamieson, *A Churchless Faith*, London: SPCK, 2002.

Walter Kaufmann (editor and translator), *The Portable Nietzsche*, New York: Penguin, 1976.

Frank Kermode (editor), *Selected Prose of T.S. Eliot*, London: Faber, 1975.

John Lloyd and John Mitchinson, *The Book of General Ignorance*, London: Faber and Faber, 2006.

Alison Morgan, *The Wild Gospel*, Oxford: Monarch Books, 2004.

Michael Moynagh, *Changing World, Changing Church*, Oxford: Monarch, 2001.

Michael Moynagh, emergingchurch.intro, Oxford: Monarch, 2004.

Stuart Murray, *Post-Christendom: Church and Mission in a Strange New World*, Carlisle: Paternoster, 2004.

Stuart Murray, *Church After Christendom*, Carlisle: Paternoster, 2005.

P.A. Mickey, 'Kingdom of God' in David J. Atkinson and David H. Field, *New Dictionary of Christian Ethics and Pastoral Theology*, Leicester, Inter-Varsity Press, 1995.

Lesslie Newbigin, *Truth to Tell: The Gospel as Public Truth*, London: SPCK, 1991.

Lesslie Newbigin, *The Gospel in a Pluralist Society*, London: SPCK, 1989.

Lesslie Newbigin, *Foolishness to the Greeks: The Gospel and Western Culture*, London: SPCK, 1986.

Richard Niebuhr, *Christ and Culture*, London: Faber and Faber, 1952.

The North West Development Agency, *Faith in England's North West*, www.faithnorthwest.org.uk.

Prayerworks, The Manual, Authentic: Milton Keynes, 2005.

Philip Richter and Leslie Francis, *Gone But Not Forgotten: Church Leaving and Returning*, London: Darton, Longmann and Todd, 1998.

George Ritzer, *The McDonaldization of Society*, Thousand Oaks, CA: Pine Forge Press, 1991

Martin Robinson and Dwight Smith, *Invading Secular Space: Strategies for Tomorrow's Church*, London: Monarch, 2003.

P. Sampson (editor), *Faith and Modernity*, Oxford: Regnum, 1994.

The South East of England Faith Forum, *Beyond Belief*, www.hitc.org.uk/cms/downloads/publications/beyond_belief.pdf.

John Stott and R.T. Coote, *Down to Earth: Studies in Christianity and Culture*, Grand Rapids: Eerdmans, 1980.

Richard Tiplady, *World of Difference: Global Mission at the Pick 'n' Mix Counter*, Carlisle, Paternoster, 2003.

David Wells, *Losing Our Virtue: Why the Church Must*

Recover its Moral Vision, Leicester: William B. Eerdmans, 1998.

Andrew Walker, *Telling the Story: Gospel, Mission and Culture*, London: SPCK, 1996.

Rob Warner, *Twenty-first Century Church: Why Radical Change Cannot Wait*, Eastbourne: Kingsway, 1998.

Robert Warren, *Signs of Life: How Goes the Decade of Evangelism?*, London: Church House, 1996.

Malcolm Waters, *Globalisation*, London: Routledge, 2001.

Ravi K. Zacharias, *Deliver us from Evil: Restoring the Soul in a Disintegrating Culture*, Dallas: Word, 1996.